The Greatest Raid

GILES WHITTELL

THE GREATEST RAID

ST NAZAIRE, 1942:
The Heroic Story of
Operation Chariot

VIKING
an imprint of
PENGUIN BOOKS

VIKING

UK | USA | Canada | Ireland | Australia
India | New Zealand | South Africa

Viking is part of the Penguin Random House group of companies
whose addresses can be found at global.penguinrandomhouse.com.

First published 2022
001

Copyright © Giles Whittell, 2022

The moral right of the author has been asserted

'Operation Chariot – Combined Plan' on pp. 231–44 courtesy of the
National Archives, reprinted in Peter Lush, *Winged Chariot* (2016)

Maps by Evolution Design and Digital

Every effort has been made to identify copyright holders and obtain their permission
for use of copyright material. Notification of any additions or corrections that should be
incorporated in future reprints or editions of this book world be greatly appreciated.

Set in 12/14.75pt Bembo Book MT Pro
Typeset by Jouve (UK), Milton Keynes
Printed and bound in Great Britain by Clays Ltd, Elcograf S.p.A.

The authorized representative in the EEA is Penguin Random House Ireland,
Morrison Chambers, 32 Nassau Street, Dublin D02 YH68

A CIP catalogue record for this book is available from the British Library

Hardback ISBN: 978–0–241–50857–2
Trade Paperback ISBN: 978–0–241–56767–8

www.greenpenguin.co.uk

MIX
Paper from
responsible sources
FSC® C018179

Penguin Random House is committed to a
sustainable future for our business, our readers
and our planet. This book is made from Forest
Stewardship Council® certified paper.

For Ted and Fran

Contents

Contents

Illustrations

1. Commander Robert Ryder VC, naval force commander for Operation Chariot, helmed the *Tai-Mo-Shan* as his first command. (Image courtesy of Canon Lisle Ryder)
2. Operation Chariot's main task was to destroy the only dry dock on the Atlantic coast big enough for the mighty *Tirpitz*, Hitler's 43,000-ton flagship. (ullstein bild Dtl./Gettyimages)
3. Commandos training in Scotland a month before the raid. (Imperial War Museums H 17469)
4. Each commando carried a Fairbairn–Sykes fighting knife, named after the two Hong Kong policemen who designed it. (Imperial War Museums H 19269)
5. The Normandie dry dock was then the biggest in the world. (Copyright © Battlefield Historian)
6. The dock's huge southern gate, or caisson, was to be rammed at maximum speed by the explosive-laden HMS *Campbeltown*. (Image courtesy of the National Archives)
7. Lord Louis Mountbatten, head of Combined Operations. (PA Images/Alamy Stock Photo)
8. John Hughes-Hallett, Mountbatten's Naval Adviser, claimed to have spotted a fatal flaw in St Nazaire's defences. (Popperfoto/Gettyimages)
9. Robert Ryder, who could 'do everything' – he could sail, navigate by the stars, fall rapidly in love and stare danger in the face. (Image courtesy of Canon Lisle Ryder)
10. Lieutenant Colonel Charles Newman VC, military force commander, rugby player and jazz pianist. (Imperial War Museums HU 16542)

11. Lieutenant Stuart Chant of 5 Commando, a former broker's clerk at the London Stock Exchange, was tasked with blowing up the dry dock's pumping station. (Private collection)

12. Lance Sergeant Peter Harkness, a Post Office mail sorter from Glasgow. (Image courtesy of the Commando Veterans Archive)

13. Sub-Lieutenant Philip Dark drew this self-portrait as a prisoner of war. (Image courtesy of the National Museum of the Royal Navy)

14. Torpedo specialist Lieutenant Nigel Tibbits with his wife, Elmslie, at their wedding reception in Shanghai in 1937. (Image courtesy of the Tibbits family)

15. Lieutenant Bill 'Tiger' Watson led the commandos of launch 457 ashore aged nineteen. (Image courtesy of the Watson family)

16. Lieutenant Dunstan Curtis, commander of Motor Gunboat 314, who later served in naval intelligence under Ian Fleming. (Image courtesy of Christopher Curtis)

17. Lance Sergeant Arthur Dockerill, former choirboy at Ely Cathedral and here pictured with his wife, Marjorie, on their wedding day. (Image courtesy of the Dockerill family)

18. Sergeant Tommy Durrant VC was furious that his launch commander refused to put him ashore. (Image courtesy of Paul Durrant)

19. Able Seaman Bill Savage VC, formerly a brewer's boy and weightlifter in Birmingham, was the forward gunner on Motor Gunboat 314. (Image courtesy of Caroline Carr)

20. Korvettenkapitän Herbert Sohler, commander of the 7th U-boat Flotilla. (Image courtesy of Images Défenses)

21. Kapitän-zur-See Karl-Conrad Mecke, who warned his flak battalions during the air raid there was 'devilry afoot'. (PeKo Publishing/Alamy Stock Photo)

22. Sub-Lieutenant Micky Wynn was reunited at the end of the war with his chief motor mechanic, Bill Lovegrove. (Image courtesy of 8th Baron Newborough)

23. Motor Torpedo Boat 74 at high speed, with Wynn at the helm. (Ajax News & Feature Service/Alamy Stock Photo)
24. HMS *Campbeltown* was modified in Devonport naval dockyard to resemble a German torpedo boat. (Image courtesy of the National Archives)
25. The wooden-hulled Motor Gunboat 314, which led the Charioteers into battle. (Imperial War Museums HU 53260)
26. An oil painting of the river battle by the war artist Charles Pears, based on Ryder's account. (Image courtesy of Canon Lisle Ryder)
27. An earlier watercolour of the scene in the estuary as the flotilla came under fire, by Enid Campbell (Ryder's niece). (Image courtesy of Canon Lisle Ryder)
28. HMS *Campbeltown* hit the southern dock gate at 1.34 a.m. British time on 28 March 1942. (Popperfoto/Gettyimages)
29. Wearing only a blanket, Beattie was questioned by his captors after spending a night in the water and being rescued by a German trawler. (akg-images/Sammlung Berliner Verlag/Archiv)
30. Despite patches of cloud, a photograph taken by a Spitfire reconnaissance plane on 29 March shows the dock gate, in the bottom-left corner, has been destroyed. (Image courtesy of the National Archives)
31. Images of Private Tom McCormack, grievously wounded by a grenade, were used by the Nazis to try to show the raid had been a failure. (akg-images/Sammlung Berliner Verlag/Archiv)
32. Wounded commandos made to wait outside the Café Moderne. (*Süddeutsche Zeitung*. Photo: Alamy Stock Photo)
33. Captain Micky Burn, poet, *Times* journalist, former Nazi sympathizer and lover of the Soviet spy Guy Burgess. Here, he is pictured with Rifleman Paddy Bushe, also of 2 Commando. (Image courtesy of Professor Peter Stanley)
34. Survivors of launch 306 are led away from the quayside the morning after the raid. (*Süddeutsche Zeitung*. Photo: Alamy Stock Photo)

35. Churchill called Operation Chariot 'a deed of glory', but Hollywood had to invent a starring role for a Canadian major played by Lloyd Bridges to justify bringing it to the big screen in *Attack on the Iron Coast* in 1967. (Everett Collection, Inc./Alamy Stock Photo)

Maps

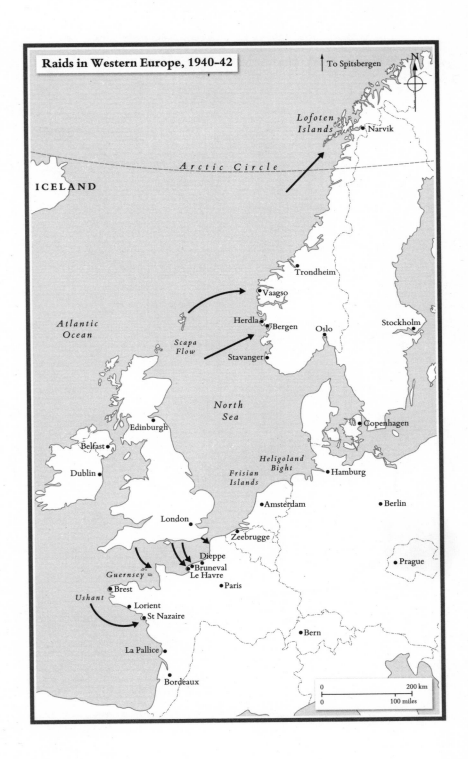

Raids in Western Europe, 1940–42

To Spitsbergen

N

Lofoten Islands • Narvik

Arctic Circle

ICELAND

• Trondheim

Atlantic Ocean

• Vaagso
Herdla • • Bergen
Scapa Flow
Stavanger • • Oslo
Stockholm •

North Sea

Edinburgh •

Belfast •
• Copenhagen

Dublin •
Heligoland Bight
Frisian Islands
• Hamburg

• Amsterdam
• Berlin

London •
Zeebrugge •
• Prague
Dieppe •
Guernsey • Bruneval
Le Havre
• Brest
• Paris
Ushant • Lorient
• St Nazaire
• Bern

• La Pallice

• Bordeaux

| 0 | | 200 km |
| 0 | | 100 miles |

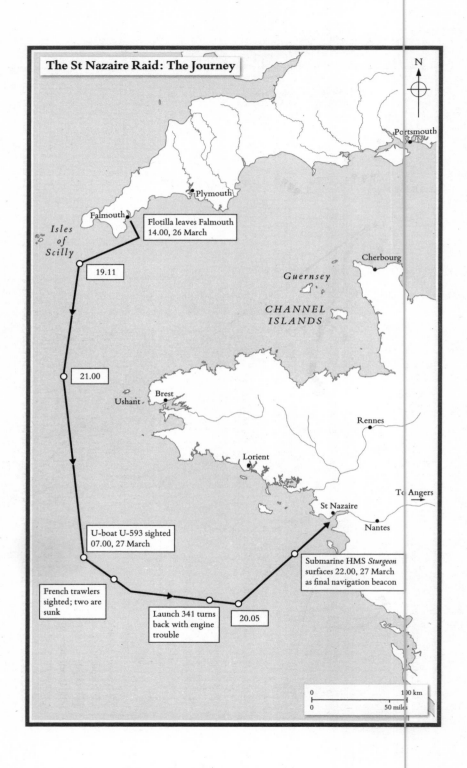

The St Nazaire Raid: The Journey

N

Portsmouth

Plymouth

Falmouth

Flotilla leaves Falmouth
14.00, 26 March

*Isles
of
Scilly*

19.11

Cherbourg

Guernsey

CHANNEL
ISLANDS

21.00

Ushant Brest

Rennes

Lorient

To Angers

St Nazaire

Nantes

U-boat U–593 sighted
07.00, 27 March

Submarine HMS *Sturgeon*
surfaces 22.00, 27 March
as final navigation beacon

French trawlers
sighted; two are
sunk

Launch 341 turns
back with engine
trouble

20.05

| 0 | | 100 km |
| 0 | | 50 miles |

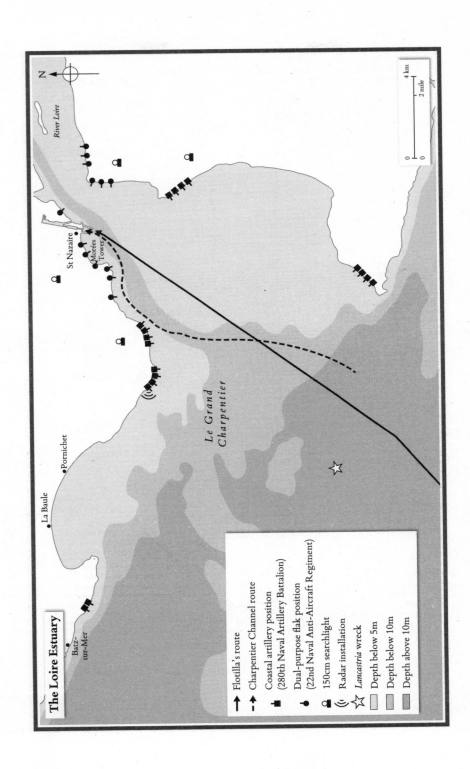

The Loire Estuary

N

River Loire

St Nazaire
Morées Tower

La Baule

Pornichet

Batz-sur-Mer

Le Grand Charpentier

4 km
2 mile
2 mile
0
0

Flotilla's route
Charpentier Channel route
Coastal artillery position (280th Naval Artillery Battalion)
Dual-purpose flak position (22nd Naval Anti-Aircraft Regiment)
150cm searchlight
Radar installation
Lancastria wreck
Depth below 5m
Depth below 10m
Depth above 10m

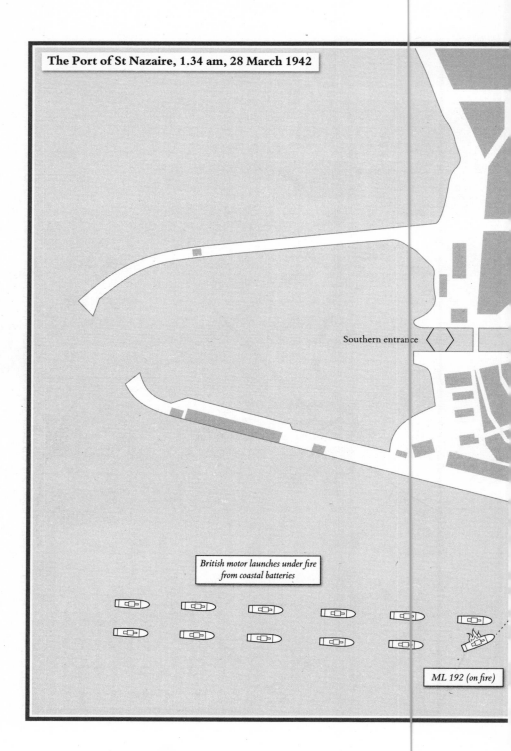

The Port of St Nazaire, 1.34 am, 28 March 1942

Southern entrance

British motor launches under fire
from coastal batteries

ML 192 (on fire)

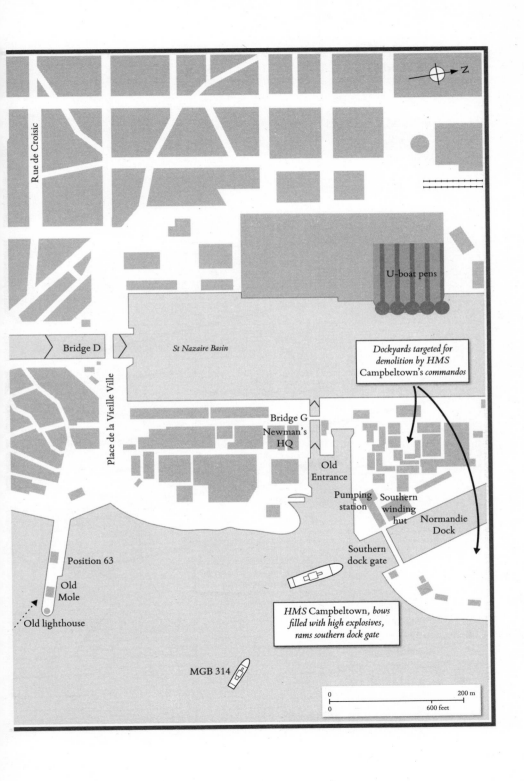

Rue de Croisic

Z

U-boat pens

Bridge D

St Nazaire Basin

Dockyards targeted for demolition by HMS Campbeltown's *commandos*

Place de la Vieille Ville

Bridge G
Newman's
HQ

Old
Entrance

Pumping
station

Southern
winding
hut

Normandie
Dock

Position 63

Southern
dock gate

Old
Mole

Old lighthouse

HMS Campbeltown, *bows filled with high explosives, rams southern dock gate*

MGB 314

0 _____ 200 m
0 _____ 600 feet

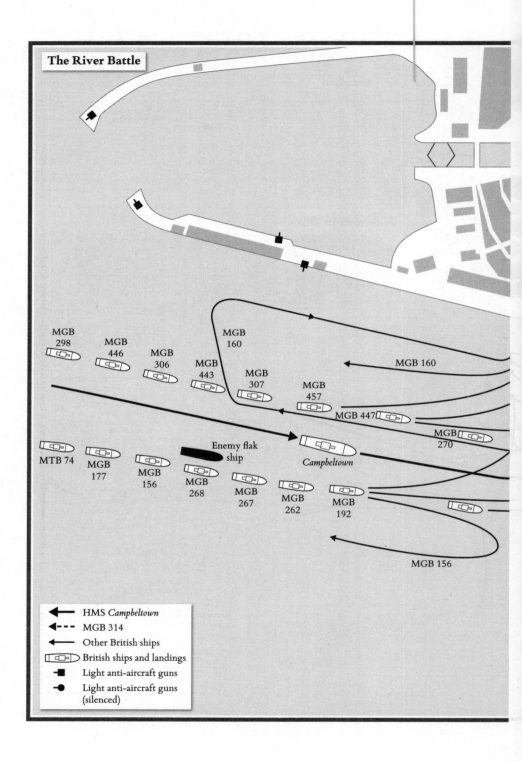

The River Battle

MGB 298
MGB 446
MGB 306
MGB 443
MGB 160
MGB 307
MGB 457
MGB 160
MGB 447
MGB 270
MTB 74
MGB 177
MGB 156
MGB 268
Enemy flak ship
MGB 267
MGB 262
MGB 192
Campbeltown
MGB 156

HMS *Campbeltown*
MGB 314
Other British ships
British ships and landings
Light anti-aircraft guns
Light anti-aircraft guns (silenced)

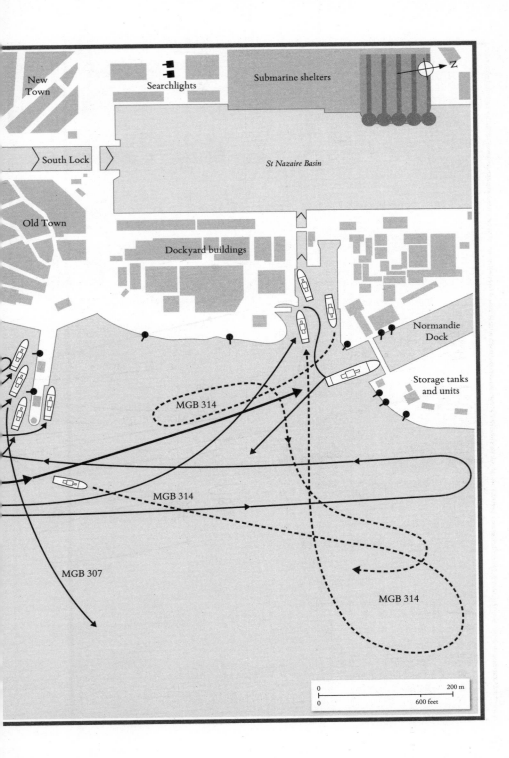

New Town

Searchlights

Submarine shelters

Z

South Lock

St Nazaire Basin

Old Town

Dockyard buildings

Normandie Dock

Storage tanks and units

MGB 314

MGB 314

MGB 307

MGB 314

0   200 m

0   600 feet

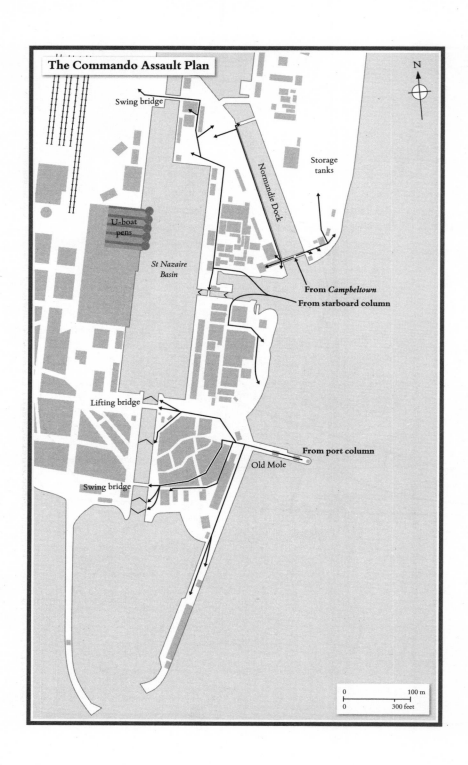

The Commando Assault Plan

Swing bridge

Normandie Dock

Storage tanks

U-boat pens

St Nazaire Basin

From *Campbeltown*

From starboard column

Lifting bridge

From port column

Old Mole

Swing bridge

N

0   100 m
0   300 feet

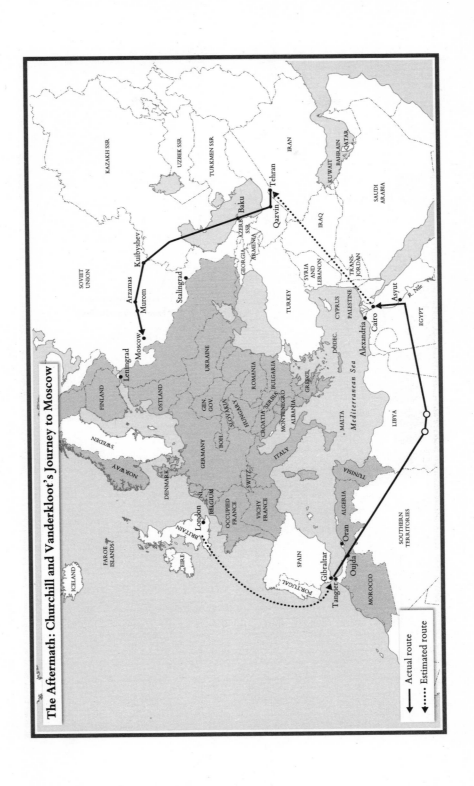

The Aftermath: Churchill and Vanderkloot's Journey to Moscow

Actual route

Estimated route

Cast of characters

In high places

Winston Churchill: British Prime Minister; ordered Mountbatten to 'initiate and sustain the offensive'

General Charles de Gaulle: leader of the Free French

Franklin Roosevelt: US President; urged Churchill to attack U-boat bases on the French Atlantic coast

Joseph Stalin: Soviet leader; demanded in vain that Churchill open a second front in Western Europe in 1942

In London

Admiral Sir Charles Forbes: Commander-in-Chief, Plymouth Command

Captain John Hughes-Hallett: Naval Adviser, Combined Operations; claimed to have spotted a flaw in St Nazaire's defences

Pedro Mones, the Marqués de Casa Maury: racing driver and senior intelligence officer, Combined Operations

Lord Louis Mountbatten: great-grandson of Queen Victoria and head of Combined Operations

Admiral Sir Dudley Pound: First Sea Lord

Group Captain Fred Willetts: liaison between Combined Operations and the RAF

Force commanders

Lieutenant Colonel Charles Newman VC: leader of Operation Chariot's commandos; told them in the middle of the battle they would have to walk to Spain

Commander Robert Ryder VC: leader of the naval force; before the war sailed a yacht the 'wrong' way round the world

Commandos

Captain M. C. 'Micky' Burn: former Nazi sympathizer and lover of Soviet spy Guy Burgess; led 6 Troop, 2 Commando

Lieutenant Stuart Chant: led the demolition unit that destroyed the pumping house

Major Bill Copland: leader of the Commando force aboard HMS *Campbeltown*

Lance Sergeant Arthur Dockerill: had ninety seconds to lead his wounded commanding officer to safety

Sergeant Tommy Durrant VC: refused to surrender on launch 306 and was recommended for an award by Kapitänleutnant Friedrich Paul

Lance Sergeant Bill Gibson: Glasgow mechanic, whose last letter to his father said the raid had 'virtually been suicide'

Troop Sergeant Major George Haines: farmer from Kent; led the only commandos to land ashore from the starboard column of launches

Captain David Paton: medic; identified the threat posed by position 63 from reconnaissance pictures before setting out

Lieutenant Tom Peyton: Old Etonian who wanted a better world for everyone

Lieutenant Corran Purdon: led the demolition unit that destroyed the northern winding hut

Lance Sergeant Don Randall: demolition man who destroyed a gun emplacement on the pumping station roof

Captain Donald Roy: held the bridgehead at Bridge G and led the advance to Bridge D

Corporal Glyn Salisbury: witness to the destruction of launch 306

Lieutenant Ronald Swayne: surrendered launch 306 to the *Jaguar*

Lieutenant Philip Walton: former teacher; led Wheeler ashore off the Old Mole

2nd Lieutenant Bill 'Tiger' Watson: first man ashore from port column of motor launches

Corporal George Wheeler: had an MSc in economics and followed Newman's escape orders to the letter

Corporal Arthur 'Buster' Woodiwiss: single-handedly destroyed two gun emplacements east of the dock gate

Royal Navy

Ordinary Seaman Ralph Batteson: rear gunner on launch 306

Lieutenant Commander Sam Beattie VC: last captain of the *Campbeltown*; directed her onto the Normandie Dock's south gate

Lieutenant Ted Burt: former Metropolitan Police detective, and commander of launch 262

Lieutenant Tom Collier: former yachting correspondent, and commander of launch 457

Lieutenant Richard Collinson: junior officer on launch 192; found refuge in a lighthouse on the Old Mole

Lieutenant Dunstan Curtis: commander of MGB 314; later worked in naval intelligence under Ian Fleming

Sub-Lieutenant Philip Dark: junior officer on launch 306; distributed morphine to survivors

Able Seaman Herbert Dyer: footballer and survivor of the destruction of launch 457

Lieutenant Leslie Fenton: Hollywood film star and commander of launch 156

Lieutenant Ian Henderson: former insurance underwriter, and commander of launch 306

Chief Motor Mechanic Bill Lovegrove: installed a new engine in MTB 74 at the last minute; saved his captain's life

Sub-Lieutenant Mark Rodier: commander of launch 177; had a premonition he would not survive the raid

Able Seaman Bill Savage VC: forward gun layer on MGB 314; came close to silencing position 63

Lieutenant Nigel Tibbits: explosives expert who turned the *Campbeltown* into a bomb

Lieutenant Bill Tillie: former secretary to Robert Ryder, and commander of the ill-fated launch 268

Sub-Lieutenant Chris Worsley: junior officer on MGB 314; had to throw a severed leg overboard on the gunboat's escape run

Sub-Lieutenant Micky Wynn: 7th Baron Newborough, and commander of MTB 74; lost an eye when his torpedo boat was destroyed

Family and friends

Cécilie Birney: rally driver and wife of David Birney

Captain David Birney: crack shot who was supposed to lead the first commandos ashore

Sir Clive Burn: Secretary of the Archives of the Duchy of Cornwall and father of Micky Burn

Alex Gibson: father of Bill Gibson

Ella van Heemstra: friend of Micky Burn and sometime Nazi sympathizer

Jennifer Newman: oldest daughter of Charles Newman; was in the scullery at her boarding school when word came that her father was missing

Elmslie Tibbits: adventurer and wife of Nigel Tibbits

Germans

Korvettenkapitän [Corvette Captain] Lothar Burhenne: the first German officer to report the approach of the flotilla

Vizeadmiral [Vice-Admiral] Karl Dönitz: commander of German U-boat fleet, visiting St Nazaire on the night of the raid

Kapitänleutnant [Lieutenant Commander] Gerd Kelbling: commander of U-593, which failed to report the flotilla's approach

Kapitän-zur-See [Captain] Karl-Conrad Mecke: commander of the flak battalions defending St Nazaire

Enno Mengers: Acting Port Commander of St Nazaire who twice insisted St Nazaire was not under attack

Kapitänleutnant [Lieutenant Commander] Friedrich Paul: commander of the *Jaguar* torpedo boat

Korvettenkapitän [Corvette Captain] Günther Prien: legendary U-boat commander in whose memory the 7th U-boat Flotilla acquired the 'snorting bull' emblem

Oberst [Colonel] Hans Hugo von Schuckmann: infantry commander; denied Sohler's request for immediate army support

Korvettenkapitän [Corvette Captain] Herbert Sohler: commander of 7th U-boat Flotilla; promised Dönitz the British would never attack St Nazaire

French

Antoinette Loréal: teenager who heard the battle for the Old Town Square from her air raid shelter underneath it

Paul Ramadier: former Resistance fighter and first Prime Minister of the Fourth French Republic

Gilbert Renault, also known as Colonel Rémy: legend of the Resistance who flew plans of the St Nazaire docks to Britain the month before the raid

Prologue

A few minutes before midnight on 27 March 1942, Major Bill Copland of the Prince of Wales' own South Lancashire Regiment and 2 Commando invited the officers in his command to join him in the wardroom of an old destroyer. A dozen men filed in from all over the ship. They moved quietly, on rubber soles. Among them were an archaeologist, a stockbroker and a curator from the Victoria & Albert Museum in London, not that anyone would have known it from their uniforms. They all wore standard green battledress with one unusual feature (apart from their soft shoes). They wore white reflective belts.

There was gin and sherry in the wardroom, but this was not the time. Some of Copland's guests had taken Benzedrine instead, a mild amphetamine, to help conceal their fear.

The destroyer was approaching the west coast of France. She'd been built in America for the First World War and disguised as German for the Second. Her name was HMS *Campbeltown* and she was making twelve knots through light mist under a full moon.

On the bridge, Lieutenant Nigel Tibbits peered out through a slit in the extra armour plating welded onto the outside of the superstructure for this, the *Campbeltown*'s last voyage. Tibbits was considered shy by his superiors, but no one doubted his expertise. He was a torpedo specialist, twenty-eight years old and married with a young son. He didn't join Copland's team below because he was a navy man and they were all commandos. But there was another reason: his work on this mission was in a sense already done. With long rolls of copper fuse and four tons of Amatol explosive – the kind used in depth charges to blow apart the pressure hulls of submarines – he had turned the ship into a giant floating bomb.

The *Campbeltown* was sailing north by north-west, trailed by fifteen smaller vessels. Three more led the way. All were loaded with commandos who had spent the past thirty-six hours eating, sleeping and contemplating the odds that they were soon to die. There were professional soldiers among them, but not many. Most were not long gone from civvy street: bank clerks, shipping clerks, motor mechanics, a rugby blue and a midfielder from Scarborough Town FC. There were three newspapermen, at least two shop managers, one Etonian and one bona fide film star. Some were armed with machine guns, some with explosives. One carried thirty-six grenades stuffed into his pack.

A medic who had joined the expedition late remarked when briefed on its target that it was a suicide job. Its planners certainly expected heavy losses. The commandos had all been given the option of staying behind but none had taken it. They had all written letters to their families instead, to be delivered if they failed to return.

'Dad dearest . . . don't worry and don't be too unhappy,' Sergeant Bill Gibson wrote. 'I can only hope that by laying down my life the generations to come might in some way remember us and also benefit from what we've done.' Rifleman Tommy Roach urged his father to 'remember what you always told me – to keep my chin up'.

They were dressed for battle in clean underwear to reduce the risk of infection when the shrapnel started flying. Many would be wounded – that was known. In the wheelhouse of each smaller vessel, surgical instruments and syrettes of morphia were laid out on fresh muslins.

Tibbits did not expect to live. He and his wife, Elmslie, had found time for a picnic in the hills behind Falmouth the previous weekend. There, in beautiful spring sunshine, he had asked her gently to get used to the idea that he'd be killed.

In the wardroom Copland went over plans that his officers had already memorized. Their mood, he wrote later, was calm and confident and cheerful. He ended the meeting with a polite request: 'Action stations, please, gentlemen.'

Copland returned to his assigned position on the foredeck. For another hour the flotilla continued undetected. To the east, German submarines attacked the Allies' shipping lanes as they had every night for two and a half years, to starve the British Isles into submission and save Hitler the trouble of an invasion. Ahead lay the wreckage site of the RMS *Lancastria*, strafed and sunk with 3,000 souls as she tried to evacuate the British Expeditionary Force in the tenth month of the war. Beyond the *Lancastria*, in the port of St Nazaire, the inner harbour was flanked by U-boat pens with concrete roofs eight metres thick. And beyond them lay occupied France, the annex of a Nazi Reich that would soon stretch to the Volga.

The sensible approach to St Nazaire was up a channel dredged for ocean liners that hugged the north bank of the Loire. But the *Campbeltown* would not be taking the sensible approach. At half past midnight Lieutenant Commander Sam Beattie ordered a few degrees of starboard rudder and left the channel for the shallow waters of the estuary.

In two places the destroyer touched bottom, slowing to five knots as its propellers churned up silt. A mile out, the commandos smelled land and knew they would be within range of shore batteries built to deter battleships. Distracted by an air raid warning, the big guns let them pass. For the time being the destroyer's disguise – two raked funnels and a counterfeit German flag – was working.

In the leading motor gunboat a young sapper went below to change into his kilt, to go out a Scot if his time was up. In the destroyer, Tibbits briefly left the bridge to check his fuses.

At 1.28 a.m. the flotilla was caught in searchlights. It was challenged and its cover blown. All hell broke loose. The shooting started with multicoloured tracer but proceeded quickly to heavy-calibre explosive shells. On the bridge of the *Campbeltown* two men at the wheel were quickly cut down by machine gun fire. As a third stepped forward, Tibbits said, 'I'll take it, old boy.'

The plans that Copland's officers had memorized were then torn to shreds in two hours of savage fighting and desperate confusion. The commandos' white belts helped them see each other in the dark but, even so, nearly half the 623 soldiers and sailors who took part in the raid on St Nazaire were killed or wounded. Of the sixteen motor launches, thirteen were destroyed or sunk. Of the troops who went ashore, not one came back, and those evacuated to the nearest field hospital had to take their chances with surgeons who wore red rubber aprons to disguise the blood.

Their mission was conceived as an attempt at the impossible; a plan so audacious the enemy would consider it madness and would therefore not expect it. Their target was a dock, but no ordinary dock. Excavated from the north bank of the Loire as a launch pad for mighty ocean liners, the Forme Écluse Joubert was the biggest dry dock in the world – and the only one on Europe's Atlantic coast big enough for Hitler's most fearsome battleship, the *Tirpitz*. Hitler himself had decided to keep her in Norwegian waters and continue to rely on U-boats to attack Allied shipping between the Old World and the New. But in Churchill's mind the *Tirpitz* had become the single most important chess piece in the Battle of the Atlantic. If she could not be destroyed – and all efforts so far had been in vain – then she had to be denied the freedom of the seas.

A century earlier Lord Tennyson wrote of the Light Brigade at Balaclava, 'Theirs not to reason why, / Theirs but to do and die'. The same was broadly true of the commandos. They prided themselves on thinking on their feet, but most never got the chance. Captain David Birney was supposed to be the first ashore but he drowned between his launch and the quayside, heavily laden, covered in oil and too slippery to be helped. Eighty years on his daughter said of the raiders: 'They didn't know what the hell they were doing.'

And in many cases this was true. Advance briefings were strictly need-to-know, and dozens who were taken prisoner had no idea what they had accomplished until after the war. But one person knew exactly what he was doing. Not quite single-handedly, the quietly spoken Tibbits made sure that Operation Chariot would be a triumph in spite of everything. Five of those who took part won the Victoria Cross, the highest gallantry award for British military personnel. No other raid in the war was honoured with so many. Tibbits wasn't one of the recipients, but he embodied a combination of understatement, guile and bravery that was the basic requirement for taking part. Thanks to these qualities, the operation can still safely be called 'the greatest raid of all'.

PART I

Before 1.30 a.m., 28 March 1942

1. Planning

As Nigel Tibbits went below to set his fuses, Micky Burn came up to sniff the air. Burn was a romantic. Heading into a fight he knew might end his life, he couldn't help being swept up in the excitement of the moment. 'I went on deck and saw white waves breaking in the dark to starboard, and thought incredulously, "this is the coast of France, forbidden France",' he wrote afterwards. 'We're about to enter France!'

Tibbits and Burn were on different boats and they were very different people. Tibbits, on the *Campbeltown*, was upright, meticulous and married to the great-granddaughter of a hero of Trafalgar. He had a Brylcreemed parting and a grand future in the navy if he could only defy the odds that night.

Burn was a rucksack of competing impulses. He was a soldier in peak physical condition who believed he was self-healing, at least for minor bullet wounds. Beneath his muscles and his battledress he was a poet, a journalist and a bisexual who'd converted to Catholicism in order to confess his urges. He'd also been an admirer, not many years before, of Adolf Hitler. This was true of many young idealists trying to fathom the upheavals of the thirties, but Burn had actually met the Führer — twice — as a young reporter keen to make his mark. He'd been twenty at the time and easily impressed — a dupe, he said.

In fact he was quizzical and clever. With 'a touch of the great English eccentrics', as one of his men put it, he was not an obvious leader — but then nor were many of those deemed officer material mainly because they'd been to a private school. He had been to Winchester, then Oxford, dropping out before getting his degree to ghost-write a memoir for a well-known racing driver. He was now in charge of twelve commandos on Motor Launch 192, approaching the French coast off the *Campbeltown*'s starboard quarter.

The launch was built entirely of wood: two thin mahogany hulls with a lining of calico between them. It was propelled by twin 850hp petrol engines and carried two extra 500-gallon tanks on deck. The plan was to drain these tanks and fill them with sea water on the run-in to St Nazaire. Some crews remembered to do this; others didn't, leaving their deck tanks full of fuel or fumes, and explosive either way.*

Within two hours, launch 192 was a flaming wreck, drifting out of control across the intended line of attack of the *Campbeltown* and its flotilla. Burn had one chance to get ashore, when the bow of his launch hit a breakwater jutting into the Loire estuary. The breakwater was a short distance upstream of the main entrance to the port, perpendicular to the current and wide enough to drive a tank onto. It was known as the Old Mole, and it was not where 192 was meant to be. Burn jumped, and nearly drowned, dragged under by his pack. Another commando jumped with him – a lance corporal named Arthur Young who'd volunteered for special service from the Gordon Highlanders. Young landed awkwardly and broke his foot, but at least he was on hard ground. He had fetched up at the bottom of a flight of steps on the seaward side of the mole. From there he managed to reach forward far enough to grab Burn's arm and pull him in against a wicked tide. Above them, German soldiers were spraying the launch and the water around it with machine gun fire. Burn and Young saw another member of their group drift by, face down on the water. Burn recognized it as the body of a friend.

---

* The launches were equipped with petrol engines because of a critical shortage of diesel ones, but petrol fumes are impossible to eliminate and heavier than air. Even without the deck tanks, the risk of an invisible explosive cloud enveloping the launches was ever-present.

'What do we do?' Young asked.

Burn said they had to leave him, but Young couldn't move. So he left them both and ran up the steps. At the top he beat a German soldier insensible with the handle of his Colt 45 and disappeared into the night.

The scene he left behind was a turkey shoot; a massacre, foreseeable and foreseen. For most of the past eighty years the question asked of the raid on St Nazaire has been 'how?' – how did it play out as it did against such daunting odds? – and much of the reason for this approach to the story is that it ends with a bang; a finale that has encouraged propagandists and historians to call it a win for the raiders, and even a strategic turning point. In many ways it was a disaster, and a better question to ask now is Tennyson's. In a word, 'why?'

Ahead of Micky Burn as he ran off the mole into old St Nazaire, on the far side of a basin the size of several football pitches lay the U-boat pens. They were the refuge of submarines that were strangling Britain to death, but they were not his target, not least because they were impregnable. Nothing the Allies could drop on their massive concrete roofs had made the slightest impression, or would for the rest of the war. And if Bomber Command couldn't destroy the pens, the thinking was that a few commandos wouldn't have much chance either. The dock that it was Burn's mission to attack lay elsewhere, on the other side of the basin, separated from it by a tongue of land covered with warehouses that would give him cover from searchlights if he could get into their shadows.

The Forme Écluse Joubert, also known as the Normandie Dock, was built for the construction of the *Normandie*, the greatest transAtlantic liner of her age. From the air it looks like an enormous salt-water lido. Up close, when emptied out, it's a void deep enough to give you vertigo and long enough for the world's largest cruise ships. Its gates – one at each end – are colossal feats of engineering in their own right: both the size of a large building on its side, rolling in and out of concrete slots on rails.

Tibbits's task was to destroy the southern gate, and for this he packed the *Campbeltown* with Amatol. Burn's was to help immobilize the northern one. Both tasks were close to suicidal, but Churchill had no doubt that the risks were worth it.

Simply by existing, the *Tirpitz* had become an obsession for the Prime Minister and his strategists. Her sister ship, the *Bismarck*, had helped to sink the British heavy cruiser HMS *Hood* with the loss of 1,418 men in May 1941 before being sunk herself later that month. The *Tirpitz* was her resurrection. Her wardroom had a grand piano and space for forty senior officers to dine in art deco splendour. Her engines consumed 60 tonnes of fuel a day *just to keep the lights on*. Above decks she menaced everything within a twenty-two-mile radius with eight guns that fired shells weighing a ton apiece. She was a sea monster who transfixed the Admiralty with every turn of her enormous screws, even though they never took her very far.

'The destruction or even the crippling of this ship is the greatest event at sea at the present time,' Churchill wrote to his Chiefs of Staff in January 1942. 'No other target is comparable to it.'

The public rationale for the raid on St Nazaire was to deny the *Tirpitz* a repair dock on the Atlantic coast and thereby prevent her attacking Allied convoys from America. In reality the chances of the *Tirpitz* ever venturing into the Atlantic were already slim. By March 1942 Hitler had decided not to let his last battleship stray far from Norway, where he believed the outcome of Germany's confrontation with Britain – at the very least – would be decided. 'Norway is the place where our destiny in this war will be played out,' he told his most senior admiral in mid-January. 'I demand unconditional compliance with my orders concerning the defence of this territory.'

In London, those who needed a strategic imperative for the St Nazaire raid were told it was the *Tirpitz*. Ever since, in the same way, those who have needed an explanation for loved ones lost or fathers killed before they met their children can say it was the

Tirpitz – but in reality that was no more than a shorthand. There was a deeper reason for the raid on St Nazaire; less specific but even more urgent. The real reason was that Britain was losing the war and desperate to show it could still fight.

On 27 March, the day before the raid, the U-boat pens that Burn could see across the basin had been bustling with activity. From the Arctic, Kapitänleutnant Joachim Berger and the crew of U-87 had arrived in the early afternoon after a long cruise defending the Norwegian coast. Half an hour later Kapitänleutnant Victor Vogel returned after forty-four days' hunting and sinking Allied shipping in the western Atlantic. Vogel had only four months to live – his submarine would be sunk with all hands by a Canadian corvette in July – but for now he and Berger were flesh-and-blood heroes of the Reich. To welcome them home Vice-Admiral Karl Dönitz, commander of all the Nazis' submarine forces, had made a special trip to St Nazaire from his headquarters on the Baltic.

In pictures taken that afternoon Vogel stands out on his conning tower in a white peaked cap. His arrival brought the total number of U-boat captains in St Nazaire to nine, since seven more submarines of the 7th U-boat Flotilla were already in the pens being prepared for their next missions. One was U-96, commanded by Heinrich Lehmann-Willenbroch, who'd returned from American waters the previous Monday, 23 March, having sunk four ships and damaged two beyond repair in the space of three weeks. It was no more than was expected of him. In five earlier missions Lehmann-Willenbroch had sent twenty more Allied freighters and tankers to the bottom. He was the true star of the 7th flotilla, greeted on his return to St Nazaire by cheering lines of maintenance workers, nurses, telegraphists, fellow submariners and schoolgirls waving posies. He would survive the war, to be portrayed much later by Jürgen Prochnow in the film *Das Boot*.

On the evening of the 27th Dönitz held a dinner in his captains' honour at a hotel a few miles up the coast. They spoke of absent comrades, including three more captains who had left St Nazaire for the hunting grounds of the US eastern seabord during the previous week. Although Dönitz would send submarines to Norway when ordered, he strongly believed in concentrating on the western Atlantic while shipping there was still virtually undefended. His strategy seemed to be paying off, though he was not complacent. As the food was cleared away, he asked the flotilla's commanding officer, Herbert Sohler, what he'd do if the British came to St Nazaire. Sohler had known Dönitz for many years, having first served under him in 1934. He was fiercely proud of his flotilla and had named its base the Prienheim after Günther Prien, one of its first heroes. In the second month of the war, Prien had sneaked into the Royal Navy's northern refuge at Scapa Flow, in the Orkneys, and sunk the battleship HMS *Royal Oak* with seven torpedoes fired at the dead of night. His crew didn't like him but they feared him, and they said he resembled a bull when hunched over chart tables or grasping the handles of his periscope. He was killed in 1941, but in his memory the flotilla adopted a snorting bull as its emblem, and Sohler practically snorted at the idea of a British attack on St Nazaire. It was inconceivable, he said.

'All our specialists have reached the same conclusion. The only approach deep enough to reach the port passes close to the north side of the estuary where the old battery has been reinforced by our own coastal artillery troops.'

That battery was one of more than thirty trained on the approach from both sides of the estuary, Sohler continued. In the unlikely event of an attack there was a plan in place to evacuate all the U-boat crews at a moment's notice and to destroy the submarines themselves.

Dönitz advised Sohler not to be so sanguine, and retired to bed.

It was entirely reasonable to think the British would not attack somewhere so heavily defended, but they attacked nonetheless – and in a small way it was thanks to Micky Burn.

★

In his previous life as a reporter Burn had been a protégé of Geoffrey Dawson, editor of *The Times*. Dawson is remembered nowadays mainly as an appeaser, but once Britain was in the war he favoured winning it. In mid-1940 Burn was beginning to feel guilty about spending all his time training with the Independent Companies, forerunners of the Commandos, rather than fighting. 'We began to hear the word Commandos,' he wrote, but traditionalists at the top of the armed forces seemed to be dragging their feet over approving any new sort of special force. Even the use of the word 'commando' prompted 'a farrago of reasonable misgivings, stale bigotries and personal jealousies', he wrote. So he made an appointment to see Dawson in his office on Printing House Square. His aim was simple: get *The Times'* support for using commandos in meaningful military actions.

They met on the morning of 20 August. That day Dawson went on to lunch at 10 Downing Street with Churchill and the Archbishop of Canterbury. Dawson noted in his diary that the talk had turned to commandos at both meetings. Five days later Churchill wrote to his Secretary of State for War to insist on the recruitment of 5,000 paratroopers and 5,000 more elite soldiers 'capable of lightning action'. That was one thread in many leading to the raid on St Nazaire. A second was a handwritten letter Churchill received from Stalin the following year, begging him to open a second front. A third was Churchill's personal fondness for raiding ever since the First World War. Then, as Minister of Munitions and a former First Lord of the Admiralty, he called the amphibious raid on the Belgian port of Zeebrugge 'the most intrepid and heroic single armed venture of the great war'. Now, as Prime Minister, raiding was one of the few options left to him.

Because the truth is, nothing else was working. Britain had tried all the conventional responses to Hitler's aggressions and had been humiliated. France fell in six weeks to the Wehrmacht in the spring and early summer of 1940. The evacuation of the British Expeditionary Force from the beaches of Dunkirk looked gutsy at the time and inspirational with hindsight – but it was still a pell-mell retreat. In April Britain sent another expeditionary force to Norway to see if it could put up more resistance there. It couldn't. The following spring Greece fell to a combined German–Italian force. British and Greek troops hoped they would be able to withstand the airborne invasion of Crete by massed paratroopers. But no.

In 1941 pin-prick commando raids on the French and Norwegian coasts – carefully filmed by Pathé – boosted morale even if they barely altered the Axis–Allied balance. That balance was determined by grander concerns. The Japanese attack on Pearl Harbor on 7 December brought the US into the war, but it would be years before American smelters turned out enough steel and aluminium to drive the German army from Western Europe. In the meantime Rommel had the Allied Eighth Army in full retreat in Libya, and Japanese forces were sweeping through South-East Asia. They were converging on Singapore, the island outpost that for more than a century had served as proof that British ships and men in shorts could rule the world's oceans and dominate its commerce.

Singapore's place in the British imperial world view was front and centre. Few Royal Navy officers had not stepped ashore there in brilliant ceremonial white at some point in their careers. Churchill no more wanted to give it up than his twenty-first-century successors want to give up Scotland. In a terrifying memo to his Commander-in-Chief in Delhi, dated 10 February 1942, he wrote that since British and Australian forces on the island should outnumber the advancing Japanese, there must 'be no thought of saving the troops or sparing the population'.

Churchill continued: 'The battle must be fought to the bitter end at all costs . . . Commanders and senior officers should die with their troops. The honour of the British Empire and of the British Army is at stake. I rely on you to show no mercy to weakness in any form.'

The unlucky Commander-in-Chief, Archibald Wavell, replied that he'd passed on the PM's sentiments to the general in charge of Singapore's defence, but that morale was 'not good'; training to counter the Japanese troops' ruthless jungle warfare techniques was insufficient; and efforts to produce 'a more offensive spirit and optimistic outlook' had not been entirely successful. Singapore's defenders were suffering, he said, from an inferiority complex.

On 15 February 1942, Singapore fell to the invaders. The navy had lost its biggest base east of Gibraltar. The most important British staging post en route to Hong Kong was no longer British. Churchill said it was the largest capitulation in British history. Jack Webb, a lance corporal who served as a junior medic on the St Nazaire raid, called it an almost unbelievable disaster. And it was the second in a week.

Four days earlier, two German battlecruisers slipped through a British blockade at Brest and sailed up the English Channel in broad daylight, escaping to the safety of the Baltic. These were the *Gneisenau* and the *Scharnhorst*, almost as central to Hitler's naval strategy as the *Tirpitz*. They had been penned in at Brest for eleven months. To keep them there or sink them were considered vital tasks for the Royal Navy and RAF throughout this period and their 'Channel dash' seemed to represent a miserable failure on both counts. In purely strategic terms it was a German retreat from the Atlantic to home waters, but the headlines in London were awful. Even the generally supportive *Times* quoted Admiral Sir Roger Keyes – in bold capitals on its first page of news – calling it a humiliation for the navy. If Singapore had shown up an army that lacked fighting spirit, the escape of the battlecruisers showed up an air force and a navy – especially its Coastal Command – that were asleep on the job.

It was especially galling for the Honourable Michael Wynn.

On the night of the 27th, Micky (to his friends and family) was to be found bringing up the rear of the St Nazaire flotilla in what he reckoned was the fastest boat in the British navy. It was smaller and lighter than all the others in the raiding party, and it looked extremely odd. Two enormous torpedo tubes were mounted inelegantly on its forward deck. Below, it had five giant V8 petrol engines; three Packards and two Fords, delivering between them the thrust of five Spitfires. At full power Wynn's boat could plane at forty-five knots. At tick-over – on the Ford engines alone – she chugged along at five. At any speed in between, Motor Torpedo Boat 74 was almost impossible to control, making its orderly presence in the flotilla an accomplishment in itself. But the truth is it was never really supposed to be there at all, since Wynn had built it expressly to sink the battlecruisers at Brest, on a mission from which he did not expect it to return.

Wynn was a son of landed gentry with a boredom threshold so low that peace would have driven him crazy. War gave him a sense of purpose: it made putting one's life on the line an almost normal thing to do. Judging by his letters home, his chief preoccupations, apart from defeating Germany, were speed and girls. His father, an army colonel and Welsh baron, was devoted to his son but considered him a liability. When he first heard that Wynn Jr might have been involved in the St Nazaire operation – which was after it was over – he wrote to the parent of one of his son's girlfriends: 'If this is so, Miccy [sic] has committed [the] most serious offence it is possible for anyone in the services to have done, as by so doing he would have imperilled the lives of every single man in the expedition.'

Wynn's boat was largely of his own design. Her genesis, by his account, was a drunken guest night at a Royal Naval Volunteer Reserve officers' mess soon after he had become an officer in the Reserve himself. (His commission was a thank you from the Admiralty for service at Dunkirk, where he'd rescued five loads of soldiers off the beaches in a thirty-five-foot motor yacht borrowed from the Fleet Air Arm.)

That night in the mess, Wynn came up with an idea for destroying the *Gneisenau* and the *Scharnhorst*. He would approach them at night in a rowing boat and drop a depth charge underneath their hulls. He was not proposing to row all the way across the Channel but to be deposited at the mouth of the harbour by a submarine.

In the cold light of day the idea still seemed to Wynn worth presenting to the Admiralty. He put it in writing and to his surprise was summoned to explain it. Asked if he was serious, the young sub-lieutenant said he was indeed, if his superiors thought it might help sink the ships. They told him to think about it over lunch. He did so, with a friend and a 'very strong whisky', and went back and confirmed he was ready to give it a go.

'Well, good luck to you,' the navy brass said. 'Go down to Commander-in-Chief Plymouth and everything will be put at your disposal.' So off Wynn went.

The fact that the Admiralty gave Wynn the time of day says much about the society into which he'd been born, and the state of its war effort. He had no formal naval training. He was not a technical genius, nor especially athletic. But he had had an expensive education, excellent connections in Whitehall and the forces, and a birthright to 20,000 acres in Snowdonia. As important were his patriotism, his appetite for adventure and what seemed in a concrete sense to be a suicidal sort of courage. In the winter of 1941–2 that was more than enough to get a young man into the fray – but it was not enough to sink a battlecruiser.

From a long way above the waterline to a long way below, the *Scharnhorst* and the *Gneisenau* had broad belts of steel armour-plating more than a foot thick, running most of the length of their hulls. A depth charge heaved over the side of a rowing skiff might have done some serious damage even so – the charges were designed to break a ship's keel and open a void beneath it into which the vessel would collapse. But it was a long-odds proposition.

Down at the Devonport naval dockyard (which would also play a vital role in the raid on St Nazaire), Wynn was told he needed a bigger boat and a bigger charge. 'So we went from a rowing boat to a speedboat and a speedboat to a bigger speedboat, and then we went on to a pre-war torpedo boat with one torpedo tube,' he said. But one torpedo was not enough for two gigantic ships. Eventually he was entrusted with a high-speed Vosper torpedo boat on which he mounted two forward-facing torpedoes designed to leap 150 feet before they hit the water. The leap was powered by compressed air. It would come in handy, Wynn hoped, for surmounting the three protective booms that surrounded the battlecruisers.

Even then there was a catch: once submerged, Wynn's torpedoes wouldn't travel far. He said after the war that most of their propulsion equipment had been removed and replaced with extra explosive to have a better chance of penetrating the armour plating. This meant he would have to get very close to his target.

It was obvious, he wrote, that in most circumstances 'we would ultimately be blown up with our weapons if we were to achieve our objective'. The idea was to sacrifice the torpedo boat and somehow find another vessel on which to get home, but everyone involved knew they would have to be exceedingly lucky to pull it off.

On the night of 10 February, Wynn and his crew staged a practice run across the Channel to the mouth of the harbour at Brest. Undetected, they turned around and got back to home waters on the misty morning of the 11th. They turned on the ship's wireless for the eight o'clock news and learned that the *Scharnhorst* and the *Gneisenau* had that night slipped their moorings and were already halfway up the Channel. They had, in a strange way, saved Wynn's life, but they had also left him with a wildly overpowered boat in search of a new mission. And they had humiliated the Royal Navy in the eyes of a public conditioned to think of it as invincible.

The state of the war for Britain was now desperate. If it hadn't been, the raid on St Nazaire might never have been approved. As it was, Churchill did what he always did when cornered: he resolved to attack. He promised Roosevelt more raids and reshuffled his

Combined Operations staff to make them happen. They in turn demanded an updated list of targets the length of Europe's Atlantic coast. St Nazaire had been considered the previous autumn and rejected as too dangerous. Now it was reinstated, and Captain John Hughes-Hallett, Naval Adviser at Combined Operations HQ, put the word out that he needed a 'really first-class man' to lead the raid. He was offered Captain Robert Ryder, who by 11.30 on the night of 27 March was on the bridge of Motor Gunboat 314 at the front of the flotilla.

'Ryder could do everything.'

That was the abiding impression of a younger man (Jason Beattie, grandson of the captain of HMS *Campbeltown*) who met him after the war. And in a *Boy's Own* sense it was true. Ryder could sail. He could navigate by the stars. He could paint. He could endure. After the war he became a Conservative Member of Parliament and set up a chain of corner shops. Throughout, he proved a capable leader, not so much by inspiration as by example. He could be the straight man for other people's jokes but he could also be straightforwardly dour. He disliked being the centre of attention but did much to attract it. In particular he had extensive experience of getting sunk.

Ryder's first appearance in the respectable British press was triumphant. He was the self-appointed skipper of a forty-five-foot ketch that starred much later alongside Stellan Skarsgård and Pierce Brosnan in the film version of *Mamma Mia*. Ryder commissioned her from a Mr Cock of the Hong Kong and Whampoa Dock Company in 1932. Harold Rouse of the Royal Hong Kong Yacht Club was consulted on design. Ryder's plan was to sail home from Hong Kong, where he and four other young naval officers had been enjoying the inter-war party scene and occasional low-risk reconnaissance forays into the South China Sea.

Many junior lieutenants had had similar ideas. None had won the Admiralty's blessing, but there was something purposeful and unusual about young Ryder's proposal: he intended to sail back the 'wrong' way, via Japan, the Kurile Islands and Alaska. They would use the Panama Canal rather than the Suez. Their home stretch would be via Nassau and Bermuda. The early legs, island-hopping up the western Pacific, seemed to offer scope for some old-fashioned spying in waters almost never visited by the Royal Navy. The Admiralty gave Ryder the nod.

In the autumn of 1932 one of Ryder's crew members, Martyn Sherwood, placed an ad in the *South China Morning Post*: 'Gentleman requires cooking lessons, evenings four to six.' He was taught by the Swiss chef of the Peninsula Hotel, and food aboard the *Tai-Mo-Shan* – for that was the yacht's name, borrowed from Hong Kong's highest mountain – was said to be exceptional.

She sailed on 31 May 1933. In the end she didn't do much spying. Her crew was waited on by geisha girls in Yokohama and granted an audience by an amused Bette Davis in Hollywood. Their voyage was written up as an evolving adventure story by reporters from Acapulco to Dartmouth, where they were welcomed home after a year at sea by hundreds of small boats and a telegram from the King.

Shore leave had been plentiful. Ryder fell hard for four different women on that voyage (one of them married) and he would spend long hours on later journeys brooding over whom to marry. In truth he was probably never happier than on watch, alone with nature, in the cockpit of the *Tai-Mo-Shan*. He dreaded the idea of a desk job and was thrilled on arrival in Dartmouth to be told he'd been chosen from a field of 200 to captain an expedition vessel to the Antarctic. The expedition filled the next three years and won him the Polar Medal. If he ever feared death with the coming of war, no one could say he hadn't lived.

His seamanship was reckless, at least by the standards of captains who advance by not making mistakes. On one occasion he anchored the *Tai-Mo-Shan* off a lee shore in the Bahamas. A storm blew up and stranded the yacht on a beach for a fortnight before

she could be floated off by good Samaritans. On another, Ryder
nearly smashed into a much sleeker racing yacht while being
blown out of control across Nassau harbour.

Ryder's first naval command in the war was of a Q ship, a heavily armed troop ship disguised as a freighter and tasked with luring
submarines to the surface, where they could be destroyed. Her
name was HMS *Willamette Valley* and she was sunk by a German
submarine with three quarters of her crew in June 1940. The only
survivors apart from Ryder himself were a group of crew members assigned the role of 'panic party'. Dressed mainly – and almost
unbelievably – as Greek women, their job was to scramble into
lifeboats to fool the submarine into thinking the captain had
abandoned ship. According to his biography, Ryder managed to
grab a lifebuoy as the ship went down. Another account says it
was a floating card table. Whatever it was, it kept him afloat in a
patch of oil that nearly blinded him. In all he spent four days adrift,
alone, 300 miles off the south-west coast of Ireland.

He suffered horribly, not just from the oil but from exposure
and thirst. But he was lucky. He was picked up by the last tanker
in the last convoy to be routed to the south of Ireland before they
were given more northerly routes for their own safety.

By chance, the senior officer in the panic party, an acting lieutenant in the RNVR called Bill Tillie, knew Ryder almost
intimately: he served as his secretary on the *Willamette Valley*, and
saw his mail. By another coincidence, Tillie went on to command
one of the motor launches in the raid on St Nazaire. Ryder was, he
said, 'a completely and utterly outstanding man . . ., immensely
brave'. He was austere by nature 'but by Jingo there wasn't a single
man out there who wouldn't have volunteered to do anything
again with him'.

Tillie saw Ryder's private side. While chasing U-boats between
naval bases on both sides of the Atlantic he was also trying to sustain a long-distance relationship with a fiancée called Frances
Woods. Woods was unhappy with the arrangement. 'She was

being very difficult in some of these letters,' Tillie remembered. 'He'd grab them, tear them open . . . and he was in a frightfully bad mood for about ten days until the next letter arrived, and he was more cheerful then.'

There may have been another reason for Ryder's moods. His beloved older brother, Lisle, was missing. Ryder did not know it yet but a month before the *Willamette Valley* went down, Lisle had been executed by the SS along with ninety other members of his regiment in a field behind the beaches at Dunkirk.

Lisle's death was not confirmed for many months. Even so, there was much for Ryder to reflect on as he recuperated from the sinking of his Q ship. He did not like to dwell on loss or risk or what might have been, but the waste of life on the Q ships project (a doomed revival of a First World War experiment) troubled many who survived it. 'How could they have been so bloody stupid?' Tillie asked later, infuriated that the Admiralty took so long to admit that the U-boat captains could see the traps being laid for them the moment they raised their periscopes.

At least Ryder could recover in comfort. He was the guest of Admiral Sir Reginald Plunkett-Ernle-Erle-Drax, Commander-in-Chief of the navy's West Indies station. They had met in Bermuda, where the admiral was still posted – but Lady Drax was at the family home in Dorset and so were their two teenage daughters, who fussed over their sunburnt visitor for several weeks. Ryder took a shine to the younger of them (he had dumped Woods by this time), but the war's relentless momentum swept him on to the command of HMS *Prince Philippe*, a converted Belgian ferry.

On 15 July 1941 the *Prince Philippe* collided with not one but two other ships in the space of less than two hours in the strait between Scotland and Northern Ireland. There was fog, but no excuse. Ryder's next job was behind a dreaded desk. And it was from this desk that he was relieved to be summoned seven months later to an urgent but unexplained meeting at Combined Operations HQ on Richmond Terrace.

He was late.

'I thought it was just going to be an ordinary low-power meeting,' he said years later. 'But when I went into the room I could see at once that I was confronted with a formidable array of senior officers with a good deal of gold lace about.'

Ryder sat down at the back of the room. He saw his name on the agenda as the suggested naval force commander of an operation about which so far he knew nothing.

'Is that all right, Ryder?'

It was the famously strangulated voice of the man chairing the meeting, Lord Louis Francis Albert Victor Nicholas Mountbatten, great-grandson of Queen Victoria, future Admiral of the Fleet.

The date was 26 February 1942. Mountbatten knew as well as anyone that the raid as then proposed would be a death sentence for many of those involved. This didn't diminish his enthusiasm for it one bit. Mountbatten was a cheerful soul, but he was of one mind with Churchill about the need for sacrifice to win the war.

He felt its defeats personally. In particular, he was more affected than most by the escape of the *Scharnhorst* and the *Gneisenau*, because something uncannily similar had occurred in 1914 when he was a naval cadet. Two German cruisers, the *Goeben* and the *Breslau*, gave the Royal Navy's Mediterranean fleet the slip a few days after the outbreak of the First World War. They escaped to Constantinople through the Dardanelles. This minor setback would not have troubled most thirteen-year-olds, but Mountbatten's father was First Sea Lord at the time. Worse, he was part German and was being blamed for the escape in the press. The navy stood behind him but he resigned anyway. Mountbatten's burning ambition from that moment was to avenge his father by becoming First Sea Lord himself. And that ambition, combined with an unsentimental acceptance that victory would come only at terrible human cost, meant that Combined Operations was going to be busy on his watch.

Anyone who had worked for Mountbatten before knew this already. Dickie, as he was known to friends, was rich and glamorous, but above all he was driven. As commander of a flotilla of destroyers early in the war he pushed his crew to the limit of their endurance in the hunt for U-boats in the Mediterranean. Half of them drowned when his ship, HMS *Kelly*, was sunk by the Luftwaffe off Crete in May 1941. Mountbatten came up singing 'Roll Out the Barrel' and insisting that the other half join in.

He was offered a cruiser next. He held out for an aircraft carrier, and got one. It was being fitted out in Norfolk, Virginia, so he flew there to inspect it (calling in on President Roosevelt on his way down to Chesapeake Bay). But he barely had time to sniff the carrier's decks before being recalled to London to take charge of Combined Operations – in other words, of raids.

To traditionalists the new job was not obviously a promotion; nor was it obvious that he deserved one. Admiral Andrew Cunningham, Commander-in-Chief of the Mediterranean Fleet, lavished praise on Mountbatten to his face after the sinking of the *Kelly* but said moments later to another junior captain: 'The trouble with your flotilla, boy, is that it was thoroughly badly led.'

As for Combined Operations, the navy high command saw it as a faddish irrelevance. The army tried to argue that raiding was its responsibility because the Channel was really a no-man's-land between two giant land-based forces. But Churchill was adamant: Dickie's star was rising and his role was of critical importance. It had two parts: to plan for the eventual invasion of France and to 'be offensive'. At Chequers, the Prime Minister's country residence, Churchill told Mountbatten in October 1941: 'You are to give no thought to the defensive. Your whole intention is to be concentrated on the offensive. Train for the offensive. Work at a craft, the equipment, the tactics, the administration and everything else needed to initiate and sustain the offensive.'

These were the words from on high that set in train the decisions leading to the raid on St Nazaire. Churchill did have the *Tirpitz* on his mind, but he had much else too. He had to convince the British that they could still fight and win. He had to convince the American public that Europe's war would inevitably be theirs too. Perhaps most urgently he had to convince Stalin, whose country was being overrun by three million German soldiers and the biggest tank force in history, that he was serious about a second front. For now, urging Dickie to be offensive was the best he could do.

Mountbatten got the message. On 19 February, John Hughes-Hallett, his Naval Adviser, came to him concerned that the St Nazaire plan was starting to look overly dependent on wooden motor boats with explosive fuel and outdated weapons.

'We could lose every man,' Hughes-Hallett said.

Mountbatten shrugged.

'I'm afraid you're right, but if they do the job we've got to accept that.'

It was a week later that Mountbatten breezily asked Ryder — who was by now married to a beautiful vicar's daughter he'd met in a Bagshot nightclub — if taking command of the naval portion of this raid would be 'all right'.

Ryder said it would.

2.   Preparation

The shell that hit launch 192 at 1.30 a.m. on 28 March probably came from a gun that should have been pointing at the sky. Instead it was pointing at the river, and this spelled disaster.

An essential part of the plan for the raid was an air attack by RAF bombers to distract attention from the boats, but the air raid failed. The flak guns were dual purpose. They could be lowered in seconds, and they lit up the boats like torches. Churchill was furious when he heard what had happened, and he apologized personally after the war. Why it happened is a question that reaches back into the memories of affronted military men with turf to defend and upstarts to put in their places. The short answer to the question, though, is simply that the best-laid plans go wrong, especially in war, especially when the clock is ticking.

For Ryder it started ticking at the Combined Operations meeting in Richmond House on 26 February. As the meeting wound down he asked the person sitting next to him: 'Where the hell is this place?'

'Didn't they tell you? It's St Nazaire.'

Ryder's spirits soared. He felt his whole career had been building to this point. His neighbour was practically beside himself with excitement too. The two men hadn't been properly introduced, but this was Lieutenant Colonel Charles Newman of the Essex Regiment of infantry, commanding officer of 2 Commando. When finally allowed to brief subordinates on the plan of attack he called it 'the sauciest thing since Drake'. He was a civil engineer by training and an army reservist answering his country's call. There was not an ounce of Sandhurst in him. One young officer who served under him said he looked a bit like an old elephant, 'with cauliflower ears and a great big nose'. Never without a pipe, he was genial, avuncular, hungry for action and to all outward appearances impervious to fear. He was thirty-seven, married with one daughter. By some miracle he would live to have three more.

Newman would lead the assault troops on the raid: the demolition experts and those deputed to protect them as they strapped explosive charges to St Nazaire's strategic ironmongery. He and Ryder were not so much chalk and cheese as bread and butter. They got on. Except at one critical point in the heat of battle, they seemed to find it impossible to disagree. 'They were solid gold,' said Brigadier Charles Haydon, mastermind of the commando project; 'each in his own way a model of the finest type of English gentleman.' (Newman played the jazz piano too.)

In a sense the Germans were ready for them: in the Wehrmacht's war directive number 40, coastal commanders were warned that 'political considerations may lead the Allies to take decisions which, from a purely military perspective, may seem absurd . . . Coastal assets valuable to the war economy will be tempting targets for surprise attack. Because clever camouflage and overcast conditions may give the enemy scope for surprise attack, all units which may be exposed to such actions must be constantly on alert and ready to counter-attack.'

The only place on the Atlantic seaboard that the occupying forces were reasonably confident would *not* be attacked was St Nazaire. As Herbert Sohler reminded his sceptical commander on the night of the raid, the approach from the sea was a gauntlet of heavy artillery. The only dredged channel ran close to the biggest guns. And 10,000 troops could be summoned within minutes to the port's defence.

Mountbatten liked to say – before and after the event – it was the fact that it was considered impossible that made it possible. And the Germans were of course right to think no sensible adversary would attack St Nazaire. Their mistake was to think sensible was any part of the Churchill–Mountbatten mindset. More pressing factors were desperation, hubris, blind courage and sheer mischief. Mountbatten especially felt a compulsion to experiment and defy the odds; to do the undoable because they said it couldn't be done.

In early 1942 he was distracted by the filming of *In Which We Serve*, the patriotic Noël Coward hit about his captaincy of the *Kelly*. But he made time for everything by working fourteen-hour days, and he brought a new can-do intensity to Combined Operations. He hired new people with no regard to cost or office space. In the six months from October 1941 the headcount at his HQ on Richmond Terrace rose from a few dozen to 400. The influx included a new cadre of specialists, many of whom had one thing in common. They were Mountbatten's chums.

Society was already well acquainted with Pedro Mones, the Marqués de Casa Maury. He was a snooty-looking racing driver and founder of the Curzon cinema chain. Now Churchill's war machine would get to know him as Mountbatten's intelligence chief. Robert Henriques, the novelist, was hired as a military adviser. Harold Wernher, who'd married into exiled Russian aristocracy, came aboard to do logistics. In fairness, they acquitted themselves well, but the new operation was still mocked by those who wouldn't have minded seeing it stumble (Lord Lovat called it HMS *Wimbledon* – 'all rackets and balls'). It depended heavily on a few solid professionals.

Hughes-Hallett was one of these. He was a keen cyclist and intellect who'd joined Combined Operations from the navy in December. When Mountbatten passed on Churchill's instructions to increase the number of raids, Hughes-Hallett proposed one a month till August. Targets included Dieppe (twice), Bruneval (a radar station on the Cherbourg peninsula), St Nazaire, and Alderney in the Channel Islands. The most important thing about them was that they had to be within reach and susceptible to stealth attack.

'We were not so much concerned at this stage in the intrinsic value of objectives on a particular raid, but rather with the feasibility of reaching the place undetected,' Hughes-Hallett wrote after the war. Going out of his way to torpedo the conventional justification for the St Nazaire raid, he continued: 'It has frequently been asserted that St Nazaire was chosen because of its great dock – the only place where the *Tirpitz* could be docked on the Atlantic coast. In fact this is not so. We first chose St Nazaire because we wanted to surprise the Germans by one or two raids on the Atlantic coast. St Nazaire happened to be the most distant objective which could be reached by a raiding force with only one daylight period on the voyage. We thought that with luck and careful timing the force might get there unobserved . . .'

Hughes-Hallett claimed to have spotted 'a fatal defect' in St Nazaire's defences. This was the fact that the wide, shallow waters of the Loire's outer estuary might allow an approaching force to avoid all but one of the coastal artillery batteries, providing it could get across the shallows without running aground.

From the start Hughes-Hallett favoured using a suicide destroyer as the spear-tip of the mission. The idea was that it would be big and strong enough to withstand incoming ordnance as it approached its target, while riding just high enough in the water to clear the sandbars in the estuary.

A plan had been drawn up the previous year. Now it was dusted off. It depended on three things: finding at least one expendable destroyer; finding someone to make the destroyer look German; and, crucially, finding someone to turn it into a bomb.

Elmslie Green found him first. She was fourteen at the time, confident and athletic. She had brown hair, broad shoulders, and a proud and penetrating stare.

Elmslie played tennis for Hampshire. It was at a tennis match that she first met Nigel Tibbits and he wasn't much good at it (she was better than him at squash as well). She found him boring, but they were both from old Winchester families and they kept bumping into each other as they grew up and became more interesting.

Around 1935, aged twenty-three, Elmslie asked Nigel to marry her and he said yes. Socially, it was a good match; he was naval royalty, the son of an admiral. Financially, Elmslie was taking a risk. For generations there had been money in her family – from sugar in Mauritius on her father's side and a lucrative Canadian sinecure on her mother's. Also, further back, a little state-sanctioned piracy; besides fighting at Trafalgar, Elmslie's great-grandfather did some privateering in the Mediterranean during the Napoleonic Wars. But in Nigel's family, for all the brocade, there was not much in the way of wealth.

It didn't matter. By now they were besotted, writing to each other several times a day if they were apart, in a language all their own. The past forms of think, drink and stink were fence, drench and stench, and Nigel threw in cryptic hieroglyphics for good measure: 'I am,' he reminded her, 'your $\bigcirc$'al fiancé.'

'I think she completely adored my father,' their son said eighty-five years later. 'And I think the feeling was entirely mutual.'

By then Nigel was a lieutenant in the navy. He may have been poor by aristocratic standards but the world was his oyster, and it certainly held no fear for Elmslie. When he was posted to China to patrol the Yangtze River in a gunboat (HMS *Gannet*), she booked passage to join him there. The journey took thirty-four days but was no real hardship. Her mother, who was something of a snob, paid for her to travel first class on the luxurious new SS *Scharnhorst* of the Norddeutscher Lloyd line (a steamship, not to be confused with the battlecruiser later stuck in Brest).

Installed in a hotel in Shanghai, Elmslie employed runners to carry messages to and from the *Gannet*. Shore life was a whirl of sightseeing tours and cocktail parties interrupted by occasional air raids, as Chiang Kai-shek's war with the Communists gathered pace. Elmslie and Nigel were married in Shanghai cathedral and not long afterwards, pregnant with their son, Elmslie set off back to England via Hanoi.

Nigel had to stay with the *Gannet*. Letters between them now took a month to arrive, taking the overland route along the Trans-Siberian railway. In one, Elmslie warned Lieutenant Tibbits that his father was 'concerned about the amount of drinking you are doing'. The admiral needn't have worried. From the very start Nigel was an exemplary young officer. He had passed out top of his class from Dartmouth Royal Naval College, won a prized mid-shipman's position on the battleship *Nelson* and immediately found himself being mentored by senior officers who were themselves on the fast track for promotion. On page 1 of his immaculate mid-shipman's log he notes being instructed in gunnery on 8 September 1930 by a 'Lieutenant Commander [John] Hughes-Hallett'.

When the time came to assign someone the task of packing the *Campbeltown* full of explosives, Tibbits was the name suggested by the navy's Director of Torpedoes and Mining, and Hughes-Hallett accepted at once.

Finding a destroyer to blow up was less straightforward. The first plan for an attack on St Nazaire had been vetoed the previous October by Sir Charles Forbes, Commander-in-Chief, Plymouth Command. This version was too ambitious for its own good. It targeted the U-boat pens as well as the Normandie Dock, and Forbes didn't rate its chances. Second time around, he was not much more impressed with the idea of sacrificing a ship on the dock's southern gate.

Forbes was on the glide slope to retirement after a grand career spanning the First World War – Gallipoli, Jutland – and the imperial zenith of the 1930s. He was acutely aware of how far he outranked Mountbatten, which may be why Mountbatten so enjoyed telling the story of Forbes's role in the meeting of 26 February at which Newman and Ryder's paths first crossed.

The scene – to recap – is Combined Operations HQ on Richmond Terrace, between Downing Street and the Thames. It's bursting by now with Mountbatten's oddball recruits. Mountbatten has put the revised attack plan to the Chiefs of Staff and Churchill, and they have approved it. Forbes's co-operation is now essential because only he can supply the boats, so he has been invited from his Devon fiefdom.

'He came up, a bit disgruntled to be summoned by a young captain who had served under him when he was Commander-in-Chief,' Mountbatten recalled. 'And I remember he started the meeting by saying, "Well, Dickie, old cock, if you're prepared to lose all your soldiers and all your ships, I suppose you can take on this task which I regard as absolutely impossible." I said, "Sir, before you go on making any further encouraging remarks, may I introduce you to the army force commander, Colonel Newman, and the naval force commander, Commander Ryder?"'

At this point Mountbatten turns to the two younger men. '"And I'd like to tell you two that in spite of what the Commander-in-Chief says . . . I personally think you'll succeed. I think you'll both come back, and if you do I'll put you both up for a Victoria Cross."'

That shut Forbes up (Hughes-Hallett said he even blushed). As for Newman and Ryder, they had little choice but to accept Mountbatten's view of their chances and get on with the job.

Ryder hadn't packed for the night. And so, deep in thought, he took an evening train back to Salisbury and told his wife what he could about his new assignment – which wasn't much. Next morning he cleared his desk at HQ Southern Command, at Wilton House, and went back up to London. He found it incredibly difficult to get anything done there. Despite the urgency and complexity of his task, 'No one seemed interested in getting me what I wanted,' he said later. 'All I could find was an antagonistic atmosphere between the Admiralty and Combined Operations.'

The latest version of the attack plan involved one destroyer, four motor launches, one torpedo boat and a gunboat with special navigation equipment. Hughes-Hallett liked it because the smaller vessels would be able to use the destroyer to shelter from the worst of the incoming ordnance. As Mountbatten said, the plan had been approved. March the 28th had been pencilled in for the attack as the night of a spring tide that would cover the shoals at the mouth of the Loire with twelve feet of water. By the end of January the *Campbeltown* had been provisionally earmarked as the sacrificial vessel – but that was not the same thing as handing Ryder the keys.

For a week Forbes dragged his feet. To this day it's not clear exactly why. He and their Lordships at the Admiralty were at pains to stress that warships were in short supply, but this wasn't true. The Royal Navy was 1,400 ships strong, including support ships and minor vessels. It was by far the biggest in the world, and this number didn't include ships like the *Campbeltown*, one of fifty First World War-vintage American destroyers handed over early in the war in return for US access to British naval bases in the Caribbean.

So Forbes had plenty of ships. In deciding to hold one back he may simply have been sulking, or he may have meant exactly what he said about the likely human cost of attacking St Nazaire. He knew the plan had been agreed but he may have been hoping that having been shelved once it could be shelved again and quietly forgotten.

It wasn't. Instead, Ryder and Newman called Forbes's bluff. Increasingly frustrated about not having their basic hardware needs met with less than a month to go, they told Hughes-Hallett they were thinking of mounting the whole operation with motor launches alone – no destroyer needed. Hughes-Hallett knew this would be suicidal.

'We pointed out that motor launches were made of wood and driven by petrol and the chances of achieving surprise with an armada of coastal craft were slim,' he wrote. 'And hence they would all most probably be blazing wrecks before they got along-side at all. Yet such was the deference paid to Newman and Ryder simply because they were going to do the job that they nearly got their way.'

This was Hughes-Hallett being wise after the event, but he was wise at the time, too. To prevent Newman and Ryder getting their way he went round them to Mounbatten, who went over Forbes's head to the Admiralty. He played the *Tirpitz* card, which was the ace of spades with navy people even though the *Tirpitz* wasn't going anywhere. He told them: no destroyer, no raid.

At last, on 3 March, the *Campbeltown* was ordered to sail from Portsmouth to Devonport for a makeover. Ryder followed her down there and was delighted to find people keen to help at last. One was Sam Beattie, an old friend from naval college, called up as captain of the *Campbeltown* for her last voyage. Even better, the refit was to be supervised by another friend from a pre-war stint on the battleship *Warspite*.

In nine days, a crew of expert metal workers would remove two of the *Campbeltown*'s four funnels, bevel the tops of the others in the style of a German Möwe-class torpedo boat and take out everything inside her – except food and drink – that was not essential for forward movement. They had two main goals: disguise and weight reduction. The *Campbeltown* needed to be as light as possible for speed and clearance – speed because she had to hit the dock hard, and clearance because her normal twelve-foot draught wouldn't get her over the sandbars in the outer estuary of the Loire, even with a high spring tide. Yet that is where she would be going to avoid the guns trained on the normal approach route – the dredged Charpentier Channel. A third goal was to give her maximum firepower consistent with a German-looking silhouette. So the Devonport workers removed her ancient 4-inch guns and replaced them with eight Swiss Oerlikon anti-aircraft guns on raised octagonal platforms. A beefier 4-pound 'pom-pom' gun was installed on the fo'c'sle. She wasn't supposed to fool anyone in broad daylight; the hope was that the disguise would make St Nazaire's gun crews hesitate when forced to make a split-second decision in the middle of the night.

Any German spies in Devonport would have had plenty more reasons to be suspicious of the *Campbeltown*. There was, for one thing, the fact of so much attention being paid to such an ancient ship. Her keel had been laid in 1918 3,000 miles away, far up the Kennebec River on the rugged Maine coast. The British were later a little rude about her handling, but at the time she was a fine example of American prowess in mass production and straight-line speed – one of five Wickes-class destroyers ordered by the US Navy from the Bath Iron Works with the idea that they would be ready for the First World War. The war ended before she was commissioned, but she was still built in a record time of twenty-seven weeks and she performed superbly. Initially named the USS *Buchanan* after the Confederate Civil War admiral Franklin Buchanan, she 'took to the chilly Kennebec on 2 January 1919 following a private launching ceremony which featured Mrs Charles P. Wetherbee as sponsor', the official historians of the Bath Iron Works record. 'A few weeks later, *Buchanan* flashed through her preliminary acceptance trials with ease, reaching a maximum speed of 35.7 knots.'

Mrs Wetherbee's husband, the dockyard's superintendent of engineering, would have been proud. Thirty-five knots is easily fast enough to pull a water-skier and an astonishing speed for a steel wedge displacing 1,260 tons of water. It was made possible by a pair of mighty steam turbines powered by boilers designed in France and made in America on terms personally negotiated by Wetherbee on a trip to Europe fifteen years earlier.

The *Buchanan* started life with four of these boilers. When she joined the Royal Navy (now technically a Town-class rather than a Wickes-class ship; one of a small group named after towns on both sides of the Atlantic), she had two of them removed to make room for more fuel for convoy protection duty. This meant a drastic loss of speed, and at Devonport she lost her lifeboats too. The glass was taken from the windows on her bridge. The windows were closed up into narrow slits. Splinter mats were positioned round the Oerlikons to protect against shrapnel, and steel plates were welded vertically to her decks amidships to create low protective walls. These were for the commandos, because the deck would be full of them. Operation Chariot – as it was now called for those who needed to know – was suffering from mission creep.

The plan to use just four motor launches had been rejected in favour of sixteen. Newman reckoned that if a job was worth doing it was worth doing well, and Ryder agreed. 'It was natural,' he wrote, 'that any attack contemplated on the port should also consider what damage could be done to the U-boat base.' The U-boat pens themselves were invulnerable. Nearly half a million cubic metres of concrete went into them, poured by German and East European work crews into mouldings for walls as thick as cars. Most of the construction was carried out in 1941 by the Todt Organization, which had grown into an engineering colossus over the course of the 1930s using forced labour to build autobahns and concentration camps. The Todt crews worked night and day, razing the quayside buildings of the Compagnie Générale Transatlantique and covering what had been open water with a brutalist Valhalla. They called it the U-Box and it was bomb-proof.

So the raiders had to go after something else. There was a diesel depot on the peninsula east of the great dock but it was half buried and heavily fortified, so they left that alone too. Instead they concentrated on lock gates and bridges – not just at either end of the dock but at each end of the basin facing the pens. Knock them out and you could render the basin tidal, forcing the U-boats to come and go at high tide only. But this meant nine extra demolition targets. That in turn meant more demolition crews, more assault troops to clear the way for them, more protection units to enable them to do their work, more commandos hitching a ride behind those steel panels on the *Campbeltown*, and more motor launches to bring them out. There would be 265 commandos and demolition men in all.

Newman was a planner. Beneath his genial exterior was a soldier who didn't like leaving things to chance. He divided the 265 into three groups: one to arrive on the *Campbeltown* and destroy pumps and winding gear around the dock; one arriving in the port column of motor launches to take care of bridges and lock gates round the Old Town; and one arriving in the starboard column to do the same for the man-made island covered with warehouses between the two. Each group was subdivided twice – not just into assault, demolition and protection units but into more than one of each in each group. And each sub-group had its own orders as to exactly where to go ashore, what to attack and where to re-embark for the journey home.

These orders were the product of long days of intense thinking and scribbling by Newman, locked in a room in Richmond House with his pipe and a detailed tabletop model of St Nazaire. In principle the orders took account of the fact that the raid would provoke a furious response from a numerically superior enemy: the first job for each group's assault teams was to establish defensive perimeters. In practice, for two of the three groups, Newman's plans were overtaken by events within seconds of launch 192 being hit.

At some level Newman must have known this would happen, but he wasn't going to let his future spoil his present. He envisaged a symphony of surgical sabotage. 'It must be definitively understood by parties detailed that the task to which they are allotted is of first priority and must be carried out before any other task is attempted,' he declared. In particular he told the demolition groups to 'do their blowing up before entertaining the idea of killing Huns'. His final operational orders, issued on 23 March, filled sixty-one typewritten pages. Every officer was expected to read and internalize them all. It is poignant now to think of him writing them, especially in view of a slow-motion fiasco unfolding at the same time and largely out of his control.

From his earliest days at Combined Operations, Mountbatten had insisted there could be no seaborne raid on St Nazaire without a diversionary raid from the air. But it turned out insisting was not enough. The idea, based on a successful joint effort with the RAF in Norway the previous October, was to distract the Germans' coastal artillery crews and where possible get them to point their weapons up rather than out over the estuary. The air raid would have to be a bombing raid since St Nazaire was too far away for fighters, and in any case there was not much fighters could do as decoys; on their own, they would merely have aroused suspicion. So Mountbatten depended on the RAF's Bomber Command for aircraft as he did on Forbes for ships. But Bomber Command was busy elsewhere. At this point in the war it was focused with special intensity on destroying German cities and morale – not because its new commanding officer, Arthur 'Bomber' Harris, had a particular zeal for destruction, although there is every sign that he did, but because these were his orders.

On 5 February 1942, the Air Ministry told Bomber Command it had 'priority over all other commitments' assigned to the RAF. Nine days later came the target list: eighteen German industrial cities within 350 miles of RAF Mildenhall in Suffolk. St Nazaire ticked none of these boxes. The RAF was reminded it was supposed to support Combined Operations – but not at the risk of missing its own targets, and it had a target singled out for the night Newman and Ryder planned to hit St Nazaire. On 28 March, Harris intended to obliterate the port city of Lübeck on the Baltic coast. He was assembling a force of 234 aircraft for the job, leaving few that night for anything else. He was uncooperative before Operation Chariot and unapologetic after it. 'My primary authorised task was . . . clear beyond doubt,' he wrote in 1945: 'To inflict the most severe material damage on German industrial cities. This, when considered in relation to the force then available, was indeed a formidable task. Nevertheless, it was possible, but only if the force could be expanded and re-equipped . . ., and if its whole weight could be devoted to the main task with the very minimum of diversions.'

To Harris, Operation Chariot was only ever a diversion. Without his enthusiastic support the operation needed a dynamic personality to present its requirements to the RAF. It didn't have one. Instead it had Fred Willetts, a sandy-haired group captain who preferred flying planes to desk jobs. Willetts meant well but wasn't the type of person to get his way by banging his fists on the table. On crucial occasions he missed meetings or wasn't invited, and when the time came to request a specific number of aircraft from Bomber Command the task fell to his deputy, a young New Zealander called Charles Elworthy. He, too, meant well.

On 18 March, with ten days to go, Elworthy wrote a detailed memo to the Senior Air Staff Officer serving as Harris's deputy, a handsomely moustached First World War holdover called Robert Saundby. At this stage the agreed plan was for three diversionary bombing raids: one straddling midnight, another heavier one between 1 and 3 a.m. UK time, and a final lighter one from 3 to 4 a.m. Elworthy estimated that 100 planes in all would be required.

Saundby replied immediately: 'I do not agree that such a heavy scale of attack is needed. We do not want to devastate the town of St Nazaire and kill lots of Frenchmen. The object is to create a diversion from 2330 hrs to 0400 hrs. For this we want about 20 Whitleys [twin-engined bombers with a range of about 1,500 miles] spaced out to cover the period, hanging around overhead dropping the occasional bomb. Please show this to the C-in-C.'

The C-in-C was Harris, who wrote on the same day: 'I agree.'

The number of planes that would cover Operation Chariot's arrival at St Nazaire was not agreed until three days before the flotilla sailed. Even then the final order to take off was almost never sent. An obsession with security meant none of the pilots knew why they were flying the mission, and their rules of engagement were so restrictive that some of them wept with frustration when told the full story on their return.

Throughout his involvement in the planning process, Newman had a bad feeling about the bombing raid. As for Mountbatten, he assumed it would take place as requested and would mitigate some of the risk to the attackers down below. Even so, he was under no illusion as to how serious this risk was, as he'd made clear to Hughes-Hallett. As he got to know Newman better he was more candid with him, too.

They bumped into each other on the steps of Richmond House just as Newman was about to drive down to Falmouth for the last time on Friday, 13 March. Mountbatten seized the moment for a final pep talk.

'I want you to be quite clear that this is not just an ordinary raid,' he said, according to a 1958 account by C. E. Lucas Phillips. 'It is an important operation of war. It is also a very hazardous operation. I am quite confident that you will get in and do the job all right, but, frankly, I don't expect any of you to get out again. If we lose you all, it will be about equivalent to the loss of one merchant ship; but your success will save many merchant ships. We have got to look at the thing in those terms.'

Mountbatten went on to say that Newman should pick no married men to join him on the raid. And he should give them all a chance to back out once briefed.

If Newman felt any apprehension, he didn't show it. If he noticed the difference between Mountbatten's optimism in front of Forbes on 26 February and his brutal realism now, he put it to one side. In Lucas Phillips's account, based on detailed question-naires filled out by most of the raid's leading participants, Newman at this point was not so much daunted as suffused with pride.

The situation in the Atlantic was dire. The day before, Church-ill had cabled Harry Hopkins, the United States' Secretary of Commerce, to express his deep concern at the loss of sixty tankers in US coastal waters along the Atlantic seaboard in the previous two months. He implored Hopkins to make the case to Roosevelt for more US escort ships in the Bermuda–West Indies area. A week later Roosevelt suggested in unusually terse language that the shipping catastrophe was as much Churchill's problem to solve as anyone's: 'Your recent message to Mr. Hopkins on this subject impels me to request your particular consideration of heavy attacks on submarine bases and building and repair yards, thus checking submarine activities at their source.'

Roosevelt wanted Churchill to bomb the U-boat bases from the air. That was not on Churchill's to-do list because it had proved pointless, but he hoped Combined Operations under its dynamic new chief would impress the White House anyway.

In Falmouth preparations were gathering pace. Ryder set up a temporary headquarters at the Tregwynt Hotel on Cliff Road. He was obsessed with security and saw German spies round every corner, but the navy had commandeered the whole hotel and this made him feel more comfortable. He was given the use of a wraparound conservatory with sweeping views of the English Channel. 'It was filled up with a chart table and sufficient office equipment to enable us to study our intelligence and issue our orders,' he wrote. 'In addition to this we acquired a small store for various special explosives, signal rockets, German ensigns, and other secret matter which we did not wish to disclose.'

Up the coast in Plymouth, Admiral Forbes had stopped being gloomy and started making things happen. 'Not much good being a Commander-in-Chief if you can't get what you want,' he told Ryder. There was even a hotline to Whitehall for specialist logistical requests. Newman told David Paton, a senior medic, that if he lifted a red phone in naval headquarters and asked for 'Cabinet annex' he could have anything his heart desired. Paton tried it. 'I wanted a pound of sulfanilamide powder [to curb infection],' he wrote, 'and sure enough it came on the next train from London.'

A list of items delivered to Newman himself includes, besides a sizeable arsenal of machine guns and explosives, two twelve-inch megaphones, twenty luminous watches, eighty Bergen rucksacks, ninety torches with belt clips, 220 self-heating tins of soup, twenty-four light metal ladders and for some reason six folding Raleigh bicycles.

He took delivery of 100 phosphorus smoke grenades, 432 2-inch mortar bombs, 354 magazines for Colt 45 automatics, 700 for Bren light machine guns and 15,000 Tommy gun rounds.

Yet there was still a problem with ammunition, particularly for Ryder. Try as he might he couldn't scare up as much as he needed for the quick-firing 20mm Oerlikon guns being mounted on the *Campbeltown* and most of the motor launches. This would haunt the expedition, but at least he would have plenty of commandos to put ashore. They arrived in Falmouth Harbour on 13 March in a converted ferry, the *Princess Josephine Charlotte*, officers and men together, Micky Burn among them.

Only a month before, Burn had been at a loose end. Frustrated at not having been in action after nearly two years of arduous commando training, he was wondering if he should become a spy. One morning, from a taxi on the Mall, he saw Charles Newman walking towards Whitehall. He knew Newman well as CO of 2 Commando and guessed important business must have brought him to London; otherwise he'd be in Scotland with his soldiers. Burn jumped out of the taxi. Newman was delighted to see him.

'You've got to come back,' Newman said. 'This is it.'

Any commando would have known what he meant. No more exercises. No more going through the motions. At last a big show was in the offing. It didn't matter where, and of course Newman couldn't say. What mattered was that it was happening.

In the previous year commandos had taken part in raids on Spitsbergen, the Lofoten Islands and Vaagso, all in Norway, but these were baby steps. Before that, in July 1940, they had raided Guernsey, and the operation was a humbling lesson for future planners.

Four hundred and sixty-nine Germans had landed on the island, which is in the English Channel, much closer to France than England. According to a British spy sent ashore from a submarine, the enemy had set up machine gun nests along Guernsey's cliffs and could get troops to anywhere on its coast in twenty minutes. Churchill personally ordered up a night raid to kill or capture them. One of its leaders was Lieutenant John Durnford-Slater of 3 Commando, who would later play a central role in commando operations on D-Day. He planned the Guernsey raid with Captain David Niven, on a break from Hollywood as a staff officer at Combined Operations HQ.

They decided the goal should be to take the airport as well as round up the Germans. The raid was postponed at the last minute and the plan was being fine-tuned right up to the afternoon of departure from Dartmouth. It unravelled quickly. Two boats broke down crossing the Channel. A third went to the wrong island. A fourth was so damaged by rocks trying to land its troops that it had to be sunk.

Durnford-Slater's launch took him off an escort destroyer at one in the morning and set off at first for France rather than Guernsey because its naval officers were too busy looking at their compasses to realize they were heading 180 degrees off course. When he eventually got his men ashore they saw no Germans or German activity until racing back to their rendezvous with the destroyer. Durnford-Slater woke the enemy by setting off his cocked pistol as he fell head over heels down a flight of steps to the beach. At this point three commandos admitted they could not swim and had to be left behind. They spent the rest of the war as prisoners.

The raid was 'a ridiculous, almost comic failure,' Durnford-Slater wrote. 'We had captured no prisoners. We had done no serious damage. We had caused no casualties to the enemy . . . There had been no machine gun nest . . . We had cut through three telegraph cables. A youth in his teens could have done the same.'

Churchill, whose idea it was, was not amused. 'Let there be no more silly fiascos like those perpetrated at Guernsey,' he fumed. 'The idea of working all these coasts up against us by pinprick raids is one strictly to be avoided.'

There was a concerted effort after Guernsey to focus on clearly defined goals. Between them the Norwegian raids destroyed a radio mast, a fuel depot and two fish oil factories. An hour spent searching army offices on the Vaagso raid yielded valuable code-books that helped Ryder at St Nazaire. But none of the Norwegian operations of 1941 proved much in terms of offensive capability. Nor did they expunge the humiliation of the first Allied adventure in Norway in the spring of 1940.

Newman had been in Norway as a company commander. Burn had been there too, 'completely outmanoeuvred' by Austrian mountain troops in white suits with automatic rifles. They swooped down on his poorly equipped reservists from snow-clad mountainsides north of the Arctic Circle and turned what was supposed to be an orderly covering operation into a rout.

Corporal Glyn Salisbury was there. He would sail for St Nazaire in launch 306 and return with a scarcely believable story of carnage and defiance. From Norway he remembered 'retreating all the time, soaking wet, no sleep at all'. He saw Gloster Gladiators sent by the RAF and shot down straight away, and the bodies of dead comrades whose bandoliers he had to pick up for ammunition because he'd run out of his own.

They were all lucky to get out alive, and Burn was furious with the government that had sent him. Two years later lessons had been learned. The official story of Combined Operations, published in 1943, put a positive gloss on them. The retreat from Norway and the fall of France the following month created an opening, it said. 'Here was an opportunity to engage in a kind of amphibious guerrilla warfare to which the British were, by temperament and tradition, peculiarly suited. The national love of the sea could be combined with a national love of the chase.' Never mind that the British were the ones who had been chased out of Europe and the sea was serving as their moat. The point was to go back to the drawing board and train for a new sort of war.

There was one difficulty. To begin with, no regular-army troops and virtually no weapons could be spared from 'the paramount task of organising the defence of the British Isles against invasion'. The solution embraced by the commandos was to take volunteers from the Independent Companies and turn them into super-soldiers without worrying too much about equipment. The emphasis was on stamina, resilience and resourcefulness.

The Independent Companies had been formed early in 1940 for the Norwegian campaign. There were ten of them, each made up of reservists from the ten Territorial Army divisions then based in Britain, topped up with officers from the regular army and – when their commanding officer decided they needed extra training in mountain and irregular warfare – from the Indian army too. Half went to Norway; half did not. But all ended up in training camps in Scotland and Northern Ireland by the first summer of the war.

The 'Independent Company' label didn't stick. At first they were renamed the Special Service Battalions, but Churchill wanted something that sounded even more special, and it was Lieutenant Colonel D. W. Clarke of the Royal Artillery who came up with 'commandos'. The name was borrowed from Boer guerrilla units that had made life difficult for General Kitchener in South Africa before the First World War. The new British commandos quickly became known for a radically new sort of training that valued initiative almost as highly as fitness.

Salisbury gave an example. 'A troop will come off parade at, say, 3 p.m. and is then told that the next parade will be at 6am on the following morning at a place sixty, seventy, sometimes a hundred miles away. How each commando gets to that place is his own affair.' It wasn't cheating to hitch-hike or take the train, even if the 'enemy' considered it unfair. 'Unfairness was the point,' Burn wrote. 'The Nazis had been unfair in France and Norway.'

Officer recruitment was idiosyncratic. One candidate interviewed in the drawing room of a Scottish mansion shortly before the St Nazaire raid listed the questions fired at him by those he would fight alongside if successful:*

---

* He was. Donald Gilchrist joined 4 Commando and fought at Dieppe, though not at St Nazaire.

What sports do you play?
Can you drink beer?
Can you swim?
Do you play any musical instruments?
Have you a sex life?
Were you a Boy Scout?

There were no barracks, even for the most junior commandos. Instead they were paid an allowance of six shillings a day for sub-sistence and accommodation in boarding houses of their choice. If they performed satisfactorily they were spared most of the drills and parade ground square-bashing of the regular army, but extreme mental and physical toughness was taken for granted. Twenty-mile route marches with heavy packs were a standard morning's – or night's – work. When they were over, ten more miles might be ordered for the hell of it. Sixty miles in twenty-four hours was not unheard of.

Commandos were taught rock climbing, unarmed combat and street fighting. They carried fighting knives in leg sheaths and scared each other witless in live-fire exercises that occasionally entailed actual bullet wounds. Morgan Jenkins, the son of a South Wales miner, took a Tommy gun round in the thigh trying to grab the gun from a soldier ordered to detain him on an ambush exer-cise near Totnes. 'The next thing I remember was that I was on the floor,' he told the court of inquiry. It didn't hurt his prospects; by the time of the raid the following year he was a lieutenant.

The training was 'comprehensive, vigorous and designed to make the fullest and most intelligent use of that spirit of attack which is the secret of the warrior', said the Ministry of Information.

David Niven trained as a commando at Inverailort in the West-ern Highlands. 'Two months running up and down mountains . . . crawling up streams at night and swimming in the loch with full equipment' left him, he said, unbearably fit. Corran Purdon was a cherubic young sub-lieutenant so Aryan-looking that his comrades told the Germans he was a member of the 'Churchill-Jugend' when they were taken prisoner. He learned to use his fighting knife to kill and skin highland sheep, which he was then expected to eat. ('Of course they were as tough as hell.') Glyn Salisbury, with 1 Commando, spent a fortnight living rough and eating mainly blackbirds.

To what end? The truth is no one quite knew. As a result, minds raced. 'With us, any crackpot project had a chance,' Burn wrote in his memoir. He never did walk to France along the sea floor in a diving suit, although that was put forward as a serious proposal. He did wade ashore at St Nazaire, and this was something no amount of training could have prepared him for.

Ryder and Newman did their best. Most of the commandos had no experience of motor launches, and most of the launch crews had no experience of combat. In what little time was left the two commanders tried to fill in these gaps. They were especially worried about seasickness and searchlights, so exercises were arranged to get used to them. The first was a two-day trip to the Scilly Isles, which sit off the western tip of Cornwall taking the full force of any Atlantic swell. The Fairmile B launches chosen for most units weren't good in heavy weather. Conceived by the Australian-born motor racing pioneer Noel Malkin, they were to become victims of their own success. Malkin had foreseen a need for large numbers of affordable new coastal defence craft and had started building them on spec at his Fairmile estate in Surrey – hence the name. They were kit boats, each one assembled from six fifteen-ton lorry loads of flat-packed wooden parts. Once the Admiralty caught up with Malkin's thinking it bought all the kits he could produce and eventually requisitioned the whole Fairmile estate. In the meantime it expanded the range of tasks the B variant could be assigned, from inshore patrol and submarine-chasing to spying missions and now, for the first time, long-range attack.

Within their wooden hulls the launches had an engine room

amidships, inboard fuel tanks and officers' accommodation towards the stern, and a mess deck, galley and radio room under the wheel-house. Crew quarters for fourteen were in the bow. They were nearly thirty-five metres long – about the length of a modest superyacht – but without automatic stabilizers or the ability to cut through waves. In high seas they pitched and rolled like corks. Ryder knew the moment they cleared Lizard Point that they were in for a rough time.

Part of the point of the trip was for the commandos and naval crews to get to know each other, but there was little fraternizing. Bill 'Tiger' Watson, a young lieutenant on launch 457, said his strongest memories of those thirty-six hours were the mingling smells of stew and vomit.

The second exercise was a dummy night attack on Devonport naval dockyard. It was a mess. Everything that could go wrong did. The searchlights blinded the launches' skippers. Several overshot the landing places. None of the radios worked, and the attackers were either beaten back with hoses and potatoes or captured. Ryder made light of it at the time – he told Forbes more had been learned than would have been if it had gone well. And he made light of it later: the real point of the exercise, he suggested, was not to prepare for St Nazaire but to strengthen a cover story that they were going some-where else entirely. For the benefit of Falmouth's probably fictitious German spy, he spent a long time putting it about that the flotilla growing in the harbour was the 10th Anti-Submarine Striking Force, bound first for Gibraltar. He even made a show of ordering sun helmets for all participants.

But the Devonport exercise was not just about the cover story. It was a dry run for an attack that Ryder knew would kill a large number of his sailors, and he did hint that he was rattled. Chris Worsley, a junior lieutenant on his gunboat, returned to the bridge as the exercise was winding down to overhear him hoping aloud it wouldn't 'be quite so bad on the night'.

★

Everyone had reason to be worried. By now they knew roughly what was in store. All thirty-eight commando officers on the raid were briefed on the evening of 18 March in the wardroom of the *Princess Josephine Charlotte*. Locking the door behind him, Newman described the attack almost as if he'd lived it, right down to the orderly re-embarkation of twenty-four separate teams of commandos from the battlefield they had chosen, stormed, secured, destroyed and bid farewell. There were gasps at the audacity of the plan, and a chill in the room as people realized what it really meant. Burn broke the tension by passing a note to Newman asking if he could go back to his unit.

Newman briefed the men the next morning – not on the target, even though some had already guessed it, but on the type of job. For the demolition crews especially, it made sense: night and day for several weeks they had been conducting dummy demolitions on dockside equipment in Cardiff and Southampton until they could place and detonate the charges with their eyes shut.

Ryder briefed his launch captains and their junior officers separately. He used the scale model of St Nazaire and a torch to indicate moonlight and shadow. It didn't take long. Unlike Newman, Ryman had not written an exhaustive order booklet. He had decided to deal in broad strokes. 'I relied more than ever on the initiative and enterprise of each commanding officer and instructed them to brief their coxswains, gun crews and officers in the same manner,' he wrote. Perhaps there was no alternative. Initiative was certainly a big part of the commando philosophy, so Ryder's approach may have felt appropriate. And if he assumed that well-laid plans would go up in smoke at first contact with reality he was right. But what then? Were the launch crews given any guidance on what to do or where to go if things did go wrong? They were not.

They could not be told the name of the target because some were still allowed ashore and word might have got out, but there were rumours. Worsley heard the one about St Nazaire and ignored it as obviously ridiculous. David Paton, the doctor who ordered sulfanilamide powder from the Cabinet Annex, took the rumours seriously and had a more practical response. He'd paid close attention to the officers' briefing, at which Newman had pointed to a pillbox halfway along the Old Mole, the breakwater upstream of the outer harbour. Newman said it was not a gun emplacement and told Paton he could use it as a first aid post. Paton said it looked to him from reconnaissance pictures as if there was an anti-aircraft gun on top of the pillbox. 'I was overruled by a WAAF specialist in photography,' he wrote later. 'How wrong she was!'

Paton's recollection of this episode has been questioned because it's unlikely that a WAAF specialist – from the Women's Auxiliary Air Force – was aboard the *Princess Josephine Charlotte*. There is certainly no mention of one being there in other accounts. But it's true that WAAF officers were among the best, most trusted reconnaissance photo analysts. Many of them worked at RAF Medmenham in Buckinghamshire, where Constance Babington Smith was the first to pinpoint the coastal launch ramps of V1 flying bombs in 1944. Others worked at RAF St Eval on the north Cornish coast, among them Ann McKnight Kauffer, the daughter of a well-known American graphic artist who produced posters for the Tube. McKnight Kauffer arrived at St Eval in February 1942 and it was there that reconnaissance pictures of St Nazaire, taken by high-flying Spitfires, were first analysed. She will have seen all the images used by Ryder and Newman in their planning, even if she never went aboard the *Princess Josephine Charlotte*. If she or anyone else did peer down through a magnifying glass at the pillbox halfway along the Old Mole and decide it was not armed, that is significant. It might have been an accurate assessment right up to the afternoon of 25 March, when the final pre-raid pictures were rushed by dispatch rider from St Eval to Falmouth. But forty-eight hours later it was emphatically and tragically out of date.

The weather in Falmouth was sunny and warm. Fearing it might not hold, Ryder brought the operation's start date forward by a day. Even so, after all the briefings and exercises, there was time to think. Those not naturally inclined to contemplate their own mortality were reminded of it nonetheless. Officers told them to update their wills and suggested they write last letters to their families, just in case. Bill Gibson's became famous. He was a Lance Sergeant in Burn's 6 Troop of 2 Commando, from Glasgow and the Gordon Highlanders. Before that he'd been an engineer.

Gibson had a gift for mischief as well as language, passing himself off as an invented twin brother when necessary for a visit to the pub. His real younger brother, Alex, had been killed already in the war. His close friend Peter Harkness was with him on the raid.

'My dearest Dad,' he wrote, sitting out on the deck of the *Princess Josephine Charlotte*, at anchor in the harbour:

'By the time you get this I shall be one of many who have sacrificed our unimportant lives for what little ideals we may have – my own ideals I can thank you for.

'The job we have been on has been something worthwhile – it has virtually been suicide but the repercussions after we finished our task will be very far reaching inasmuch as the raiders who sink so many of our merchant ships will be put out of action for at least six months – so the food line from America should be unimpaired. Peter and I will be together – our task is just a wee bit dangerous, but if we can hold Jerry off it will mean the saving of the lives of a lot of our pals . . .

'Tomorrow morning I am going to Holy Communion – the first communion I have ever been at – but I know God will help us all he can, and I pray, Dad, that he will help you, and bless Betty for all she has been to us. My will has been made out – it seems so silly but we have all had to do it.

'I would like you, Dad, to write a note to my Irish girl and let her know what has happened. You will get her address in any of the letters – her name is Anna Brien – would you do this for me.

'The reason I'm writing this at all, Dad, is just the thought that it might be a little better for you to get this rather than the dreaded telegram.

'I don't think I have made any enemies in the world – I have made a lot of good friends, but you've been the best pal I've ever had. Your influence, plus our Alex's, has certainly helped me to pass through life with the character which, though a bit rough in some things, still has all the fine thoughts gained from both of you . . .

'It seems ever so peculiar to be writing this letter. We've just finished our tea and the sunshine is streaming through the portals. We've been on deck sunbathing all day. Peter is very red now, and I am myself, and everything seems so far removed from the job ahead of us. We have not been allowed to leave the boat for over a fortnight now except for organized parties to get some exercise. With spring in the air and everything looking so beautiful we can only now appreciate how lovely everything is – almost like condemned criminals.

'Well, Dad dearest, I'll close now. Don't worry and don't be too unhappy – remember what you always told me – to keep my chin up. I'll have done what chance has made my duty, and I can only hope that by laying down my life the generations to come might in some way remember us, and also benefit by what we've done.

'It is unnecessary for me to tell you how sorry I am at not being able to do a lot of the things I have longed to do to pay you back for the chance you gave me. In a time like this I turn to you, Dad, and God – I hope there will be peace for everyone soon. Give my love to everyone – I'll remember you.

'Your loving son, Bill.'

Years later Burn recalled that strange, warm day on the deck of the troopship, so full of possibility and dread. At one point, as his men wrote their letters in the sun, he had a hideous shock. 'For a moment I saw Bill Gibson's face, and knew that he knew he would be killed,' Burn wrote.

Maybe there is such a thing as premonition. Maybe in that moment it came to both of them. A slightly different interpretation is that what Burn saw in Gibson's face, and felt himself, was a realization that death was likely for all of them. That this wasn't just another Vaagso. That the national jeopardy, the shame of Singapore, the pressure from above to be offensive and the impatience from below to do more for the war effort than run up and down Scottish mountains were all coming together and would find expression in a bloodbath and a lottery.

Rifleman Tom Roach (a shop manager in his previous life) told his father he was going into 'the biggest raid of all times' and if the worst happened it would be for 'the best country in the whole world'. Maurice Harrison, a commercial artist from South London, confided to his diary that 'being so full of life it was hard to think of what I would write if I were dead'. Tom Peyton had plenty of ideas. He was the only Etonian among the commandos and his letter became a plea for social justice; for a 'new British Order' that would make sure of jobs and pensions for the poor.

They were all from 6 Troop; Micky's boys. A separate group managed to get off the boat for a final swim further up the River Fal. Afterwards Lieutenant Harry Pennington, who'd played rugby for Oxford, remarked matter-of-factly while drying off that England was worth dying for. How many of the raiders would have agreed in so many words is impossible to say, but one of them, looking back, said the atmosphere in Falmouth in those last few days was like something out of Nevil Shute: 'You could feel something was up. It was the calm and peacefulness of it all . . . the end of everything.'

The commandos were all told, in a final meeting with Newman on the *Princess Josephine Charlotte*, that if they had reservations about going they could say so and withdraw without fear of shame or criticism. The reaction was silence, according to one officer present – 'a relaxed silence, one of acceptance despite the risks . . . Even so, we understood well what he was trying to convey to us. We were expendable.'*

---

* This is how it was remembered by Lieutenant Stuart Chant, who sailed on the *Campbeltown* as head of a four-man demolition unit. C. E. Lucas Phillips,

The navy men were not offered a get-out. They were following orders and could only hope those orders attached a reasonable value to their lives. Lieutenant Richard Collinson wasn't sure they did. He would be the number three officer on launch 192 carrying Burn and others into battle. But he was one of the few in the whole flotilla with any experience of combat with the German navy. Once he'd heard from his commanding officer what they were supposed to do, he found it hard to project the required confidence. 'I felt a complete fraud,' he wrote. 'The rest of the time passed very slowly for me, with the possibility of being killed or wounded seeming very real . . . I kept hoping ignobly, but in vain, that bad weather would blow up and cause the cancellation of the operation.'

Another person hoping providence would intervene was Elmslie Tibbits. Having married in Shanghai and travelled overland to Hanoi she'd hitched a ride home, according to family legend, on a tanker. Her husband, the promising young naval explosives man, would follow. She gave birth to their son in Winchester in 1938 and continued to live there when Nigel returned from the Yangtze to take up a wartime posting at HMS *Vernon*, the navy's torpedo and mining school in Portsmouth. By March 1942 they were a busy young family whose lives were enmeshed in the war. They had a certain status. It might even have been enviable but for the uncertainty surrounding Nigel's latest assignment – which he could not explain even to his wife.

'Good morning my Swede Frwoggie [sic],' he wrote to her on 7 March, on embossed notepaper from the Royal Naval Barracks at Devonport. 'I have just got here but I am away again this evening. I expect to be . . . in London on Wednesday. Please tell nobody, if possible, not even Whiskers, of my movements.'

---

the brigadier whose account of the raid in 1958 set the tone for many that followed, offered a different version in which the commandos rejected the idea of pulling out with a great guttural roar. Chant was there, and heard no such thing.

Tibbits was in possession of one of the most sensitive secrets of the war at that point – his own design for the *Campbeltown*'s explosive charge. There had been proposals for devices that would detonate while the commandos took cover nearby. He had rejected them. With a confidence that seemed to reassure everyone who might have doubted him, he proposed instead a bomb made from off-the-shelf explosives, wood, steel, concrete and two sets of fuses. Twenty-four standard 300lb depth charges were lowered into a huge concrete box subdivided into six smaller ones and encased in steel plate. The concrete was to protect the charges from incoming shells and the ship's impact with the dock. The steel was to make the whole package look like a fuel tank. The wood was in the form of bungs used to keep the fuses in place. One set of fuses, known as time pencils, had a 2.5-hour delay and could be activated by a switch hidden in the leg of a card table in the boardroom. The other was an acetone–cellulose fuse linked to six of the depth charges – one in each subdivision – with an 8.5-hour delay, in principle. In practice it always seemed to go off two hours late.

The charge was positioned above a real fuel tank and up against the support structure for the 4-inch gun on the *Campbeltown*'s foredeck. Tibbits reckoned it would be safe there until it was time to blow, and when it blew it would be devastating.

By mid-March most of his work at Devonport was done. Elmslie joined him at the Grand Hotel in Plymouth for a short holiday, and on one of those perfect spring mornings that all the survivors remembered they drove out to Dartmoor for a picnic. It was there that he told her he thought he wouldn't be coming back. 'He definitely had a premonition,' says his son. 'My mother said he did, but he was determined to go anyway. The one thing he was really scared about was that the whole operation would be a disaster because the fuses would get damaged . . . He wanted to make sure it blew up even if he blew himself up, because the entire raid would've been a failure if that happened.'

Tibbits wasn't prepared to countenance failure, but Combined

Operations headquarters wanted a Plan B. That is why, late in the day, Micky Wynn showed up in Falmouth with his torpedo boat, MTB 74. The Marqués de Casa Maury had said of Wynn: 'He's mad as a hatter but he has a very useful toy.' Ryder wasn't pleased to see him, not least because he did not think much of the toy. It had 'every form of insurmountable defect,' he wrote. The most obvious was speed – too much and too little of it.

The trouble with MTB 74 was that while its five engines were impressive on paper they were temperamental as an ensemble. 'A defect in any one seemed to upset the whole lot, and even when at the top of her form she was unable to do any speed between six and 33 knots,' Ryder went on. 'As the rest of the force could only steam at speeds between seven and 15 knots she had to devise a peculiar, leapfrog-like performance to keep in station, and was continually breaking down. Many times I decided to leave her behind, but her commanding officer pleaded for her with the eloquence of a defending counsel.'

That defending counsel was Wynn. He was desperate not to be left behind now that he had found a potential purpose for his boat after being denied one by the slippery *Scharnhorst* and *Gneisenau*. He was allowed to join the night exercise to Devonport, but returned with a blown gearbox. He promised to fix it, trusting silently that his chief motor mechanic, Bill Lovegrove, would find a way. When it turned out that he needed a whole new engine, Lovegrove promised to install it if Wynn could get hold of one. Needless to say, he could. Lovegrove worked twenty-three hours straight with improvised lifting gear to get it working in time, but the engine still had to be run in. And there was another problem that Wynn dared not tell Ryder about. He was supposed to fire his torpedoes at the dock gate if for any reason the *Campbeltown* failed to hit it, but the torpedoes needed new fuses from HMS *Vernon*, and they hadn't yet arrived.

The commandos were intensively trained but many had never been in combat. Every naval officer except Ryder was a reservist.

He had issued no contingency plans for a scenario in which it proved impossible to land troops near the docks, relying instead on 'initiative and enterprise'. The boat that would lead them into battle had to be towed there because its fuel tanks weren't big enough for the whole voyage. The Oerlikon gun crews had at best half the ammunition they needed, or by one estimate enough for three minutes' hard use. As they reached the open sea, Wynn and Lovegrove were still fitting their fuses and tuning their fifth engine. And Bomber Command, on which everyone agreed the operation depended, had not been told it had begun.

'Modern war has little use for amateurs,' the Ministry of Information stated in *Combined Operations*, its 1943 booklet. 'Impatience and improvisation seldom win battles.' And yet, when Ryder's flotilla finally slipped its moorings in Falmouth harbour and headed out into the Channel on the balmy afternoon of 26 March, there was a distinct sense of amateurs giving it a go.

3.   The voyage

The 32-pound cannonball of Napoleonic vintage was an awesome piece of ordnance. Glowing from the heat of its launch, with a muzzle velocity of 500 metres per second, it flew slowly enough for its prey to see it coming. It could ricochet around a gun deck for several seconds before coming to rest, dismembering anyone in its path. It could turn oak into splinters as lethal as shrapnel and it came preceded by a shockwave that could kill all by itself.

At the battle of Trafalgar, HMS *Royal Sovereign* was reputed to have killed or wounded 400 men with a single broadside fired into the stern of the Spanish three-decker the *Santa Ana*.* On the surgeon's table the wounded had a swig of brandy and a belt to bite on if they were lucky.

It would be hard to imagine a more frightening prospect for anyone sailing into battle than the one faced by Nelson's men – but St Nazaire provided one in 1942. Its coastal defences were a thorough and versatile killing machine that worked rather like a mangle: the closer their prey approached, the tighter they were gripped. The gun that hit launch 192 was in the shore battery at Pointe Mindin on the east side of the estuary, one of thirty-one flak and artillery batteries defending the approaches to the port.

Most guns in the Pointe Mindin battery were 37mm flak, designed to bring down aircraft but just as capable against boats. Their shells were not as big or heavy as cannonballs but they travelled four times faster and each carried half a pound of TNT. Reloading was automatic and took less than half a second,

---

* Not true, Roy Adkins wrote in his epic history of the battle, but in a sense it was repute that counted, for that was what broadcast fear.

compared with at least two minutes for a cannon. That said, one flak round was often enough.

One round, well-aimed, did for launch 192. It heaved one engine off its mountings, blew a hole in the deck from rail to rail and sent bodies 'flying into the air and overboard', as Richard Collinson recalled. The captain of the launch behind thought 192 had blown up completely.

Few of the 623 men who set out from Falmouth on 26 March had any real understanding of what lay in store. The officers had been told their target was St Nazaire. The men had not; only that they would be attacking a port where they were not welcome or, with any luck, expected. Its name was withheld from some of the launch crews even after leaving Falmouth: 'We didn't know it was St Nazaire until after we were taken prisoner,' said Ralph Batteson of the 306. Even the fact that they would have to enter an estuary came as a surprise to him. 'They didn't tell us things like that.'

As for St Nazaire's place on the grand wall map of the war, that might have inspired some Charioteers, but it didn't bear thinking about as a factor in their odds of survival. At this point, Hitler's strategy was geared towards two goals: victory in Russia and dominance in the Atlantic. And the second of these depended on round-the-clock usage of his most important U-boat bases, in Lorient and St Nazaire. To imagine catching its defences unawares was thrilling but surely delusional.

Collinson at least knew enough to be afraid. He had gone up against fast, heavily armed German patrol boats in the North Sea, and he knew the launches were plodding and vulnerable by comparison. Bill Copland, who would muster the commandos on the foredeck of the *Campbeltown*, had fought in the First World War and knew not to be surprised when the deck became slippery with blood. But most of the others who had seen action had seen it in Norway or at Dunkirk, where the risks weren't comparable. The low casualty rates on recent small-scale raids may have encouraged them to believe the enemy was overrated, and there was a natural human tendency to hope for the best or at least block out the worst. Don Randall, a Lance Sergeant who went ashore in a kilt, said when he tried to imagine the immediate future from the deck of the *Campbeltown* on the way in, he saw only 'an incalculable mental blank'. The Charioteers left Falmouth in a mixture of moods. Survivors spoke of excitement, dread, hope, denial and quiet resignation.

The launches left in twos and threes. A big formation would attract attention. By tradition, the navy men had been offered hot baths on the accompanying destroyers before departure so as to put clean bodies into their clean underwear. The commandos were told to wear navy duffle coats over their green battledress if they wanted to go up on deck in case German reconnaissance planes should fly over and become suspicious.

None did. The only aircraft in the sky as the flotilla left the English coast was a lone Hurricane escort. As dusk fell, it turned for home. Even then, Ryder kept up the pretence that he was on a submarine sweep, forming up his launches into a broad arrowhead led by the *Campbeltown*. If the German spy in Falmouth had been picking up the quayside gossip, there might have been grounds for a warning to U-boats in the Western Approaches, but the secret of St Nazaire was safe.

By this time, Newman said, 'The thrill of the voyage was upon me.' The miniature armada made a magnificent sight, Collinson wrote, even though there was no one else around to see it. As it sailed into the night, Lieutenant Commander Beattie served drinks on the bridge of the *Campbeltown*. It was making fourteen knots. Ryder had calculated that after cruising till dawn at that speed he would be able to slow down to avoid his wake attracting attention in daylight. He was there on the bridge with Beattie, Newman, Tibbits, Bill Pritchard and other officers from 2 Commando but his mood was pensive: 'Much lay ahead, and even the least imaginative of the company present, alone with his thoughts, must have speculated as to his future . . . The whole thing seemed vaguely unreal, and under the circumstances I decided to get as much sleep as possible.'

Half a mile off his port quarter, Ordinary Seaman Ralph Batteson had the same feeling of unreality. He described it as a state of suspended animation. There were obvious reasons: the quietness of men thinking about death, waiting to find out if it would come. But there was also a fear of being caught napping, a feeling, as one commando on the same launch put it, 'of some hidden eye watching us, either through a periscope or through the clouds'.

The Charioteers were all white, all male, all young, yet still a complicated slice of the country they were leaving in their wake. In their complement of 623 were poets, landed aristocrats and roughnecks who could barely sign their name. There were Catholics and Protestants, Eastenders and Ulstermen, ultramarine Conservatives and progressives dreaming of a more equitable life for everyone after the war. The social firewall between officers and men was less obvious than in the regular armed forces, but still there. It was clear who was leading whom into this death trap, and it was usually the sons of privilege leading working-class strivers.

On His Majesty's Motor Gunboat 314, which would lead the raiders into battle, the commanding officer was Lieutenant Dunstan Curtis – Eton, Oxford and the great-grandson of an admiral who as a junior officer had served with Charles Darwin on the *Beagle*. Curtis sported a dashing red-gold beard and had earned a reputation for keeping a cool head in tight spots. He'd spent a dangerous winter putting members of the French Resistance ashore at dead of night on the rocky Breton coast. Some of these agents provided intelligence that helped Newman and Hughes-Hallett plan Operation Chariot, including plans of St Nazaire's docks and maps of its surroundings. Curtis spoke fluent French and had grown up sailing the French coast in school holidays, so he knew more than most about where they were going. From the moment of Ryder's briefing aboard the *Princess Josephine Charlotte*, he'd known they were 'already embarked on an adventure from which it was obvious that many would not return'. After the war he served in naval intelligence with Ian Fleming, joining that small group of men who could genuinely claim to have been the inspiration for James Bond.

The forward gunner on the 314, Bill Savage, had a red beard too. There was mutual respect between Savage and Curtis but not much else in common. Savage had been a brewer's boy in Birmingham, the youngest of seven siblings. In among them all his mother, Kitty Savage, who had earlier been in service to the Duc d'Orléans, endured twenty-two miscarriages and stillbirths, each lifeless form carried by an older sister in a shoebox to the nearest cemetery. The family called them 'the non-starters'.

Savage's nickname on the gunboat was 'Henry VIII'. He was powerfully built, a weightlifter with beer barrels in his past life at the Mitchells & Butlers Brewery in Smethwick. He was 'a good-tempered and good-hearted man', said Curtis, but you didn't mess with him.

'I can take what comes,' Savage once wrote to his brother Jack. 'I can hold my own in my own nasty way.' In fact his family and fellow crew members saw little evidence of nastiness but plenty of strength. Mistaken once for Jack in an argument at the Beehive pub on Raglan Road, Bill decked the aggrieved parties before they realized they'd picked on the wrong brother.

His only weakness was his stomach. He was a fussy eater and felt queasy when anxious, as he was on his last home leave before the raid. 'He had his gippy tummy on,' his niece remembered. 'He was a bit offhand and quiet. He knew the odds weren't good.'

Gunboat 314 was towed into the open sea by one of two escort destroyers, the *Atherstone*. The *Campbeltown* towed Wynn's torpedo boat and carried seventy-one commandos in addition to its crew. In a sense these were the lucky ones. The *Campbeltown* was made of steel, not kindling. Her sides rode high in the water compared with the launches, and the extra steel plate welded further to the deck gave some protection from incoming fire for those who kept their heads down.

That first night at sea, the commandos were free to move about the ship but their battle stations had already been assigned. Three demolition groups were to be below decks for the attack run. On deck amidships, nearest the gunwales, would be two assault groups of ten commandos each. Inside them would be two protection squads and two demolition squads, each five men strong. The starboard demolition squad would be led by Stuart Chant, a former broker's clerk on the floor of the London Stock Exchange, with thick, dark eyebrows and a talent for rugby. He played for Wasps on Saturdays and Sudbury Stallions on Sundays and served as a reservist with the Artists Rifles, a precursor of the SAS. One of his demolition men, Lance Sergeant Arthur Dockerill, had been a choirboy at Ely Cathedral.

Dockerill was a singer, a hummer and a whistler. His talent meant he got his early education at the Cathedral Choir School. But when his voice broke, instead of moving pews to join the tenors or the basses, he left school to be apprenticed as a plumber. He was gifted at that too; a natural with lead. He moved away to Peterborough before the war to earn an extra shilling an hour, then back to Ely to get married in December 1940. 'He was a strong little fella,' said his son, 'and he'd sing his heart out if there was a singsong going.' Even if there wasn't, there always seems to have been a soundtrack playing in his head, upbeat and imperturbable, and fate and Stuart Chant would thank him for it.

Nearly three quarters of the commandos were assigned to the launches trailing in *Campbeltown*'s wake. Micky Burn commanded those in 192, the leading boat in the starboard column. His opposite number in 447 at the head of the port column was David Birney, and on paper they had a lot in common: Winchester, Oxbridge (in Birney's case, Trinity, Cambridge), conspicuous natural gifts and every reason to think the world their oyster. Birney was born in the foothills of the Himalayas and grew up shooting. He'd won medals for it at university and toured the dominions shooting for

Britain. Two years younger than Burn, he qualified to practise law in 1939, just in time for war to elbow it aside.

Birney led a small group of commandos on the Vaagso raid in 1941, blowing up a road and a telephone exchange on a day that may have planted in his mind – and many others – the idea that well-laid plans can actually go right. The previous year he'd married Cécilie Wood, a Swiss adventurer who took up rally driving after the war. They conceived a daughter in March 1942, not long before the raid.

Two boats behind Birney in launch 307 was David Paton, the medic tasked with setting up a first aid post on the Old Mole. Like most members of 2 Commando, they knew each other from long months of training and killing time in Scotland. Paton and Burn knew Cécilie too: she'd moved north to be with Birney after they married and she borrowed their landlady's Daimler to drive her husband to commando officers' social gatherings in the Southern Uplands.

Between 447 and 307 in the port column for the run-in was launch 457, skippered by a former yachting correspondent of *The Times*. His name was Tom Collier, and he impressed everyone on board with his determination not just to land his troops – per Newman's orders – but to pick them up again. 'I will not let you down,' he told them, and the result was a fight they could never have prepared for.

One of the commandos on 457, George Wheeler, was a mere corporal as far as the army was concerned but a sophisticated sort of corporal: a baker's son from Dorchester with an economics degree from the University of Exeter. He was a fan of Rachmaninov and of Appalachian country music: a polymath who could have joined up as an officer but chose to do so as a private. And he was the husband of a young wife (Madeline; they'd met at school) to whom he was quite clear he would return.

Wheeler's daughter said the family used to think he looked like Archibald Wavell, the field marshal whose portrait stared down from garrison walls across the Empire. It was true, up to a point. In uniform, with a neat moustache and faintly intimidating gaze through black-rimmed glasses, he did look like a leader. In practice he had to entrust his safety to a protection squad led by a twenty-year-old second lieutenant six years younger than he was – the baby-faced Bill Watson, nicknamed 'Tiger' by Colonel Newman because – said Newman – he looked like the cartoon Tiger Tim. (There were also too many Bills in 2 Commando to let him use his own name without causing confusion.)

Watson's own commanding officer, Bill Pritchard, was a demolition man; an expert in portable plastic explosives. Before the raid he'd been told to draw up plans for the destruction of Britain's dockyards in the event of an invasion. His father was the Master of Cardiff Docks, so he was steeped in the subject. By chance he'd been lent Combined Operations' three-dimensional model of St Nazaire on which to base a sample demolition plan, so he recognized it at once when Newman first showed the officers a map.

That was how everyone aboard launch 457 knew where they were going. When they got there, Collier watched from the wheelhouse with an Able Seaman at his side as the commandos went ashore.

The Able Seaman's name was Herbert Dyer, trained for naval work at Devonport, and for life in the English Football League. The war had interrupted a promising career for Dyer as a utility player moving steadily up eastern England from Peterborough to Grantham, Filey Town and Scarborough. There he was a part-time professional 'doing a bit of gardening for the directors to make the money up'. Dyer had left school at fourteen. Before football started paying he did deliveries for a fruit shop.

Two boats back in the starboard column, Harry Pennington was set up for a smoother path through life, assuming he survived the war. The oldest of four brothers from Wigan, he had a degree to go with his Oxford rugby blue. He was on launch 268, commanded by Lieutenant Bill Tillie of HMS *Willamette Valley*'s 'panic party'. Pennington's demolition team included Bill Gibson, author of the plangent letter to his Dearest Dad; Gibson's close friend Peter Harkness (a Post Office mail sorter and fellow Glaswegian); and Morgan Jenkins, the miner's son shot through the thigh in Devon.

Like Wheeler, Jenkins had excelled at school; unlike Wheeler he had parlayed that into a commission. He'd been spotted and promoted for his leadership potential when already in 2 Commando, even though he was afraid of heights and couldn't swim. What he lacked in those departments he made up for with the kind of courage that Churchill's doctor, Lord Moran, called a moral quality – not a gift of nature like an aptitude for games, but 'a cold choice between two alternatives, the fixed resolve not to quit'. Jenkins showed that sort of courage one night in 1941, climbing a rock face in the Lake District alone in the dark while his fellow soldiers unwound in the pub. He'd wanted to show himself that he could overcome his fear of heights.

Sergeant Tommy Durrant's gallantry was more conspicuous, manning the forward gun on launch 306 in the heat of battle. No one who saw him in action would have contested the idea that his courage was a moral quality, but it was underpinned by anger, not all of it directed at the enemy.

Durrant was born and raised in Green Street Green in Kent, then a quiet village in the Garden of England. From the very start, he was tough. Some of his primary school classmates later admitted they were afraid of him. After school he worked as a butcher's boy and builder's labourer before joining the Royal Engineers in 1937. He was a crack shot, 'a formidable character' (his commanding officer wrote), 'and was treated carefully by all ranks'.

By chance, Durrant's brother Jack had been to St Nazaire before. As a staff sergeant in the Royal Army Service Corps, he'd won the Military Medal for helping to evacuate British troops on the day the *Lancastria* was sunk with all hands in the outer Loire estuary. Tommy accompanied Jack to Buckingham Palace and gave him a pep talk before his brother stepped forward to receive his medal: 'Tell them when we go back to St Nazaire we're going to knock seven bells out of them.'

A year and a half later, on the early morning of 28 March, Tommy Durrant was antsy almost to the point of mutinous, fearing he might have missed his chance to fulfil his promise of revenge. There were several witnesses to the results, including a German destroyer captain who could scarcely believe his eyes.

Launch 306, commanded by Colonel Ian Henderson, was the second-to-last boat in the port column. By Newman's plan it would be the fifth to land troops on the Old Mole. Bringing up the rear in the starboard column was launch 177, skippered by Mark Rodier, a young sub-lieutenant in the RNVR who – like Tibbits, Gibson, Pennington and others – became more and more convinced as the battle approached that he would not survive it.

The starboard column was supposed to land its troops 200 metres upriver of the mole at the Old Entrance, a lock gate giving direct access to the U-boat pens. This gate was at the top of Micky Wynn's to-do list. Unless diverted elsewhere at the last minute, he would use his two torpedoes to destroy it.

On their first night at sea, Wynn and his chief motor mechanic, the redoubtable Bill Lovegrove, were still installing their new torpedo fuses and fine-tuning their five engines. There is not much evidence in the records of deep thinking in MTB 74, or of brooding on mortality. The boat was busy. Ryder, too, was mercifully preoccupied. From the bridge of the *Atherstone*, still towing his gunboat, he saw that the launches' wheelhouse windows were reflecting too much moonlight. He signalled to the flotilla that all glass was to be covered with grease, paint or paper by the following night. After the war he wrote that 'the weight of responsibility outweighed all fears for one's safety'.

On the *Campbeltown* there was time for minds to wander. Don Randall, with the assault group assigned the critical task of securing the south end of the Normandie Dock, remembered a fellow sergeant who just had to be alone. 'He expressed regret for not being better company,' Randall wrote. 'He always found at times of waiting in rising tension that he must get away on his own and had found isolation in a life-boat.'

Stuart Chant, the demolition squad leader, who would depend on Randall and others for protection, described 'a great opening of cupboards' on the *Campbeltown* as those aboard twigged the significance of the fact that she was on a one-way trip. Old uniforms and equipment were discovered and the result was a wild fancy dress party. The knees-up was led by Robert Burtinshaw, a monocled lieutenant from 5 Commando whom Chant knew as a capable prop forward. Refreshments included sherry, stew and purser's cocoa. For his own part, Chant wrote, 'I did a lot of quiet praying'.

Day two dawned calm. Compared with normal conditions for the Bay of Biscay it was as flat as the Round Pond in Kensington Palace Gardens, said Gordon Holman of the London *Evening Standard*. Holman had landed what must rank as one of the most dangerous assignments in the history of war reporting. Ordinarily even 'embeds' can be kept – or keep themselves – out of the worst of the incoming fire, but not this time. Once accepted as a ridealong on Motor Gunboat 314 he was at the mercy of every shore battery that fired on her, with nothing to fire back.

At first, Ryder and Newman had resisted taking a reporter. The fact that they were forced to relent (and in the end took a second, Ed Gilling, from the *Exchange Telegraph* news agency) speaks volumes about the purpose of the raid. Whatever else it achieved, it had to yield a story, and that meant someone had to tell it.

Holman was an obvious choice. He'd been with the Independent Companies in Norway. He'd covered the Lofoten Islands and Vaagso raids, and he understood exactly the mix of narrative and propaganda that suited the censors – and, to some extent, the public. An omnibus edition of his raid coverage was published in May 1942. It opened with a polite suggestion that in the early part of the war the army was slower than the navy or the air force to switch from 'taking it' from the enemy to dishing it back out. 'With all the courage and will in the world [the army] seemed to have a long way to go,' he wrote. 'Then there came whispers of shock troops – units of the British Army ready to strike at the might of German military power – of commandos! It was a sweet thought to every man, woman and child holding the front line in our tight little island.'

Who could turn down a man willing to risk his life for lines like that?

Holman joined the commandos several days before they left Falmouth and stated for the record that no man had ever been in better company. 'They knew the hazardous nature of the expedition but, without exception, they were patient, cheerful and expectant.'

At first light on the 27th they were 110 miles south-west of Ushant, the island off Brittany's western tip. Their route was still designed to fool enemy eyes into thinking they were making for the Med.

With their morning coffee they got word of a U-boat sighting to the north-east. Ryder immediately sent the *Tynedale*, his second destroyer, to take a closer look. His flotilla was not obviously British but any German report of suspicious shipping in the Bay of Biscay could wreck its chances of surprise. All the *Tynedale* could see was a conning tower 5,000 metres away. The view from there, looking in the opposite direction, was more alarming. U-593 was limping to port after a traumatic maiden voyage. For all but two of its crew this had been their first mission in a submarine. Even their captain, Gerd Kelbling, had never heard a depth charge detonate before leaving Hamburg at the start of March. Then 136 of them had exploded in the water around him in the space of eight hours, deployed by a squadron of British destroyers trying to force him to the surface in the North Channel between Stranraer and Northern Ireland.

U-593 was damaged but not sunk. Kelbling later thanked his 'wonderful crew and our good angel', and wondered if said angel 'knew it was a German crew and not a Nazi-minded one'.

Peering through binoculars at Ryder's flotilla, he assumed at first it consisted of Dutch or Norwegian boats commandeered by his own side. 'I couldn't imagine them to be English so near the French coast . . . And so I sailed away on an easterly course waiting for what would happen.' What happened was that the *Tynedale* closed to 2,000 metres flying a German ensign, swapped it for a white one and started shooting with machine guns and a quick-firing 2-pounder. The fake German flag was a legitimate *ruse de guerre*,★ as long as the white one was run up before hostilities began. It was a rule the Charioteers observed scrupulously and – later that day – with dramatic results. In the meantime the U-boat crash-dived and prepared to return fire with a torpedo from one of its stern tubes. Now above her, the *Tynedale* launched a shallow pattern of depth charges to try to force her back to the surface. Kelbling passed under the destroyer undamaged. He had a chance to fire his torpedo from astern of the *Tynedale*, but it wouldn't launch. Anticipating that it would, Kelbling had already flooded a rear ballast tank to compensate for the lost weight of the torpedo. He was suddenly stern-heavy and bow-light and shot bow-first to the surface. There was only one way to regain horizontal trim.

'All hands forward!! We tilted the boat by running through towards the bows,' another crew member recalled. Back in control of his ship, Kelbling dived again, this time to 180 metres, to hold his breath as both the *Tynedale* and now the *Atherstone* too hunted her overhead. After two hours they gave up, leaving at high speed to rejoin the flotilla. Still the U-593 didn't move, hanging off the edge of the continental shelf where the Atlantic plunges from 200

★ As enshrined in the Hague Convention of 1907, which tried and failed to establish binding laws of war but did give those who read the small print a number of ways to dupe the enemy with honour intact.

to 1,000 metres deep. 'Very tense and in total silence we waited for several hours,' the crew member wrote. 'At dinner time we surfaced and reported our observation by radio.' Those observations were: 'Three destroyers, ten motor launches, west course.'

'West' was the key word. The secret of the 10th Anti-Submarine Striking Force, Ryder's cover name for his flotilla, was still safe.

By this time the flotilla had begun a long, slow turn towards the east. In the process it ran into a shoal of French trawlers – dozens of them – which Ryder had to assume were carrying German spies.

Ryder to *Tynedale*: 'Investigate trawler bearing 060.'

The *Tynedale* did, and sank her. Ryder then asked Dunstan Curtis on MGB 314 to board another trawler and use his French to interview the crew. Curtis was quickly satisfied that they were nothing more or less than fishermen, but then he had to pass on the message that their boat was to be sent to the bottom anyway. 'The Frenchmen were a very good lot,' wrote Curtis, who'd interrupted them preparing lunch. 'When I apologised, their skipper replied without any apparent bitterness – "*c'est la guerre!*"' Both crews were taken aboard the destroyers and eventually back to England, where they joined the Free French under Charles de Gaulle and stayed for the rest of the war.

The Charioteers pressed on, riding their luck. The second trawler had at first refused to sink, leaving what Richard Collinson remembered as a 'smudgy, cinnamon-coloured column of smoke towering up in the still, calm air'. It would have been visible for miles, but the weather was closing in at last. By zero hour there would be cloud, darkness and the RAF.

That was the plan, at any rate. The reality was less reassuring. By a sequence of blunders that would not be unravelled for seventy-five years, as of lunchtime on the 27th final orders to the bomber crews assigned to the diversionary raid on St Nazaire still had not been issued.

Part of the problem was that shortly before the flotilla left

Falmouth, formal military responsibility for the raid passed from Combined Operations to the Commander-in-Chief of the Home Fleet in Plymouth – in organizational terms, the Admiralty. This should not have made any difference to who received which orders when, and yet, apparently, it did.

On Wednesday, 25 March, and Thursday, 26 March, C-in-C Plymouth issued two crucial orders: 'Prepare Chariot' and 'Carry out Chariot.' Neither one was ever copied to the RAF. It was not as if the two forces had never had to co-operate before. As Holman's dispatches made clear, they had done so very successfully at Vaagso. But even if the navy brass in Plymouth had unaccountably mislaid their contact details for Bomber Command, they should have been able to reach Group Captain Willetts, the Liaison Officer appointed by Hughes-Hallett at Combined Operations HQ. Either they didn't bother, or they forgot.

On the 26th, a second signal was issued in addition to the 'Carry out Chariot' order to indicate that the operation was indeed about to start. This was a message from Ryder confirming that the flotilla would sail that afternoon. Unlike C-in-C Plymouth, Ryder took steps to keep Bomber Command in the loop, but his cover story got in the way. For security's sake, he insisted on copying his signal to 'Air Striking Force 10' – a fictitious aerial partner of the equally fictitious 10th Anti-Submarine Striking Force – instead of to an RAF unit that actually existed. It was routed via the Admiralty's teleprinter room in London, as the historian Peter Lush discovered, 'with no priority marking and with an unrecognised address'. And there it languished.

Willetts, at least, was awake and alert at Combined Operations HQ in London on the 26th. That evening he saw Combined Operations' own copy of Ryder's signal and telephoned Bomber Command to make sure they had it too. They didn't. The flotilla they were supposed to protect had sailed and they had no idea. They weren't formally notified that the operation was a 'go' until 2 a.m. on the 27th, by which time it had been underway for twelve hours. The bomber crews didn't get their orders until nearly three o'clock that afternoon. Take-off was at 19.30. Considering the stakes, it was a close-run thing.

The launch crews and their commandos were meanwhile approaching France at about eight knots. Ryder was still worried about wake. He was also concerned by a signal from Plymouth that five enemy torpedo boats had been seen near St Nazaire, but it was too late to fret. The 10th Anti-Submarine Striking Force had been spotted by a U-boat and kept going. It had been seen by plenty of trawlers that it *hadn't* sunk, and kept going. The die was cast. The cloud cover was a blessing. 'This and our unimpeded progress thus far cheered us immensely,' Ryder wrote, 'and the nearer we got the higher our spirits rose.'

George Wheeler – of the stern gaze and black-rimmed glasses – remembered an intense feeling of calm and fatalism from his last afternoon swimming in the Fal, and he felt it again approaching France. It was 'peaceful . . . out of this world,' he said. 'The atmosphere was fantastic. There was no fear, no panic, no nothing.'

But there was fear – and the fear of showing fear, especially among the junior officers. 'I honestly don't think I was too worried at the time,' said Lieutenant Ronald Swayne of the raid itself. 'But by God I was shit scared before.'

Corran Purdon, in charge of a five-man demolition squad, said afterwards: 'I didn't know if I was going to be frightened or not. What I wanted to do was for them not to know if I was.' To keep control of their emotions the men on the *Campbeltown* and the launches spent the rest of the afternoon eating, chatting quietly and in some cases, almost unbelievably, asleep. 'I was blissfully unconscious,' Tiger Watson wrote, 'when the ships manoeuvred themselves into their assault formation, were given their final bearing . . . and began to approach the mouth of the Loire.'

4.   The run-in

At 8 p.m. the raiders stopped. It was a little before sunset; the end of a long day's sailing and the start of a hard night's work in which the odds of survival would turn out to be about twice as bad as in Russian roulette.

The sea was still eerily calm. Tibbits' great-grandfather-in-law would have recognized the conditions from Trafalgar. Dunstan Curtis brought his motor gunboat up alongside the *Atherstone* and took Ryder and Newman aboard. He started his engines, slipped his tow, and moved forward between the two columns of motor launches to take his place as guideship. It was, he said, one of the most vivid memories of his life.

Ryder signalled to all vessels to increase speed to twelve knots, and Lieutenant Bill Green, a specialist navigator, joined him and Curtis in the wheelhouse.

In London, Mountbatten had asked the Admiralty to inform him at once of any signal from the raiders received via C-in-C Plymouth. Churchill would receive an update with his usual intelligence briefing the next morning.

From seven RAF bases in Yorkshire and south-west England, a total of sixty-two Whitley and Wellington bombers had already taken off, with orders to attack St Nazaire's docks in three phases, starting half an hour before midnight and continuing until 4 a.m. To drag out the raid, they were each to drop only one bomb at a time. To limit civilian casualties, they were not to bomb at all without being able to see their targets, and in the event of cloud they were not to fly below 6,000 feet. Churchill was worried about French civilian casualties; he believed his alliance with de Gaulle and the Free French government-in-exile depended on avoiding them. The rules were restrictive but the planes were in the air. The boats had seventy miles to go. One launch in the port column broke down and its assault troops had to be transferred to the 446 as the remaining boats ploughed on. There was no thought of the flotilla turning back.

According to survivors, Japanese pilots preparing for kamikaze missions at the end of the war tended to experience a mixture of intense sadness and elation. Contrary to the propagandized version of their story, this was not – on the whole – the elation of the brainwashed cultist but of the idealist led to believe he was doing right by his family and country. That was not remote from what many Charioteers may have been feeling on the run-in to St Nazaire. Like the pilots, they were motivated by patriotism. Like the pilots, they had been encouraged to write last letters to their loved ones. And many of them remembered a strange sense of unreality about the last days and hours before the battle; of leaving the mundane behind and moving towards a mighty reckoning. There were fundamental differences too, of course – not least between the near certainty of death as a result of weaponizing life, and the hope of surviving the raid unscathed. That hope was enough for some Charioteers to compartmentalize death and stop thinking about it altogether. Richard Collinson, like Tiger Watson, managed to sleep when fear and adrenaline might have been kicking in. As the flotilla got underway again, Collinson went below, ate a plate of bacon and eggs and dozed off to the sound of launch 192's engines.

Others took stimulants instead. Two years earlier, Professor Alfred Clark, of Edinburgh University, a founder of modern pharmacology, had run an experiment in the Western Highlands using commandos as guinea pigs. He wanted to study the effects of Benzedrine – an American brand name for amphetamine – on soldiers who were already very fit. These effects were remarkable. Benzedrine had been marketed in the US since the 1930s as a decongestant and it certainly dried up nasal passages. But it also banished muscle fatigue and nervous exhaustion and cranked up stamina with no obvious side effects. Clark told a researcher to divide a group of commandos with an especially gruelling overnight march into two subgroups. One would get the Benzedrine when they started to look miserable; the other wouldn't. The case of a Major Todhunter, the researcher wrote, was of special interest. He left Lochailort on Scotland's remote north-west coast on a Monday morning carrying a twenty-eight-pound pack, and led his men over twenty-two miles of 'stiff, hilly moorland' in driving rain. They spent the night in their wet clothes, and then walked six more miles to a rendezvous where, according to the researcher, Todhunter looked 'pinched, ill and blue with cold'. He was given five milligrams of Benzedrine and within fifteen minutes looked 'quite well'. After a brief ferry ride, Todhunter marched another ten miles ending in a steep climb from sea level to 1,800 feet.

'He went up at a surprising pace as if he were perfectly fresh,' the researcher wrote. 'He still carried 28 pounds and although I carried nothing and am fit and accustomed to the hills, I had the greatest difficulty keeping up with him. At the top we started down a long slope of two miles, most of which he did at a run, saying that he "just felt that he had to". We then reached a gritty road and did the last two-and-a-half miles at four-and-a-half miles an hour. He got in feeling full of go and the next day said he felt particularly fit.'

Benzedrine was approved by the War Office in June 1941 'for issue to troops in circumstances where they are engaged in, or likely to be engaged in, active operations of a peculiar and intensive nature'. It was to be offered in pills known as 'Special Ration Tablets', and Sam Beattie, captain of the *Campbeltown*, confirmed afterwards that they were available to the Charioteers. He disapproved of them but reckoned half his ship's company took them. It's safe to assume a good many commandos did too, not to mention the bomber crews who were supposed to be approaching overhead. Soon after Clark's Scottish study, a similar one looked at the effects of Benzedrine on pilots on long night missions. It said the drug boosted their vigilance, alertness, aggression, optimism and appetite for risk. Flyers on both sides of the Atlantic – and especially over the vast ocean in between – started calling it their extra co-pilot.

An estimated 72 million Special Ration Tablets were handed out to British troops in total during the war (and their memory lingered, especially in the mind of the former naval intelligence operative Ian Fleming; Benzedrine resurfaced in the fifties as James Bond's preferred upper, often taken with chilled Bollinger and a hand-rolled Turkish cigarette).

Amphetamines don't seem to have troubled Collinson's sleep, but he woke with a start when a hand touched him on the shoulder at 10 p.m. and a voice told him his skipper wanted him on the bridge. He got there just in time to see a red light disappear beneath the surface of the water. It was a signal from HMS *Sturgeon*, a friendly submarine, dispatched to lurk as a beacon marking the final approach to the Loire Estuary. *Sturgeon* was to surface at 10 p.m. – and only 10 p.m. – to confirm to Bill Green aboard MGB 314 that he was on track and on time. Mission accomplished, she submerged and headed home. *Tynedale* and *Atherstone* had already hung back to keep station at a safe distance overnight. Collinson and Burn on 192 wished their men luck.

With forty miles to go the raiders were now on their own, up to a point. In fact those who cared to look over the side could see they were ploughing through fields of phosphorescent jellyfish. There were millions of them, Ralph Batteson reckoned, shining in the bow waves of the launches and exaggerating the strangeness of the night.

'This was the time of greatest tension,' wrote Jack Webb, the junior medic on launch 446, 'all nerves keyed taut, palms sweating and eyes straining to see through the darkness.' Two boats forward, David Paton went below to find two of his unit changing out of trousers into kilts. They explained to him that as they were probably going to die they preferred to die in kilts. For Webb and others on his launch, the tension had been briefly broken by engine failure: they'd been transferred from near the front of the port column to reserve launch 446 at the back. Their task was to deal with St Nazaire's port defences so that the demolition crews arriving after them could work without too many distractions. Their repositioning in the order of battle was to have consequences, but Ryder hadn't wanted to slow down to let them catch up. There was an air raid to synchronize with; a clock ticking in his head.

Around 11 p.m. Tibbits went down into the bowels of the *Campbeltown* to set the long fuses leading to his explosive charge. Soon afterwards, the first distant drone of bombers reached the flotilla. Like an answering call, at 11.20 p.m. British time (0.20 a.m. local) air raid sirens sounded over St Nazaire.

'Allied aircraft! We needed this!' wrote Don Randall of 5 Troop, 2 Commando, who was amidships on the open upper deck of *Campbeltown*. 'The defences would now be concentrated against air attack. If a raid could begin now and last for three hours, we might complete the destruction of the dock installations and be on our way down river with much less of the firepower concentrated on us than would otherwise be expected.'

There was no harm in hoping, but Randall didn't know about the instructions given to the air crews above. Nor did the people of St Nazaire, for whom this sounded like another raid they'd have to sit out in their cellars. Antoinette Loréal, then a teenager, lived with her parents on the first floor of an apartment building on the Place de la Vieille Ville – Old Town Square. When the alarm went off they traipsed downstairs as usual with a suitcase, like every other tenant in the building. An outside entrance to the cellar gave glimpses of the night sky. 'There was the continuous circling of the English planes and the crash of anti-aircraft guns,' Loréal remembered. 'And no bombs.' Ginette Guillerme thought she did hear a few bombs – 'and then a great silence: we thought the alert was over and waited for the all-clear. Instead came the singular sounds of gunfire.'

The first ten planes had arrived bang on time from RAF Leeming in North Yorkshire, to find 10/10ths cloud cover at 5,000 feet. Their instructions not only ruled out flying below 6,000; they also stated that targets had to be 'definitively identified before attacking'. And for a bomb aimer peering down at so much cloud there was no way of identifying anything. The aircraft stayed over the target area for fifty minutes dropping nothing, and returned to base.

All six bomber detachments sent to St Nazaire that night had the same instructions and the same miserable experience – bar one, which saw a gap in the clouds and dropped a single bomb on the north end of the inner harbour.

For the Charioteers it was dismaying. 'The air raid seemed to have petered out and the searchlights were switching off one by one,' wrote Tiger Watson. 'This boded no good. It was just what we did not want.' On launch 177 at the rear of the starboard column Mark Rodier was seized later than many with a conviction that he would not survive the night. As the boats entered the wide mouth of the estuary, still undetected, he was heard insisting that his number two, Frank Arkle, made sure his personal effects were sent to his parents.

There would be endless recriminations. Did the air raid achieve its main aim of distracting St Nazaire's defences long enough for the flotilla to get past the big shore batteries? Or did it succeed in waking every German gun crew so that they were alert and ready when it mattered? It may have done both. What's certain is that it seeded anxiety and suspicion in the mind of Kapitän Karl-Conrad Mecke, commanding officer of the 22nd Naval Flak Brigade.

Mecke was a flak nerd: an air defence specialist since before the war. It is hard to think of a more exposed or vital defensive role in the entire German war machine at that time, and he carried the burden of responsibility on a wiry frame. In a team photo from November 1941 he smiles more nervously than his more ample fellow officers, from under a pencil-thin moustache. For his head-quarters he commandeered St Nazaire's most desirable piece of waterfront real estate, the Belle Époque Château St Marc overlooking what is now the Plage de Monsieur Hulot (the beach featured in Jacques Tati's 1953 comedy about Monsieur Hulot's holiday). From the chateau, Mecke enjoyed unimpeded views of the whole Loire Estuary, commanding forty-three guns whose fields of fire stuck out into it like giant molars. Most were in fortified emplacements around the harbour and across the river. Some of the toughest to get at were on rooftops.

Mecke was not afraid to show uncertainty and he messaged his junior officers shortly after midnight: 'I do not understand what the enemy is doing; I fear deployments of parachutists.' At 00.30 he circulated an update: 'Stay vigilant, including out to sea.'

Out to sea, the *Campbeltown* and her entourage were passing the wreck of the *Lancastria*. Tommy Durrant would have known it since his brother Jack had been there, and this was their chance to give the Germans seven bells in return. Captain Bob Montgomery, with Copland near the front of the *Campbeltown*, had been there too. Whether many others knew much about it is doubtful precisely because it was Britain's worst maritime disaster to that point or since, and Churchill had used a D-notice to keep it out of the papers. It was a cover-up that Churchill said he forgot about, but a cover-up nonetheless. Dive bombers had attacked the *Lancastria* with anything from 3,000 to more than 7,000 souls on board. She had sunk in fifteen minutes. Two terrible years later it was possible that the tide of the war was starting to turn. The question now was whether British efforts would be integral to that development or a supporting act. The next few hours would suggest an answer.

In the timeline of the run-in, every second counts. Every yard gained towards the dock without being detected narrows the field of fire for the German guns.

Burn and Collinson are still in their position off the destroyer's starboard quarter in launch 192; Burn at the bow, Collinson by the rear gun with most of their contingent of commandos. Looking left they can see the front of the port column in stark silhouette: 447 carrying David Birney and fourteen assault troops, 457 with Pritchard, Tiger Watson and George Wheeler. Up front, Curtis, Ryder, Newman, Signalman Seymour Pike and Navigator Bill Green are in the wheelhouse of MGB 314, where one shell could decapitate the operation. Bill Savage, a long way from Smethwick now, is manning the four-barrelled pom-pom at the bow of the gunboat, the apex of the force.

At 1 a.m. British time a guardship north of Pointe St Gildas sees the raiding force and tries to send a Morse signal ashore by lamp, but there's a light mist and no one notices. The spotter should follow up with a radio message, but doesn't have a working radio. At 1.02 Bill Green directs Ryder to leave the safety of the Charpentier Channel and head in a straight line over the shoals. Ryder slows to ten knots to keep the *Campbeltown* as high as possible in the water.

At 1.10 Korvettenkapitän Lothar Burhenne of Mecke's 809 Flak Battalion on the south side of the estuary phones in the second German sighting. He calls the Port Commander's office, where a stand-in, Enno Mengers, is in charge. Burhenne is told to mind his own business and keep his eyes on the sky. Not so easily dismissed, Burhenne then calls Mecke direct just as Mecke is getting similar information from Pointe de Chémoulin on his own side of the river. There, lookouts assigned to the heavy coastal guns on Pointe de Chémoulin have counted all eighteen vessels in the raiding force – but too late. They are already upstream and at too tight an angle for Chémoulin to fire on.

Mecke grabs his binoculars, sees the raiders' dark moon shadows and asks the Port Commander if a flotilla is expected at this time of night. The answer comes back: no.

Soon after 1.20 Mecke warns all units to be ready for a landing from the sea.

By now the raiders are deep into borrowed time, scarcely able to believe their luck. Beyond the worst of the shallow water, they have increased their speed to eighteen knots. There are two and a half kilometres to go to the port; three to the great dock. The sound of their engines travels easily over that distance and there's nothing in the sky to mask it. Yet so far neither searchlights nor Mecke's guns have found them. At 1.22 this changes. As the boats pass the Morées tower, a disused lighthouse on the last headland before the port, they are lit up by the five-foot lens of a searchlight positioned on rising ground behind the tower. A white cone picks out the *Campbeltown* surging upriver with a giant swastika streaming from a flagpole at her stern.

It's a confounding, extraordinary sight, 'theatrical and unreal', says Collinson. Within seconds, more lights illuminate the whole flotilla. Each craft stands out clear and bright, and Ryder wonders how long the bluff can hold. More than 600 lives depend on it. Stuart Chant and Arthur Dockerill are crouched in shadow on the starboard side of the *Campbeltown*, their rucksacks bulging with thick sausages of plastic explosive. These are the last moments of pure hope for the commandos. There's not a scratch on any of them yet.

Savage's orders are to hold his fire. The first shots from the other side are tentative: warnings from a bewildered flak battalion in the Villès-Martin district between the tower and the port. At the same time Pike sees a challenge by signal lamp from a guardship anchored dead ahead. It's a standard recognition signal: who goes there? Pike has an up-to-date German signal handbook lifted from Vaagso three months earlier, and he has fluency in German Morse. He plays for time. 'Wait.' Then he sends the call sign of a German torpedo boat known to be in the area, courtesy of Naval Intelligence. Then: 'Urgent: two craft damaged by enemy action, request permission to proceed up harbour without delay.'

The warning shots pause. Some of the lights go out but there's another challenge and more tentative shooting from the north bank. Pike signals again: 'Wait! Am being fired on by friendly forces.' Again, the shooting stops. Entirely taken in, the Acting

Port Commander calls Mecke to inform him these are German vessels after all and no cause for concern. But standard procedure is for ships challenged like this to stop and confirm their identity before continuing – and they are ploughing on.

It's 1.26. Ryder has smuggled the force past four huge artillery batteries that no longer threaten it, but he still has nearly a mile to go. Mecke has a decision to make. He orders one more shot across the bows of the intruders. Ryder replies personally, with a red flare fired from a pistol brought from Falmouth for this very moment. He has it on good authority that this should serve as a last-ditch recognition signal. It doesn't. Ryder's sources have mistakenly provided him with a flare designed to be fired down from a plane, not up from a boat. And anyway, it should have been orange. The flare drops into the water and fizzes out. It's 1.27, and the game is up.

'Was this to be another Charge of the Light Brigade into another Valley of Death? We prayed that this time no one had blundered.'

Jack Webb had reason to pray. The Charge of the Light Brigade eighty-eight years earlier was a catastrophe of arrogance, pig-headedness and miscommunication that led to the slaughter of a quarter of the British Empire's proudest, bravest cavalry unit in less time than it takes to smoke a cigar. It was a function of class, pride, vanity and the crazed pursuit of military glory★ for its own sake.

The Charioteers were fortunate by comparison – in their commanders, who cared genuinely for them; and their cause, which was just. There was no Captain Nolan to strike confusion and terror into an already lethal undertaking and there was no blind idiocy to lead fine men into a death trap. But there was a death trap, and the masterminds of Operation Chariot knew it, and

---

★ 'Military glory!' – the opening words of Cecil Woodham-Smith's *The Reason Why* set the tone of an unimprovable demonstration of the simple truth that everything in history has deep roots.

they threw their commandos and launch crews into it all the same.

The onslaught, when it came, was sudden and deafening. It felt to Ralph Batteson on launch 306 like 'being trapped inside a massive dustbin crammed with fireworks at the instant someone tosses a match to ignite them'. Below decks in the *Campbeltown*, Corran Purdon's main worry so far had been that the destroyer would run aground in the outer estuary. Twice she nearly did, shuddering over the sandbanks as her twin screws bit into them, slowing the ship almost to walking speed. 'Now we felt and heard the hammering and explosions of German shells and bullets . . . A shell, glowing red, passed through the ward room as we sat there but continued without exploding.'

At 1.28 Mecke instructed all flak units to fire at will, and for a few seconds the ordnance was all one way. Then Lieutenant Commander Beattie had the white ensign run up in place of the swastika on the *Campbeltown*'s rear flagpole and it seemed that every raider with a weapon fired back.

Savage was the first to find the target, raking the guardship end to end with a long burst from the pom-pom. Bill Green told him to swing round immediately after that to take out the pillbox on the Old Mole. Savage let it have a well-aimed burst. Behind them on the *Campbeltown* the sound of return fire was 'sweet music' to Don Randall, lying next to the port gunwale, half blinded by searchlights. It wasn't obvious to the German flak commanders on shore which targets to concentrate on first, but at least one machine gun outpost aimed immediately at the destroyer's bridge. Chief Petty Officer Albert Wellsted fell dead at the wheel. A telegraph-man who stepped forward to replace him was killed too. It was at this point that Tibbits took the wheel. Beattie, standing next to him, was staring intently into the night, looking out for the Old Mole as his final landmark. It would tell him the dock was minutes away and a few degrees to port. By chance a searchlight picked it out, and Tibbits straightened up for the final run-in to the target.

Tiger Watson, who became a doctor after the war, had given in to the recklessness of youth. He was standing on the port side of launch 457 blazing away at the nearest searchlight with a Bren gun and feeling 'nothing but elation'. Kneeling to change magazines, he glanced forward to see the *Campbeltown* 'ploughing along, brilliantly lit up . . . her sides alive with the flashes of the shells which were hitting her continuously'. Over his shoulder in launch 192, Collinson felt 'curiously unafraid' at first, surfing on adrenaline. Then the first of many shells that showed exactly why the Germans thought even the British wouldn't try anything like this hit the launch amidships at 800 metres per second. It took out both engines, the steering and several of the crew. Tom Peyton – a natural leader, tall, handsome, easy-going – was doubled over dying or already dead. Collinson couldn't see anyone else. Nor could he think straight: 'My adrenaline-fuelled euphoria vanished abruptly and I felt completely nonplussed as to what to do next.'

Chaos had taken over. At the front of the 192 Burn felt only a jolt and a sense of being out of control as the launch swerved to the left, scythed through the port column and hit the mole at eighteen knots.

In an air raid shelter between the Normandie Dock and the St Nazaire Basin a German tanker crew prepared for the worst as one of their own ran in shot through the hand and breathing heavily. 'We're out of ammunition,' he said. 'And the English are coming.'

On the *Campbeltown* Beattie ordered full speed ahead and the commandos braced for impact.

PART II

1.30—3.30 a.m.

5.   On land

Sam Beattie had one job. He had to hit the southern gate of the Normandie Dock square on as fast as possible. This would not have been straightforward even in broad daylight. The *Campbeltown* was nearly 100 metres long and after all her modifications was hard to manoeuvre at the best of times. Her steering gear was by now distinctly old-fashioned and her two propellers tended to drag her off course because they both turned in the same direction. She did not handle, Beattie said, like a normal destroyer at normal speeds. At seventeen knots and above she was more predictable, but, even so, arriving in the middle of the night at full speed under intense bombardment with no previous experience of the harbour was always going to be a challenge.

Beattie nearly made a disastrous error. Reaching out into the estuary downstream of the mole are two sea walls that form the outer harbour. For newcomers they can be confusing. So much so that when French news agencies first got hold of the story of the raid they created a starring role for a fictional French pilot on the assumption that Beattie couldn't have found his way without local help. But he did. By the end he didn't even have Curtis's gunboat to follow because it had to turn out of the way to let him through. And at first he mistook the east wall of the outer harbour for the Old Mole. Turning to port at this point would have driven the *Campbeltown* uselessly ashore half a mile short of its target.

With seconds to spare, Beattie realized his mistake and ordered a hard turn to starboard, swinging out into the river. At least this meant the *Campbeltown* cleared the mole rather than crashing into it, but then Beattie – with Tibbits at the wheel – had to turn back to port by just the right amount. Too much and the destroyer could lose forward speed and fishtail at the stern. In a worst-case scenario all the Charioteers' efforts could be wasted by a split second over-correction which could cause the *Campbeltown* to bounce off the dock gate instead of ramming into it.

The gate was hard to see despite the searchlights and tracer. At this high spring tide it sat low in the water, a thin stripe a different shade of dark. Beattie spotted it with less than 800 metres to go and told Tibbits to steer a course of 350 degrees – north by north-west. Newman was watching from the gunboat's bridge. His only remaining worry was that the *Campbeltown* would snag on an underwater boom put there to defend against attack by submarines. There was one, but it didn't trouble the destroyer. 'Through the boom she cut without a tremor,' Newman wrote. 'Flying timber, smoke, sparks and flames made it impossible to see very clearly, but when these cleared away, there she was firmly wedged right through the middle of the main gate.'

The *Campbeltown* hit the dock at seventeen knots at 1.34 a.m. British time; all 1,250 tons of her. The upper part of her bow rose up over the gate while the lower part crumpled back under her own momentum. Thirty-six feet of American steel crumpled like foil. As Tibbits expected, she came to rest only when her forward bulkhead hit the gate, and that put his five tons of concrete-encased explosive right up against it.

'Well,' Beattie said, 'there we are. Four minutes late.'

The *Campbeltown*'s foredeck was already a scene of carnage. Her route over the sandbanks had taken her unscathed past every piece of heavy artillery guarding the outer estuary, but she was still a sitting duck for Mecke's flak guns, and she was on fire. An incendiary shell had taken out her main forward gun, killed the whole gun crew and torn a wide hole in the deck. The innards of the ship below were burning. Smoke billowed out through the hole and wounded men lay either side of it where others were trying to get past. On the port side, Lieutenant Johnny Proctor, who had dressed for battle in a kilt, was now immobilized with a leg half severed above the knee. On the starboard side, Lance Corporal Jack Donaldson lay mortally wounded.

Another shell had killed the gunner strapped to the starboard Oerlikon at the stern of the ship. Lying with rucksacks full of explosives directly underneath the gun platform, Stuart Chant and others were peppered with shrapnel. Chant felt no pain but realized his leg was wet and sticky and his arm was spurting blood.

Corran Purdon and his demolition team clambered up from the wardroom into a theatre of mayhem. 'The noise was indescribable and tracer was everywhere,' he wrote, 'crossing the ship and coming towards us in seemingly slow coloured arcs of whites, yellows, blues, reds and greens.' That slow look was a cruel illusion, yielding to the crack and snap of live rounds whipping past or picking victims at random.

The main deck was slippery with blood. Chant reckoned three quarters of those taking cover behind its minimal protections were already wounded. He marvelled afterwards that they were not all killed. Perhaps the enemy was distracted by the fast-moving launches downstream, or inclined to think that because the *Campbeltown* had crashed to a halt her work was done. But still: 'One burst of fire from a 20-mm cannon would have killed all of us, and what is more could have ignited the hundreds of pounds of explosives we were carrying between us.'

It was about 1.40 a.m. Chant still had some cover from the ship's main superstructure, but those in front of it had none. They were especially vulnerable to flak and machine gun nests firing down at close range from rooftops at either end of the dock gate. The commandos were lit up on an enormous, smouldering target, stuck fast and going nowhere.

What happened next is easily misunderstood as inevitable, like the outcome of the war itself. Over the course of an hour and three quarters, on a battlefield about 400 metres long by 200 wide, the commandos did what Churchill had demanded of Mountbatten.

They fought back – not on a scale to avenge Singapore or the *Lancastria*, but emphatically enough to show it could be done; and to give the French a glimpse of what it would take to end their occupation.

There were echoes of history. At Balaclava, Captain Nolan rode back through the ranks of the Light Brigade mortally wounded and giving out 'a shriek so unearthly as to freeze the blood of all who heard him'. At St Nazaire, Johnny Proctor with his shattered leg gave the commandos a final reminder that they were fighting for their lives as they filed past him on the deck of the *Campbeltown* – but instead of shrieking he cheered them on. At Trafalgar, Nelson paraded in his admiral's finery on the quarterdeck of the *Victory*, defying the musketeers in the mizzentop of the *Redoutable* to kill him. At St Nazaire that role of laughing at the odds was played by everyone who stood up and presented their profiles to the invisible gun crews behind the searchlights – but it was played especially by Bill Copland, Newman's number two, who slung a rifle over one shoulder and walked up and down the *Campbeltown*, heedless of tracer, bullets, fire and smoke, urging on the soldiers he had hand-picked for this moment.

Their task was to get ashore, keep the enemy at bay and blow up three buildings vital to the dry dock's operation: two winding huts housing the gear that opened and closed the gates at each end, and the pumping station that filled and emptied it.

Newman wanted the job done in ninety minutes; two hours at most. Much longer, and he feared his force would be hopelessly outnumbered by German reinforcements sent from nearby garrisons. 'Success was dependent on getting in and out quickly,' he wrote. That in turn depended on training and planning – and no one could accuse him of skimping on either of those fronts. It also depended on adrenaline. His soldiers were channelling two years of pent-up frustration and energy and the amour-propre that came from being a commando – but they were channelling an almighty bio-mechanical rush as well. Whether or not they'd chosen to take the artificial stimulants offered as Special Ration Tablets, every one of them was amped up on natural ones. Chant found that he could get up and lead his unit despite his shrapnel wounds. Proctor thanked Copland for a tourniquet high on his left thigh and later survived being literally thrown over the side of the *Campbeltown* into a launch. Don Randall, shot clean through the arm, felt nothing at all until two hours later.

Many officers on the raid were convinced the Germans had been tipped off before their arrival, but the truth is that the defenders of St Nazaire had no idea what was about to hit them.

By 1.30, Acting Port Commander Enno Mengers had made a fool of himself twice in half an hour. First, he had told Lothar Burhenne of the 809th Flak Battalion that he should stop pretending to have seen ships that weren't there. Then he had told Karl-Conrad Mecke of the 22nd Naval Flak Brigade that the raiding force whose existence he had denied half an hour earlier was in fact German.

Now Mengers was wide awake and in damage limitation mode. He told an orderly to phone Herbert Sohler, commander of the 7th U-boat Flotilla, to tell him a large enemy ship had rammed the outer gate of the great dock. Sohler, ten kilometres along the coast in La Baule, assumed the orderly was drunk and told him he was relieved of his duties, but the orderly stood his ground.

Sohler demanded to speak to Mengers, who came on the line and said half the port and half the town were already in English hands. It was a wild exaggeration, but it got Sohler's attention. Once he was persuaded that the English really were landing in the middle of St Nazaire, he woke his subordinates, who suggested he was the one who was drunk. He then called Admiral Dönitz, who had more or less foreseen the whole thing three hours earlier. Dönitz didn't think Sohler was drunk at all, and asked quietly about the condition of his submarines. Sohler could only say he didn't know but he was hastening to find out. He assured Dönitz that the U-boat crews, who were too valuable to be risked in territorial combat, were being evacuated to La Roche-Bernard, thirty kilometres north of St Nazaire. Then, without waiting for anyone to wake his driver, he set off for the U-boat pens at high speed in his car. Seven months earlier a 'most secret' memo from the Admiralty in Whitehall to C-in-C Plymouth had requested a feasibility study for a raid on St Nazaire, noting encouragingly at the end: 'It has been reported that German officers sleep outside the town and do not reach their offices until 8 or 9 a.m. and that a surprise attack before this hour would stand a good chance of success.' This intelligence was broadly sound. The German decision-makers were on the whole billeted out of town in requisitioned villas like Mecke's. And while he and Mengers – and now Sohler – were obviously up and about now that a battle was raging, there is a distinct sense in German reports on the raid that others were still fast asleep.

Protocols were followed but no one formed a plan. In line with standing orders, preparations were made to evacuate the U-boat crews and, *in extremis*, to destroy the U-boats. Secret documents were gathered together in case they had to be burned. The captain of one of two boats being repaired in the Normandie dry dock said he had a bottle of petrol ready for the task. Mengers said afterwards that shock troops and reconnaissance units were deployed to the St Nazaire Basin, the Outer Harbour, the Place du Marché and the railway station, as if according to well-practised routine. But that wasn't how it felt to Leutnant M. A. Franz of the 208th Naval Artillery Brigade. He heard gunfire on the Boulevard de l'océan and ran there to find twenty men of the port's own defence troops mustering in a side street with one sergeant and no other officers. They proceeded to the unit's temporary headquarters in the École Louis Pasteur to find one more sergeant, no more officers and no one even aware of the landing alert. Suspecting paratroopers were about to fall from the sky, Franz deployed troops outside to be ready for them. He received no orders from a senior officer until 5.30 a.m.

The port's defenders were caught completely off guard and

took hours to muster a coordinated response. In the meantime, chaos reigned. Because of the air raid, flak troops, minesweeper crews, port security guards and customs staff were mixed up more or less at random in air raid shelters. Most were separated from their commanding officers and unsure where to find them. To be any use in defence they needed weapons, most of which had to be retrieved from barracks.

Mecke was the first senior German officer to seize the initiative. He ordered every battery of the 703rd and 705th flak battalions on the north bank of the river to contribute personnel for as many instant combat groups as could be formed – but without depleting the gun crews themselves. That meant secretaries, orderlies and technicians with basic training but barely a minute of combat experience between them.

In the U-boat basin, three minesweeper mechanics, all nineteen or younger, rose to the occasion by casting off and repositioning their boat in front of the pens without waiting for orders. They were later congratulated for their presence of mind.

In the dry dock, there was panic. The two boats being repaired there were lightly armed German tankers, the *Passat* and the *Schlettstadt*, their weapons out of action. Their crews had moved ashore into an air raid shelter on the west side of the dock when the sirens sounded. Most stayed there but at 1.30 the *Schlettstadt*'s captain ordered his mate and four others to man a 75mm flak gun on the roof of the pumping station near the west side of the south gate. Mate Kern and company were installed there just in time to get a unique grandstand view, from upstream, as the destroyer smashed into the gate and came to rest like a beached shark on top of it. Kern said afterwards that he started firing at 200 metres and got off thirty rounds before running out of shells. He claimed to have taken the destroyer clean out of the fight. It was Kern who then ran back to the shelter with the news that the English were coming.

They certainly were.

★

For all the blood and bodies in his way, Bill Copland was not going to be distracted from his task of getting men ashore to blow things up. He had fought at Passchendaele in the First World War and he nursed a simple hatred of the Germans that the second war had done nothing to dilute. This was payback. They were 'going to get a taste of what they'd been giving us,' he said many years later. But first he had to drag the wounded aside to clear gangways to the bow so those still walking could climb down onto the gate. 'Sorry to hurt you mate,' he said, 'but my chaps MUST get through.'

First off was Corporal Arthur 'Buster' Woodiwiss, of the Queen's Royal Infantry and 2 Commando, assigned to take out the rooftop guns hitting the *Campbeltown*. Woodiwiss became a builder after the war and retired to Kent, where he seldom spoke about the raid. But he did remember his part in it in some detail. He could hardly forget. Jumping off the destroyer because his assault ladder proved too short, he rushed the closest gun emplacement on its starboard side, fly-kicking a German grenade back the way it had come. It exploded. He followed it up with a couple of stun grenades of his own, eliminated the position's sentries with 'bitter hand-to-hand fighting' and killed those left inside it with his Tommy gun. He then wrapped an explosive sausage round the German gun, blew it up and moved on, ticking off three more guns as if on a shopping list. He was supported by his lieutenant and another corporal. It took them twenty minutes.

Next off the *Campbeltown* were a kilted team of Scottish assault troops including Don Randall and his commanding officer, Captain Donald Roy, a former trader on the Liverpool Corn Exchange who in 1931 competed in the Monte Carlo Rally. Each carried backpacks of explosives and a Colt 45. Accompanied by a corporal with a Tommy gun to watch their backs, they were used to climbing on and off ships. A training exercise that Randall wrote about involved four tankers tied up side by side. The idea was to use them as pontoons to attack a Scottish oil storage complex. They started at walking pace, 'clambering from ship to ship to land, then

1. Commander Robert Ryder VC, naval force commander for Operation Chariot, helmed the *Tai-Mo-Shan* as his first command. It was a forty-five-foot teak ketch that he sailed home via the Panama Canal; years later, it appeared in the film *Mamma Mia!*

2. Operation Chariot's main task was to destroy the only dry dock on the Atlantic coast big enough for the mighty *Tirpitz*, Hitler's 43,000-ton flagship.

3. Commandos training in Scotland a month before the raid. Once the operation was explained to them, they were all offered the chance to withdraw. None took it.

4. Each commando carried a Fairbairn–Sykes fighting knife, named after the two Hong Kong policemen who designed it.

5. The Normandie dry dock, seen here with the liner after which it was named, was then the biggest in the world.

6. The dock's huge southern gate, or caisson, was to be rammed at maximum speed by the explosive-laden HMS *Campbeltown*.

7. Lord Louis Mountbatten, head of Combined Operations. Rich, glamorous and above all driven, Mountbatten knew as well as anyone that the raid would be a death sentence for many of those involved.

8. John Hughes-Hallett, Mountbatten's Naval Adviser, claimed to have spotted a fatal flaw in St Nazaire's defences.

9. Robert Ryder, who could 'do everything' – he could sail, navigate by the stars, fall rapidly in love and stare danger in the face. He once clung to a card table for four days in the Atlantic after his ship was torpedoed by a U-boat.

10. Lieutenant Colonel Charles Newman VC, military force commander, rugby player and jazz pianist.

11. Lieutenant Stuart Chant of 5 Commando, a former broker's clerk at the London Stock Exchange, was tasked with blowing up the dry dock's pumping station. 'We almost dreamt explosives,' he later recalled of his training exercises.

12. Lance Sergeant Peter Harkness, a Post Office mail sorter from Glasgow. He and his close friend, fellow Glaswegian Bill Gibson, a mechanic with a gift for mischief, went into battle on launch 268.

13. Sub-Lieutenant Philip Dark was injured on launch 306 but still tended to the wounded on both sides once aboard the *Jaguar*, a German torpedo boat. He drew this self-portrait as a prisoner of war.

14. Torpedo specialist Lieutenant Nigel Tibbits with his wife, Elmslie, at their wedding reception in Shanghai in 1937. The ship is HMS *Gannet*. The quietly spoken Tibbits made sure that Operation Chariot would be a triumph in spite of everything, embodying the essential combination of understatement, guile and bravery.

15. Lieutenant Bill 'Tiger' Watson led the commandos of launch 457 ashore aged twenty.

16. Lieutenant Dunstan Curtis, commander of Motor Gunboat 314. He had a reputation for keeping a cool head in tight spots, and later served in naval intelligence under Ian Fleming.

17. Lance Sergeant Arthur Dockerill, former choirboy at Ely Cathedral and here pictured with his wife, Marjorie, on their wedding day, led Lieutenant Chant to safety with seconds to spare.

18. Sergeant Tommy Durrant VC was furious that his launch commander refused to put him ashore.

19. Able Seaman Bill Savage VC, formerly a brewer's boy and weightlifter in Birmingham, was the forward gunner on Motor Gunboat 314.

20. Korvettenkapitän Herbert Sohler, commander of the 7th U-boat Flotilla. Sohler's monomaniacal approach to crisis management on the night of the raid was the *Führerprinzip* in action.

21. Kapitän-zur-See Karl-Conrad Mecke, who warned his flak battalions during the air raid there was 'devilry afoot'.

22. Sub-Lieutenant Micky Wynn (*left*), 7th Baron Newborough, who had no formal naval training but made up for it with patriotism, an appetite for adventure and what seemed to be a suicidal sort of courage. Here he is pictured reunited at the end of the war with his chief motor mechanic, Bill Lovegrove.

23. Motor Torpedo Boat 74 at high speed, with Wynn at the helm. When a shell flew through the engine room, Lovegrove was plunged back into crisis mode; in the middle of that furious battle, he set about fixing the broken central engine of MTB 74.

over and through a network of oil pipes . . . The distances were not great but the footwork needed to be nippy and accurate. Then we ran it, then it was run again and timed. Then faster and timed again, then with equipment and arms.' Once they got it down to under half a minute they paused for supper and did it all again in darkness.

Now they picked their way past the hole in the foredeck and climbed off the *Campbeltown*'s port bow. Nigel Tibbits, having checked his fuses one more time, was already down on the dock gate holding an iron scaling ladder steady for the demolition men, and urging them on. Randall used his own bamboo ladder because he had to take it with him to his target – the gun nest on the pumping station's roof. It was a short sprint away. The ladder snapped in two when used a second time – it had been weakened by machine gun fire – but Randall and Roy found a stairway at the back of the building. They saw three Germans running down it. These were presumably Mate Kern and his comrades from the *Schlettstadt*. And it's worth pausing to consider their retreat. It was no more than a dash back along a quayside in the middle of the night, but when else had German troops fled British ones on continental Europe since the beginning of the war? The raids on Spitsbergen and the Lofoten Islands had been demolition jobs. At Vaagso there was house-to-house fighting and prisoners were taken but no one could say the target was a stronghold. This was different. Challenged at the most heavily defended point on the Atlantic seaboard, the soldiers of the Reich had fired back – and run for it. D-Day was still twenty-six months away but that moment when Roy and Randall realized their immediate task was feasible and would not necessarily cost them their own lives was a turning point.

Randall and Roy let others pursue Kern and went up onto the roof. Fortunately a fixed ladder led up there from the top of the stairway. There they found two unmanned guns and for a few strangely peaceful moments they prepared them for demolition. 'Concentration on our task relaxed the tension,' Randall wrote. 'Tracer was floating harmlessly and colourfully past overhead.' It seemed they weren't targets because the enemy assumed the roof was still held by their own side. When both charges were ready, the two men calmly squeezed their firing mechanisms and started counting.

'There were nine seconds to cross to the edge of the roof, climb down the ladder, then down the stairway to ground level to take whatever cover was available . . . We walked, avoiding hurry, to the edge and down.' The guns blew up. There were chunks of debris but no injuries and Roy and his men might have been forgiven for thinking the fog of war was lifting.

Below, another team was already working on the pumps. It consisted of Stuart Chant, Arthur Dockerill and fellow Lance Sergeants Ron Butler, Bill King and Bill Chamberlain, all of 1 Commando. In terms of objective danger they had surely drawn the shortest straw of any unit on the raid. They had to get into the pumping station, climb down forty feet below ground level, attach explosive charges to the four big impeller pumps they expected to find there, and get out before they blew.

Detailed drawings of the pumps had been provided by the French Resistance – notably in an extraordinary haul of documents flown to RAF Tangmere on 27 February by Gilbert Renault, alias Colonel Rémy, the former film producer and legend of the Free French. The pumps were elephantine pieces of hardware, set in concrete and housed in solid iron casings eight feet across. Chant and Dockerill and company had trained on similar machines in Scotland, Cardiff and Southampton. They were supervised by Captain Bill Pritchard and were told, as he had been, that they were preparing to destroy the docks in the event of a German invasion. They practised blindfolded by day so they were comfortable feeling their way at night. 'We almost dreamt explosives,' Chant recalled. The King George V Dock at Southampton was especially useful: it was almost as big as the Normandie Dock and the commandos had the run of it because no shipping was using it for fear of being bombed.

On the night, complications piled up fast. First, Chant was wounded, then Chamberlain was hit too. Dockerill, used to carrying lead on plumbing jobs in Cambridgeshire, simply picked up Chamberlain's sixty-pound pack as well as his own. Then they found the pump house doors were locked, which stumped Chant until Captain Bob Montgomery happened by with a magnetic charge perfect for blowing locks. Montgomery told Chant to ignite it, but by this time Chant's inventory of wounds extended to his left leg, right arm and both hands. 'My hands were trembling and very sticky with congealing blood,' he explained later. 'I asked [Montgomery] to do it in case the soldiers would think I was frightened, which I was.'

The doors blew open. From the outside the building had looked familiar from the King George V Dock. Inside, it was different. 'I suddenly realised I'd got a problem,' Chant said. Even in the gloom he could make out a tangle of girders and galleries, completely unlike the pumping station in Southampton. Which way led down? He turned to his right and found a stairway. Leaving the wounded Chamberlain to watch their backs with two Colt 45s, the other four followed the stairs into almost total darkness, each holding on to the belt of the man in front.

'The whole descent was punctuated with galleries which broke off [in] several directions with no indication as to which one led down to the main staircase,' Chant wrote. They had pencil torches but each lit up an area only about a yard across. It took seven flights of steps to reach the main floor, level with the bottom of the dock. 'Nobody said anything . . . and as I went on down I got this feeling of remoteness and detachment from the battle that was going on outside. We were almost in a silent world of our own.' The only sound, they all remember, was of Dockerill whistling 'The White Cliffs of Dover'.

The pumps were familiar even if the stairways and galleries were not. Each taking one, the commandos spent twenty minutes swaddling them in high explosives: eight 5lb sausages per machine, expertly placed and connected with a ring main of Cordtex fuse and two igniters. When the charges were ready Chant sent Sergeants Ron Butler and Bill King back up to ground level with instructions to call down when they got there. They were then to get clear with Chamberlain. Dockerill stayed with Chant, who was still unsteady from his wounds and knew he'd need help on the stairs. They would have ninety seconds.

'Dockerill and I waited quietly until we heard them shout clearance; then, giving Dockerill one igniter, I took the other and said, "I'll count three and then we'll pull the igniter pins at the same time". We looked at each other as I slowly counted, one-two-three – and I pulled the pin of my igniter and Dockerill did the same . . . Not stopping for another second I ordered Dockerill to go ahead of me and, clinging to his waist belt, we climbed up the stairs as quickly as we could.'

They reached the top with seconds to spare and ran from the building as it came apart behind them.

At this point, in this part of the battlefield, Operation Chariot was proceeding on time and to plan. In the time it takes to get a meal delivered in a restaurant, Newman's commandos had penetrated one of Hitler's most heavily defended fortresses, blown up some of his most valuable machinery and made it look easy.

It wasn't easy, as a separate battle unfolding at the far end of the dry dock showed. Three groups of commandos trotted down there. One, led by the superfit nineteen-year-old Corran Purdon, headed for the northern winding hut and broke it open with a sledgehammer. Working as if on auto-pilot, they primed it for destruction within ten minutes, and when the time came Purdon reduced its contents to twisted, useless metal within seconds. 'I pulled the pins of our igniters,' he wrote. 'It was a memorable sight. The entire building seemed to rise several feet vertically before it exploded and disintegrated like a collapsed house of cards.'

The other two groups had the task of blowing up the dry dock's northern gate in case the *Campbeltown* failed to destroy the southern one. The plan was to do this by lowering explosives into a yawning cavity between the gate's two walls. A roadway lay across the top of the gate, thought to be of timbers that could be moved aside to access the cavity, but it had been laid with tarmac. The groups were led by Lieutenants Gerard Brett, the historian of Byzantium and curator at the V&A, and Robert 'Bertie' Burtinshaw, who went into battle with his monocle, humming 'There'll Always be an England'. As they tried to get access to the cavity through a manhole cover they came under withering fire from six flak guns on towers across the inner Penhoët Basin, and another on the *Passat* in the dry dock. They never did get their explosives into the cavity, and had to lower them into the water on the upstream side of the gate instead. In the process Brett was hit at least twice. Burtinshaw and six others were killed on the gate. The *Passat*'s captain claimed in his report that one of his lieutenants, positioned on the fo'c'sle, killed four commandos with a single grenade.

The casualties were regrettable – but Newman knew they could have been worse. He said afterwards he would have been willing to take losses from bombs dropped by his own side if that was the price of 'getting in'. They'd got in, destroyed the pumping house and both winding huts and at least damaged the inner dock gate. The wreckage would take months if not years to repair. Until then the gates would not roll in or out. Within half an hour of the *Campbeltown*'s arrival, whatever happened with Nigel Tibbits's bomb, the dock had been put out of use.

For Herbert Sohler the big dock was a small consideration. All that mattered were his submarines, because they were all that mattered to Admiral Dönitz, because they, in St Nazaire, were all that mattered to Hitler. Sohler's monomaniacal approach to crisis management that night was the *Führerprinzip* in action.

At around two in the morning Sohler pulled up on the outskirts of St Nazaire. Behind him were two truckloads of reinforcements from Mecke's outlying flak posts that had been dispatched in a rush to the port. Sohler could see at once from the low-flying tracer patterns that the enemy had indeed arrived from the sea and not the air, and he was desperately concerned. He ordered the trucks to clear and hold the road to the U-boat pens, and followed to inspect their contents. All nine submarines had been primed for destruction with explosive charges. The troops guarding them were awaiting further orders but as far as Sohler could tell the base was not under attack. He phoned Dönitz to tell him his U-boats were intact.

Across much of St Nazaire the phones and power were down. The blackout heightened a general sense of alarm and confusion, and may explain why some junior German officers had to wait all night for orders.

Without instructions from above, they acted on their own initiative. In the St Nazaire Basin directly in front of the U-boat base, three minesweeper crews cast off and positioned themselves across the tunnel-like openings to the pens where the submarines were hidden. In the air raid shelter east of the basin, the unarmed crews of the *Passat* and the *Schlettstadt* tried to regroup. The *Passat*'s First Officer formed his men into two teams. His plan was to get them back on board their ship, where they would at least have access to weapons and where their captain and a few others were under fire from the *Campbeltown*. One team made it and set up a flak gun, which they used to torment Brett and Burtinshaw's commandos on the northern gate. The other team didn't, caught in Tommy gun fire from those same commandos as they headed north to start their work.

The dockside battle was fierce but self-contained, mostly taking place beyond the massive concrete barrier of the U-boat base. The only residential district near the action was the Old Town, south of the St Nazaire Basin and reached from the mainland by two bridges, a lifting bridge to the north and a swing bridge to the south. Gérard Pelou of the *Défense Passive* – the Home Guard, more or less – showed up there soon after 1.30 in the morning. He yelled down into the basement of an apartment building where nine families were still sheltering from the air raid: 'Are you there? Whatever you do, don't move. The English are landing!' The building was a former hotel on the Old Town Square. 'We assumed we were in for a long battle,' said Antoinette Loréal, the teenager who was living there with her parents. She guessed the square would soon be part of the battlefield, and she wasn't wrong.

Across the basin, 100 more civilians had crowded into the U-boat base for shelter from the air. They would be made to stay there through the night. Further away from the fighting, Gilberte Ollivier lost her arm and her husband to a stray shell from the far side of the river. Most Nazairiens suffered less but still were left bewildered. During a pause in the fighting, Loréal's father crept upstairs to look out across the estuary and rushed back down to say the river itself was on fire. Others looked up and saw the flames reflected in the clouds. When word got about that an English destroyer had impaled itself on the Normandie Dock gate the question why was hard to answer. Was this how the liberation started? If so, what next? If not, what had possessed them? There were no obvious answers. As Ginette Guillerme's neighbour said after peeking out of his attic window on the Place de la Gare and seeing tracer arcing low over the river, 'C'est très curieux.'

Buster Woodiwiss had no time for contemplation. At 2.30 a.m., forty minutes after he'd left the *Campbeltown*, his commanding officer announced it was time to fall back to Colonel Newman's temporary headquarters. It wasn't. The plan said that the rendezvous was at 3.15, but the officer, Lieutenant John Roderick, had mistaken red and green tracer for the red and green flares Newman was supposed to use to signal re-embarkation time. Not that it mattered. Despite suffering four serious casualties, Roderick's team had succeeded spectacularly. Having taken out four gun positions they'd dropped some hand-held incendiary bombs into oil storage tanks east of the dock and were now just holding territory.

Their route to Newman's mustering point took them back over the outer dock gate, where the *Campbeltown* blocked the way. There was no way round her. Woodiwiss and company had to climb back over the destroyer, and his account of this part of the action belongs in the pantheon of soldierly sangfroid.

'Lieutenant Roderick ordered withdrawal. I covered this so that our survivors could recross to the ship and regroup. I then climbed the lashed ladder up to the bows and pulled this up to prevent pursuit. A burst of fire indicated a counter-attack. A large group of Germans were forming to cross the open area we had just left. Lying abandoned on the deck behind the shrapnel shields were Brens [machine guns] with 100-round magazines which had been fired as we sailed up the Loire. I set up three of these behind the shields and began firing each of them in turn to prevent their advance and forced them to withdraw . . . I dropped all the spare weapons I could find into the Loire, collected all the Tommy magazines I could carry, rejoined my section and shared out the ammo.'

While fighting this one-man rearguard action, Woodiwiss knew about the four-ton charge beneath him, but not when it was set to blow. (No one knew; not even Nigel Tibbits. His acetone–cellulose fuses had such a wide margin of error that they could detonate any time from five to ten hours after activation, or more, or not at all.)

Chant and Dockerill had meanwhile narrowly missed being crushed by falling masonry as the roof of the pumping station lifted off and redistributed itself in chunks on the quayside. Their 160 pounds of explosive charges had utterly destroyed the pumps, but their combined force still had to be channelled somewhere, and there was nowhere for it to go but up. Chant's orders were then to go back into the building and take care of the electric motors that drove the pumps from two floors above them – but the floors had pancaked on top of each other and taken the motors with them. 'So we just did a little quiet wrecking with sledgehammers and incendiaries,' Chant wrote, before calling it a night.

Newman's masterplan called for an orderly re-embarkation

from the Old Mole. All being well, the first launch-load of assault troops would clear the mole of Germans and hold it until all demolition tasks were complete. The launches would then line up to take the soldiers back to England.

This presented a particular challenge for the *Campbeltown* commandos and others assigned tasks in the northern part of the docks. The only way to the Old Mole from there was via a narrow bridge between the Old Entrance to the St Nazaire Basin and the basin itself. Known as 'Bridge G' on Newman's maps, this had to be held at all costs. Holding it was the second main task for Captain Roy's men after dealing with the gun nest on top of the pumping house, and hold it they did, for an hour and a half.

Throughout this time Roy's men were under heavy fire from guns on the roof of the U-boat pens across the basin. Their only cover was a low brick wall near the bridge. If they stood, they were targets from the waist up. Roy's men remembered him standing the whole time, patrolling the northern edge of the Old Entrance looking out for returning demolition troops and their protection parties. Somehow he survived unscathed. So did Arthur Dockerill, arriving from the pumping house with Chant and the wounded Sergeant Chamberlain. Chant was now limping heavily. Dockerill, whose good fortune would perplex him for the rest of his life, was completely uninjured.

Roy's men waited because there had to be dozens from other units to be shepherded across the bridge. And yet for long periods no one came. 'Time passed and we were taking casualties,' Randall wrote. 'Some of these were beyond us to cope with, but most were not life-threatening; a 20mm ricochet made a hole in my left forearm but had not broken a bone and I saw [the bullet] fall out.' After a while Roy asked Randall to join him walking up a dark road which led between warehouses to the north end of the dock. A small pinpoint of light appeared, getting nearer. A tense moment, eased by an exchange of challenge and password, revealed the sole figure of Captain Micky Burn.

6. Atonement

After the war Burn told a story that was typically unbelievable and as far as anyone could tell completely true.

In the mid-1930s he had become friends with – and briefly the lover of – a Dutch baroness, Ella van Heemstra. She was married to an Englishman and had a daughter with him. As war approached, they divorced and mother and daughter moved to Arnhem, where, in the late spring of 1942, Van Heemstra spotted Burn in a German propaganda newsreel at the cinema. He was in an unfamiliar context – battle-weary, being marched at gunpoint through the streets of a French port – but it was definitely Micky. Van Heemstra was delighted. It meant he was alive, whatever military disaster he had been a part of. She knew the owner of the cinema and together they paid a secret visit to the projection room to clip three frames out of the newsreel to prove to Burn's parents he was alive. She then managed to get a message to him at his POW camp. They kept in touch throughout the war, and afterwards, when shortages in newly liberated Holland were more acute than ever and daily life a struggle even for minor aristocracy. In October 1945 Van Heemstra wrote to Burn to say her daughter – then sixteen – was gravely ill with jaundice, anaemia and malnourishment. Could Micky send cigarettes to trade for penicillin, which doctors said might make the difference between life and death? 'I sent loads,' Burn wrote in his memoir, 'and she wrote back that the barter had saved the child's life.' Burn was posted to Vienna for *The Times* and they fell out of touch. Years later he opened a Sunday newspaper to see a feature from Los Angeles on Ella and her daughter, who by then had recovered, and flourished, and changed her name to Audrey Hepburn.

Fans of *Breakfast at Tiffany's* owe Burn a debt of gratitude. But if

Hepburn was lucky to survive, Burn was luckier. More than half the commando troop he led were killed on the night of the raid. Only seven out of twenty-nine got back to England before the end of the war and he was the only one to get further inland than the Old Mole under his own steam. Over the course of about ninety minutes he walked the full length of the dockyard and back, alone, looking for trouble if that was all there was, but anxious above all to carry out his mission. His orders were to eliminate two gun positions on rooftops at the far north-east corner of the St Nazaire Basin; and then to prevent any German reinforcements getting over a nearby bridge from the mainland. In the circumstances he could honourably have stayed with Collinson and others, who found shelter in a lighthouse on the end of the mole and waited there until captured. But something drove him on even though he had only his revolver and a single hand-grenade to fight with, and it's not a stretch to think that that something may have been a yearning for atonement.

Seven years earlier Burn had been so infatuated with Hitler that, as he confessed to his mother, 'I cannot really think coherently.' He was in Nuremberg at the time, strung out on fascism after a week spent covering the massed Nazi rallies of September 1935. 'It has been so wonderful to see what Hitler has brought this country back to and taught [it] to look forward to,' he wrote. 'I heard him make a speech yesterday at the end of it all which I don't think I shall ever forget.'

What he omits to say about Van Heemstra in an otherwise painfully honest autobiography is that Nuremberg is where he met her – for at that point she was a Nazi sympathizer too. She and her first husband – Hepburn's father – were also supporters of the British Union of Fascists. Separated from him now, she felt free to cavort with the passionate young Burn in a high-summer fling she later told him was 'a holiday from yourself'. Nor was she the only well-connected Hitler fan in his address book. On paper at least Burn was at Nuremberg as a Nazi-certified member of the pro-Nazi Rothermere newspaper group; he was using an extended summer holiday from a junior reporting job on the Rothermere-owned *Gloucester Citizen* to try and land a scoop that would impress *The Times*. For that, more useful than his press card was his connection with Unity Mitford, 'who had become a friend in the smart social life of London'.

The six Mitford sisters, daughters of the Second Baron Redesdale, were all natural provocateurs. But even by their standards Unity was bold. She was a virulent anti-Semite who had fallen in love with Hitler and found that stalking him was neither hard nor doomed. By the time Burn caught up with her in Munich in August 1935 she was unquestionably his favourite Englishwoman. (Her only rival was her sister Diana. She was about to marry Sir Oswald Mosley, leader of the British Union of Fascists, but as singletons she and Unity had turned heads across Nazi Germany. 'Tall, flaxen-haired and cornflower-eyed,' Burn wrote, 'they strolled through the lounges of privileged hotels like a pair of off-duty caryatids.')

Unity showed Burn that to meet Hitler all you had to do was spend time at his favourite restaurant, the Osteria Bavaria on Schellingstrasse. In a sense he was only doing what his father had raised him to do: 'Always go to the top.'* How much higher could you go in search of a story in 1930s Germany than to Hitler's table? But when the moment came Burn disgraced himself.

The words are all there in a letter to his father which, steeling himself, Burn printed in full in his memoir:

Munich. 26th August '35
Dear Daddy,

I have justified my extended holiday and met Hitler. He came to lunch in the same restaurant as Unity Mitford and I, and I went up

---

* Sir Clive Burn practised what he preached. An inveterate social climber with a kind heart that tended to get him into debt, he eventually found a congenial niche and a knighthood as Secretary, solicitor and Keeper of the Archives to the Duchy of Cornwall.

to him among his adjutants and told him he was very popular with young English people, in German. He thanked me and told Unity Mitford afterwards that he thought me pleasant and he could always tell an Englishman from an American. She said she had forbidden me to speak to him in that abrupt way and he said he was very glad that I had, and would give me an autographed photograph and meet me again. I have been asked to the great Nazi Party demonstrations at Nuremberg which begin on the 9th and last a week. All expenses are paid. Mr Bell sent a telegram to say I could stay. Now I must go and see a labour camp.

The camp was Dachau. It had already been open for two years. Prisoners had already died there. Burn was shown a Potemkin version, naturally. Like many, he was taken in, wilfully blind to the cruel reality behind the spruced-up bunk rooms and workshops he was shown. He chose to believe the camp was part of Hitler's solution to unemployment. In an unpublished write-up of his trip he even went out of his way to soften the impact of an admittedly detailed description of punishment beatings at Dachau, by noting that the beatings were supposedly not handed out more than once to the same prisoner and that the cat-o'-nine-tails was 'not yet obsolete in England'.

In his memoir he was disgusted with himself. 'What sort of person was I then,' he asked, 'to write from so sickening an attitude, and attempt such monstrous exculpations, such contortions to excuse the inexcusable?' Well, there was an answer. He was the sort of person to impress Geoffrey Dawson at *The Times*. Even the *Gloucester Citizen* didn't print anything Burn wrote in Munich, but in 1937 its editor wrote him a glowing reference and he was taken on as a glorified copy boy in the Imperial and Foreign News Department of the grandest paper in the world.

Burn was young. He was less worldly than he pretended to be, except perhaps in his experience of 'the twilight youths who hung about the West End of London [and] were not there for the late-night shopping or the theatres'. By his own account he quickly re-educated himself on his return from Germany, reading reports on the Nazi phenomenon by (mainly American) journalists who knew what they were doing; who knew to ask what was happening to Jews, Communists, dissidents, trade unionists; who understood that totalitarianism's default strategy with numbers is to make them up, and with treaties to tear them up. As a result Burn rejected not only Nazism but the idea of appeasing it. Dawson was – notoriously – an appeaser, but he liked Burn even so, handing him opportunities that established *Times* names could only dream of. There was something about the devil-may-care Burn style that appealed to an editor who was considered stodgy.

So it was that Burn was sent to Canada and the United States in 1939 to cover a royal tour. This was not just any royal tour. It was a trans-continental train tour by the principals, the King and Queen, on a mission to win over the New World to the appeasement the government as well as *The Times* endorsed. And Burn turned out to be not just any correspondent. He was still only twenty-seven, decades younger than most of the travelling press. But he charmed them as he'd charmed Dawson. Once, he became the story. Tommy Thompson of the *Express* profiled him from Banff in the Rockies, where he had become the 'mascot of the pilot train'.

'Young, tousle-headed, debonair, and in the habit of breaking into a Serge Lifar dance in the middle of a station platform, he did not tie up with my memory of the London *Times*. All the Americans loved Michael Burn, although half of them could not understand what he said. His accent was so veddy Briddish [that I had to act as interpreter.'

This, to be clear, was by one reporter about another who should have been a rival. It was unheard of.

By the time the royal party got to Washington, Burn's reputation preceded him. The *Times'* resident White House correspondent, Sir Willmott Lewis, introduced the travelling tyro to the President.

'Why!' Franklin Roosevelt declared, leaning across the Resolute desk in the Oval Office to extend a hand. 'Mr Michael Burn, from the London *Times.*' Burn wrote later that FDR's charm was overwhelming. In New York, Thompson and his wife threw a party for Burn at which a braless Tallulah Bankhead asked him: 'What can I do for you?' He had no words.

In London, Dawson was so delighted with the political and journalistic outcomes of the tour that he asked Burn if he would like to go back to DC to be trained up as a full-fledged foreign correspondent. He declined; unlike his boss, he believed diplomacy was doomed and war was coming. He told Dawson he'd joined up with the King's Royal Rifle Corps and wrote later that 'enlistment became my reaction to his foreign policy'.

It didn't bring contentment. Sex put paid to that. Burn was drawn to one-night stands with men (having turned down the offer of something steadier with Guy Burgess, the Soviet spy). He also wanted to have what he called a profound experience with a woman. But his flirtations with women went nowhere and 'unhappiness began to seep, and then surge, into my hitherto rather happy nature'. This was the multi-talented, mercurial creature who bumped into Charles Newman on Buckingham Palace Road barely a month before the raid on St Nazaire; and who emerged out of the gloom with his blue pencil torch two hours after the raid began in earnest.

He'd found his gun nests – but no one in them. He'd pulled a pin from his one grenade but thought better of killing anyone with it and thrown it into the basin. Apart from a chance encounter with Major Copland, who was inspecting the docks like a registrar on ward rounds, he'd seen no one in all this time. 'I was leaving an isolation in which I had led no one, destroyed nothing, protected no one, hindered no enemy movements,' he wrote. He felt a failure.

Roy directed Burn to a tall building on the other side of Bridge G. This was the rendezvous point chosen by Newman, who was beginning to wonder why more soldiers hadn't joined him there. The always cheerful colonel was in a slightly disconcerting bubble. He'd brought a skeleton headquarters staff with him, including a radio specialist, but the equipment wasn't working. For more than an hour no one had replied to requests for updates. He'd also brought a supply of signal flares to tell the demolition crews and their protection teams when it was time to withdraw. But the flares had been lost in the battle. The Regimental Sergeant Major carrying them had been shot and drowned in the Old Entrance trying to get ashore. Outwardly at least, Newman was unperturbed. There was plenty of evidence things were going well.

'A large explosion on the other side of the Old Entrance was the first indication of good work being done,' he wrote after the war. This was the southern winding hut. The pumping station took longer for Chant and his crew to prepare for demolition, but Newman noted that explosion with satisfaction too. By this time 'buildings were going up right and left in the dry dock area' and soon the teams responsible were trickling over the bridge to be congratulated in person. (Some trickled under it instead. Chant decided it was safer to cross Bridge G by swinging hand-over-hand along the girders beneath it. His whole team got across this way, including the wounded Chamberlain.)

'Next to arrive was Major Copland,' Newman wrote. 'His report that all had been well with the *Campbeltown* and the wounded [including the critically injured Johnny Proctor] was a great relief to me.' In the meantime Newman's own team had dealt briskly with a German unit that had chosen to take cover where he wanted to set up his own command post (a few grenades sufficed), and Troop Sergeant Major George Haines, one of the most fearless and experienced of all the commandos, had methodically pummelled the German gunners on the roof of the U-boat pens with 2-inch rounds from a portable mortar.

The only cloud on the horizon was the arrival of Captain Burn without any of his men. Copland confirmed quietly to Newman that this was because none of the others had got ashore, but even that didn't seem to bother the colonel unduly. It simply meant the time had come to withdraw Captain Roy and his bridgehead and get back to the Old Mole. *This* would have been the time for one of the red and green signal flares. Since they were lying at the bottom of the Old Entrance, Newman sent a runner instead. Dashing across Bridge G and back through increasingly heavy gunfire, Corporal Jack Harrington of 2 Commando and the Royal Ulster Rifles delivered the withdrawal order and rejoined Newman's party just as it was leaving the rendezvous point.

The Old Mole was 300 metres away. It was separated from the Old Entrance by warehouses and railway sidings with goods wagons that provided useful cover and obscured the view. Newman, Copland, Burn, Chant, Dockerill and the others moved carefully through the shadows, keenly aware from sporadic shouting and gunfire that they were encircled by a growing number of German troops. There is no indication that when the commandos reached the quayside north of the mole at about 3.30 a.m. any of them knew what to expect.

Randall had caught up by now, to see the river lit up by burning launches. 'Two were visible to me as the last view I had of the flotilla that was to take us home,' he wrote. 'They were end-up in the water, slowly sliding beneath the surface, their flames dousing as they went under, leaving only burning petrol on the surface to lighten the darkness of the night.'

'Good heavens, Bill,' Newman said to Copland. 'Surely those are ours?'

7. At sea

Rewind two hours. The *Campbeltown* is churning over its final thousand yards to the dock. Launch 192 is scything across the flotilla, about to crash into the sea wall south of the Old Mole. The other launches are coming up behind and abreast of her at eighteen knots, two a minute, entering a field of fire not much bigger than the Serpentine in Hyde Park; a dozen or so football pitches. Their gunners and captains are looking for targets and landing places but are blinded by searchlights. They're running on high-octane petrol, which is explosive. They've been advised to empty their reserve tanks but their main tanks below decks are half full for the return journey, and are completely unprotected.

After 192, the first two launches in the starboard column overshoot. Further back in the port column two more do the same. By the time they realize their errors yet another two – one in each column – are crippled and in flames. One of these, launch 447, is carrying David Birney, whose commandos are supposed to clear the Old Mole of enemy troops and hold it so the next launches in line can land their soldiers safely. But Birney is drifting south of the mole and preparing to abandon ship. Next to arrive at the north side of the mole is 457 under Tom Collier. He has promised to get his men ashore, and does, despite intense machine gun fire from not one but two pillboxes on the mole itself. The group that jumps off 457 includes George Wheeler and Tiger Watson and is led by Captain Bill Pritchard, the explosives expert who has already led them all a merry dance through most of the important docks in England. They assume Birney and his team have cleared the mole. To double-check, Watson fires a burst from his Tommy gun into the closest pillbox. He hears nothing, but smells fresh cement.

The smell is a clue that these gun positions have recently been reinforced. It's another sign that David Paton, the medic, was right to anticipate defences where he has been tasked with setting up a first aid post. Watson and Pritchard are wrong to assume it has been dealt with. It's identified on German maps as position 63. It has a clear shot at everything afloat in two ninety-degree quadrants either side of the lighthouse at the end of the mole, and it will torment the launches until they've all fled or been destroyed.

Those that escape punishment from position 63 will get it from Mecke's flak emplacements on both sides of the river; from the closest of the heavier artillery posts, the number two battery of the 280th Marine Artillery Battalion at Le Pointeau; or from any of the twelve armed tugs, minesweepers and harbour defence boats moored in the St Nazaire Basin.

It all happens very quickly: within fifteen minutes of the *Campbeltown*'s ramming of the dry dock, the front four launches in the starboard column of Ryder's doughty force have been blown up or are burning. In the port column the first two are sunk and the next four withdraw without landing troops. Of them, two are subsequently lost. Of the remaining five, four are destroyed or scuttled. So when Newman peers out from the shadows near the mole and muses that 'those are ours', he's right. They were, but the remnants he can see have been burning for an hour and a half and they're going nowhere.

Most wars are longueurs of boredom and frustration interrupted by intense and disorientating bursts of action. The campaigns of attrition on the Western Front in the First World War were an exception and a formative one for Churchill. His reaction to their prodigious human cost was: never again. The early raids of the Second World War, including Chariot, were in a sense a return to the kinetic combat he knew from his twenties in India and South Africa. Once again there is a seductive parallel between St Nazaire and Balaclava: the Charge of the Light Brigade, from the moment the Earl of Cardigan began his imperious trot down the Valley of Death to the moment he regained the Causeway Heights (miraculously unscathed), took all of twenty minutes.

The Light Brigade was doomed by the mutual loathing of Lords Cardigan and Lucan. The Charioteers weren't doomed, but their commanders did choose to have their only recorded argument in the heat of battle. Dunstan Curtis had steered their gunboat as planned in a wide arc to starboard to get out of the way of the *Campbeltown* as she approached the dock. For a few minutes Ryder and Newman could only watch as the launches ran into the full force of the German guns. Ryder must have seen the fourth launch in the starboard line explode. This was launch 268, commanded by Bill Tillie and carrying a large contingent of Burn's 6 Troop commandos. Fifteen of the seventeen aboard were killed, including Harry Pennington, the rugby star from Warrington and Oxford; Morgan Jenkins, who'd conquered his fear of heights behind a Lakeland pub; Bill Gibson and his dear friend Peter Harkness – all killed in an instant; a bright orange flash.

Ryder will have seen it but there was no time to dwell on it. He was more concerned about the guardship anchored off the east mole of the Outer Harbour, which seemed to be coming back to life despite the pasting Bill Savage had given it two minutes earlier. His anxiety was heightened by the fact that Curtis's radio antenna had been shot away. If he wanted to give new orders he would have to do it by loudhailer. C. E. Lucas Phillips, the military historian, later reconstructed the tense exchange on the gunboat bridge verbatim, after consulting with both parties:

Ryder: Charles, that ship has got to be sunk. I must find a
    torpedo motor launch at once.
Newman: No – you simply must get me ashore first.
Ryder: Not until I have sunk that ship.
Newman: Look here, Bob; your job is to get me ashore, and
    as quickly as possible.

Ryder: It's also my job to sink that ship before she does any
 more damage.
Newman: For heaven's sake, Bob, put me ashore first and
 sink your ship afterwards.

Ryder gave way, and even at this distance it seems significant that he
did. The improviser was giving way to the planner. Not only were
Ryder's operational orders to his launch captains much shorter than
Newman's to his officers; they lacked a contingency plan. Now that
landings were proving impossible at the Old Mole and Old
Entrance, next steps were anyone's guess. Ryder's reliance on the
initiative and enterprise of each commanding officer was being put
to the most brutal test. In principle it was obvious they were heading into chaos in which the simplest plan would probably be
forgotten at first contact with reality. In practice some discussion of
alternative landing places or holding patterns might have helped.
Even without a shot fired there were going to be traffic jams at the
Old Mole and Old Entrance simply because the boats were arriving
so fast. But there had been no such discussion. On the contrary, the
combined plan issued on Ryder's and Newman's behalf by Admiral
Forbes stated that 'even damaged launches were to do their utmost
to reach their landing positions even if this may be some time after
the main assault'. And now Ryder found that when he wanted to
exercise his own initiative he couldn't impose his will on the man
with the plan – even though, once Newman got ashore, he had
little to do for at least an hour but wait.
 From Ryder's own point of view, at that moment there wasn't
time to argue. Curtis brought the gunboat neatly into the south
side of the Old Entrance and there Ryder and Newman shook
hands and wished each other luck. Holman the reporter was
watching and said it was 'a happy, cheerful man who dashed
ashore from the motor gunboat accompanied only by his adjutant and two or three commandos'. Ryder then told Curtis to
turn round and move to the north side of the Old Entrance,

where he was immediately distracted by wounded survivors from the *Campbeltown* looking for a ride home. He also had questions at the back of his mind about the *Campbeltown* herself. He felt he had to make sure she was stuck fast and properly evacuated so that when she blew – assuming she would blow – she wouldn't take any of his people with her.

Ryder need not have worried. Copland and Captain Beattie were both busy taking care of the destroyer. But he set off anyway on foot with only Signalman Pike for company on a quixotic trip to inspect her. The upshot was that whatever happened next at the Old Mole, he would be unaware of it.

The plan for the port column was meticulous; a management consultant's approach to organizing war. After 447 had cleared and held the Old Mole, another boatload of assault troops would head briskly south to eliminate any gun positions on the eastern break-water of the Outer Harbour. Then 457's commandos would trot through the Old Town to the northern lock gate of the southern entrance to the U-boat basin and the bridge next to it.

The next four launches in the column would complete a sequence of demolition jobs on the rest of the southern entrance (there were two more lock gates and another bridge) before withdrawing in orderly fashion to the north side of the mole. There the launches would be waiting 'bows outward under the orders of the piermaster'.

On paper it made perfect sense. Tantalizingly, it might even have played out as Newman dreamed if surprise, preparedness and hunger for the fight were the only factors: we now know these were all on the Charioteers' side despite the low cloud cover and its impact on the air raid. But the fact that the raid petered out so soon was not ideal. From the fifth boat in the line Ordinary Seaman Ralph Batteson saw the result clearly: 'They were all at their guns, ready to have a bash at us as we got in.' The engine failure of the second launch in the column earlier in the day left half the group's assault troops at the back of the line instead of near the front. The demolition troops who now had to go ashore without their help had only Colt 45s for self-defence. And having satisfied himself that they really were English rather than German, Karl-Conrad Mecke had told his batteries to fire at will.

Ablaze and out of control, launch 192 cut across 447's bow soon after 1.30 a.m. Seconds later both 447's deck-mounted Oerlikon guns were hit at close range and their crews killed. By the time the 447 turned left to approach the north side of the mole only six of Captain Birney's fourteen commandos were not dead or wounded. Birney was still eager to get ashore and there were two ways to do this: up a gently sloping slipway or a flight of steps a few feet closer inshore. Birney's skipper seemed to have run aground trying for the slipway so he backed out to try again. For a moment the launch had been directly under position 63 and too low for its guns, but now it was a sitting duck again. Its engine room took a direct hit and caught fire. The launch drifted backwards into the path of Tom Collier's incoming 457, and then south with the tide.

Throughout the night soldiers made split-second decisions with their lives at stake. Birney made one now. When the order came to abandon ship he didn't hesitate, leaving his weapons and following two of his surviving men into the water. It was cold. All the survivors said so. It may have been balmy in the Fal in Cornwall on their final days in England, but in late March the Loire carries meltwater direct from the Massif Central. Worse, this patch carried a skin of oil left by the burning 192.

One of those who went in before Birney was a strong swimmer with a powerful imagination. Troop Sergeant Major Ted Hewitt of the Essex Rifles and 2 Commando struck out for the north bank and eventually reached it despite the current, sustained by a vision of Jesus walking on the water at his shoulder. Birney was not such a powerful swimmer, or believer. He called for help. David Paton, who considered him a dear friend, heard him from launch 307. 'We managed to lock hands,' he wrote, 'but then the boat's propellers gave a great surge in reverse and our hands were torn apart because of the oily water.'

A few of those too badly wounded to leave launch 447 were rescued as she burned. But sixteen of her sailors and commandos were either killed or drowned. Birney expired in the water. His body was found the next day on the beach at La Baule, where Admiral Dönitz and his U-boat captains spent the night.

The battle had a dreadful in-built momentum. Behind launch 447 the others were closing on the mole and the Old Entrance at most 400 yards apart, a new one arriving every minute. As 447 backed out its skipper was already yelling at Paton's, two boats back down the line: 'Don't go in! It's impossible to land!' Further back, Ralph Batteson could already hear and smell the 'crackle of burning mahogany' from 192. Then the petrol tanks of 447 exploded and the sea itself caught fire. Batteson said he saw men burn alive in the petrol that covered the surface, 'while others sank in the bloody foam as they succumbed to their wounds'.

At the front of the line Collier was landing his troops under a hail of stick grenades and machine gun fire from position 63. Tiger Watson was one of the first ashore. He'd heard screams from the withdrawing 447 but assumed that Birney and his men had landed even so. Watson was annoyed to find the forward gun crew hadn't lowered a handrail at the bow to make it easier to jump off. 'Then I realised that [Sub-Lieutenant Kenneth] Hampshire and his men were lying round their gun either dead or wounded,' he wrote. 'There was no time to lose getting the rail down ourselves.'

Back in the wheelhouse Able Seaman Herbert Dyer, the Scarborough Town footballer, thought he'd felt the launch touch bottom – just as 447 had. 'First off I said to the skipper, "Is it shallow here sir?" He said, "No it's not, it's hand grenades."' He sent Dyer below to see if the commandos had left any weapons, because the launch's own twin Lewis machine gun had jammed and they had nothing else to fire back with. Dyer came up empty-handed to find the grenades still coming. 'And one dropped right in amongst us on the bridge and it cleared them right out,' he said. 'It took the captain's leg off and it took my Scotch boy – took his insides out.'

The 'Scotch boy' was Ordinary Seaman Leith Scott-Dixon from Aberdeen, twenty years old and now mortally wounded. Collier's leg was practically severed but he was still coherent. Dyer, miraculously, was unhurt. Collier's plan was to get to a place of relative safety in midstream and wait there till required for the pick-up. But the whole estuary was now a free-fire zone, criss-crossed by searchlights that left no hiding places. Losing blood and in fearful pain, Collier manoeuvred for half an hour under attack from both banks of the river, then tried to head back towards the mole. The closer he got to it, the fiercer the pounding from position 63. It was only a matter of time before the boat caught fire.

In that half-hour the second and third launches in the starboard column surged upriver past their designated landing place in the Old Entrance. They resorted to loudhailers to ask each other where the hell they were, and circled back to try again. Launch 262, in front, was commanded by a former Metropolitan policeman with a young wife and daughter and an instinct for self-parody. His name was Ted Burt – 'dismal' as a vacuum cleaner salesman, 'abortive' as a would-be Post Office engineer and reconciled to policing before the war like many other 'ex-public schoolboys who had failed to make the grade elsewhere'. On the night of 28 March he showed another instinct – for selflessness – that saved lives but also ended up costing them.

At about 1.40 he nosed into the Old Entrance and put his commandos ashore on the upstream side. Their target was Bridge G, once Captain Roy's team had seen everyone else across it. It wasn't far, but they still never got close to it. As Burt was backing out he saw them running back to the quayside in the face of lethal cannonades from the harbour defence boats in the U-boat basin. Burt went back in to pick them up. Minutes later more commandos appeared out of the night, scrambling over barbed wire on the upstream side of the Old Entrance. This was a demolition unit led by Lieutenant Chris Smalley. Far from retreating, they were looking for a quick ride home having already completed the demolition of the dry dock's southern winding hut. Burt went back for them too, even though his forward gun was jammed and the fire from the boats in the basin was as furious as ever. 'I loaded up with as many commandos as I could, until the motor launch looked like a Thames pleasure steamer on a bank holiday, cast off and started to make my way downstream amid a hail of everything from machine gun bullets to 3-inch shells – most unhealthy as I soon found when the microphone with which I was directing what was left of our armament was literally shot out of my hand.' As 262 made for open water for a second time it was hit in the stern, the funnel and the engine room, but somehow kept moving.

Unlike Ryder, still busying himself with the *Campbeltown*, Burt was aware of the disaster unfolding near the Old Mole. He will also have read his orders, which instructed commanding officers not to stop for survivors, especially if it would put their own boats at risk. Then Burt saw the limping remains of 457.

'As we approached, I saw a crumpled figure on her bridge and took my boat alongside to take him off. It was her captain, who, though mortally wounded, had ordered her crew to abandon ship without him.' Collier begged Burt to keep moving for his own sake. It was too late. As Burt recorded:

'The next thing I knew was that a 3-inch shell hit my bridge, ploughed through the crowded personnel there and out the other side where it burst. By the grace of God all I got was a chip taken out of my backside, as I had obviously been shielded by the press of sailors and soldiers around me . . . This was followed by two more shells, one in the engine room and the other down aft near the magazine . . . The [launch] was now ablaze, and with 2000 gallons of aviation spirit in the fuel compartment it was a matter of minutes before she blew up.'

He was right about that. He gave the order to abandon ship, and what was left of his crew began helping the commandos into the 262's few life rafts. The launch was drifting by now, close to Collier's, whose crew had not in fact abandoned him entirely. Dyer and Scott-Dixon, the Scottish lad, and Signalman Albert Jones were still aboard with him. Now Dyer and Jones threw a raft over the side and helped Collier and Scott-Dixon onto it.

'The skipper came, the signalman was hanging on, the boy with his wound was lying on the raft and the tide was taking us out,' Dyer recalled. They managed to get a line round the mast of a shipwreck as they were swept past it, but Dyer was a lonely witness to the fact that staying in place was not the same as staying alive. 'The skipper you could see wasn't very good. He just let go and went under. The signalman, he wasn't dead [but] he said "cheerio" and he went under. By morning the Scotch boy was gone too.'

Fifteen of those who set out on Collier's boat were killed or drowned. Fourteen were killed on Burt's. None of those he stopped or went back to pick up made it back to England before the end of the war. The launch that followed Burt up the river, skippered by a lawyer who brought a rugby ball with him in case there was time to play while waiting to re-embark the commandos, was shot to pieces in the Old Entrance with the loss of nine men. Sixteen more had perished with Birney from the 447.

Nine of the seventeen launches, gunboats and torpedo boats in the flotilla were destroyed in the first desperate hour of the battle. Five more sank later or had to be scuttled. They were thrown deliberately at hardened landing points and there was no plan B. On the contrary – in Newman's words – 'Our chances lay in the fact that the landing places chosen, the Old Mole, the Old Entrance and the Dry Dock itself, were the most unlikely that the enemy might consider for landing operations, *as there were excellent landing beaches on both sides of the Dock Area.*' So he knew there were alternatives. The whole point was to look the other way. The point was to do the impossible, as Mountbatten loved to say. The trouble was, it proved to be just that. In Lord Louis's defence, ramming the dock with a destroyer did offer a proof of his theory that doing the impossible made it possible, but storming the rest of the port with wooden speedboats made that same thing look ridiculous. For the launches and everyone on them 'the impossible' was a simple description of reality. As Lucas Phillips wrote without quite enough irony: there were no failures, only impossibilities. He even suggested the launches 'stood up wonderfully to the cannon-fire of Oerlikons and even to the shells of Bofors [anti-aircraft guns]'. This is completely wrong, and an especially peculiar thing to say at the end of a book that shows in detail just how wrong it is. The launches did not stand up well and there were failures – of planning, tactics, communication and design – that played out from the first second of the battle to the last. To pretend otherwise ultimately distracts attention from the most remarkable aspect of Operation Chariot, namely the equanimity of its participants in the face of death.

Lucas Phillips, in 1958, may simply have wanted to avoid offending the many planners of Operation Chariot who were still alive. One of the most candid takes on the launches' performance came from one of their own skippers, Kenneth Horlock. He nursed launch 443 all the way back to Falmouth and wrote afterwards about the moment he got to the front of the port column and grasped the two pillboxes on the mole were still undamaged despite everything. 'It was then that I realised that this part of the operation was a flop,' he said in his report. The Australian historian Peter Stanley offered two simple insights: i) the success of the *Campbeltown*'s part in the mission was the overwhelming priority; ii) 'Everything else was secondary, but almost everything else went wrong.'

This may seem unfair on the commandos who blew up the pumping station and the winding huts, but they were delivered by the *Campbeltown*. Stanley's assessment is a useful corrective to the idea that the launches somehow defied the odds. They didn't. Their crews were unimaginably brave, but as attack boats the launches were worse than useless.

8. On land

Only one launch from each column of six landed any troops ashore. From the port column it was Collier's commandos: fifteen men in three small groups that were confused, dispersed and then effectively decapitated. In the circumstances they performed heroically.

Tiger Watson led the way, twenty years old and with a burning desire to prove himself. His instructions were to make sure the mole was cleared of the enemy before proceeding, so immediately on landing he scrambled up a ladder onto the flat roof of position 63. Crucially, he found it deserted. What's more, he'd seen a row of German helmets running off the Old Mole into the Old Town, hands raised as if in surrender.

Was it a ruse? There was no reason to think so, and in any case the other two groups of commandos were off the launch and itching to get down to business. One was led by Philip Walton, a schoolmaster in peacetime. In training he had teamed up with Micky Burn and Tom Peyton to give some wealthy fugitives of the blitz at their Devon hotel 'something to remind them of us'. It involved slabs of TNT, fifty broken windows and a dressing down. The other group was led by Captain Pritchard, the explosives expert, who could see as well as Watson that the mole was deserted.

'What the hell are you up to, Tiger?' Pritchard yelled. 'For God's sake get on!'

There was no sign of the enemy soldiers last seen running ashore, and no time to waste. Walton's men were to blow up the inner lifting bridge at the southern entrance to the basin. George Wheeler was one of them and had been assured it would be quite straightforward. He had great confidence in his training, and besides: 'We presumed the . . . assault groups had cleared all opposition away and it was dead easy. All we would have to do was to go to the lock gates with our 75 lbs of explosives, done up in their separate little packets with their detonators and their fuses, and put them in their places which we had practised for weeks . . . and come away and get on our boat and go home.'

Pritchard's men were to blow up targets of convenience and assist other groups as needed. Watson's were to blaze their trail with Bren and Tommy guns, and keep the others safe as they worked.

Watson came back down the ladder, ran past the others and kept going. It was a short distance across the quayside and some railway tracks to the Old Town Square, a long, open space leading to the lifting bridge – Bridge D. Leaving Walton's team behind, he pushed on into the middle of the square and into a cluster of French townspeople anxious to know what was going on.

'Dedans vite! C'est les Anglais!' Watson said, using prepared phrases to refer to himself in the third person. Inside quick! It's the English! If it hadn't been so tense it would have been comic. He was yards now from the basement where Antoinette Loréal said she could tell the difference between the noisy boots of the German soldiers in the square, and the 'stealthy and cautious' ones of the English. But he shattered any remaining calm by firing his Tommy gun in the air and then at the ground when the onlookers wouldn't get inside as asked. That made him a target. More German helmets appeared ahead in silhouette. He had a phrase for them too. 'Hände hoch!' Hands up! It didn't work. A stick grenade exploded to his left. He threw himself to the ground and started firing. Reaching for a grenade of his own he found his rucksack had been torn open. 'I was now being fired upon by a machine gun from somewhere behind me. I vainly scrabbled about groping for those elusive grenades with my left hand, but this resulted in another burst of machine gun fire clanging into a metal litter tin fixed to a lamppost above me . . . not wishing to be riddled like the litter tin, it seemed wise to withdraw.'

Reunited with Walton's group, which he was supposed to be protecting, Watson found that Walton himself had also dashed ahead, apparently without looking to see if anyone was following. No one was. He was now presumed dead. Wheeler later pointed out that as demolition troops they had orders to avoid heavy fire if possible — because fighting wasn't their job and if live rounds hit the explosives on their backs that could wipe them all out. 'Our whole plan,' he said, 'was based on not running into trouble.'

They were in enough of that already. Watson again alerted the enemy to his position by shouting Walton's name. 'The only answer was the clatter of more machine gun fire.' He was standing next to another member of Walton's group — Lance Sergeant Dick Bradley of 2 Commando and the Royal Berkshire Regiment. Not that anyone would have guessed it from his name or accent, but Bradley was born to German parents who had moved to Islington before the First World War and changed their name before the Second — from Goebbels. At that moment, next to Watson, he fell to the ground, shot through the lung. As Watson knelt to administer morphine he was shot too, in the backside. The young officer who not ten minutes earlier had been exultant to be in the fight was now shaken and unsure what to do. Eventually he decided it was time to send for reinforcements. He tried to send up a flare with a Verey pistol designed for the purpose, but it jammed. As a last resort he sent Wheeler off in the general direction of Newman's temporary HQ to ask for help.

Watson was angry with himself. It was dawning on him now that the enemy was everywhere, which meant he must have failed to clear the mole. He'd failed to get to Bridge D or protect anyone even though protection was his job, and his bottom was sticky with blood. When he realized he was not immobilized he decided to follow Wheeler to press his case for reinforcements. That meant heading north away from the square to thread through warehouses towards Bridge G. Creeping on rubber-soled boots up a passage-way leading to the U-boat basin, he and Private Bill Lawson realized they could hear Germans talking nearby. It might have been wise to keep as quiet as possible, but Watson couldn't help himself. 'I still had on my little plastic stun bombs tucked in my blouse so, handing my Tommy gun to Lawson I lobbed it up the passage. It went off with a gratifying bang and a dramatic orange flash only to provoke a much more violent response.'

There are times when Watson's account of that night suggests he kept forgetting he was in a real war, and being reminded of it in the most terrifying way, and then forgetting again. This time more machine gun fire kicked up clouds of dust that seemed to leave a sad huddle of inert bodies when it cleared. Watson was seized with fear that these might be the other members of his unit but they turned out to be bags of cement.

The din that seemed to accompany him everywhere he went may have served a purpose – distracting the attention of a large number of German troops. Much more surreptitiously, Pritchard led his men quickly by a different route all the way to Bridge D. Having got there they came under fire from many angles, but still managed to sneak aboard a pair of tugs moored in the basin and sink them. Leaving three of his men at the east end of the bridge Pritchard then set off on a tour of inspection of the Old Town, not unlike Copland's north of Bridge G. He was accompanied only by Corporal Ian McLagan of 9 Commando and the Royal Engineers, who described what happened as they turned away from the southern entrance and back towards the bridge:

'There was no sign of any of our men. We were retracing our steps and were trotting down a lane between [some] tenements, Captain Pritchard on the right-hand side and myself on the left-hand side, when unexpectedly Captain Pritchard reached a corner at the very moment that a German should turn the corner. The whole tragedy was over in a flash. In one second the two of them met, in the next Captain Pritchard had fallen backwards. I took a couple of paces towards the German and emptied the remainder of my Tommy gun magazine into him.'

Pritchard seemed to have been run through with a bayonet. McLagan knelt beside him. 'He was breathing terribly heavily. After a little he spoke, and his words were, "That you, Mac? Get back and report to HQ. That's an order!" He never spoke again.'

Instead of following Pritchard's last order to the letter, McLagan returned first to Bridge D, where he found the rest of his unit dead. He continued to Newman's HQ and asked for help to retrieve Pritchard dead or alive. The request was declined. Newman had hoped to have a reserve for just this sort of emergency but so few men had made it ashore that he had none to spare — not least because the twenty-year-old Watson had already been given two more Tommy-gunners for one more attempt to blow the southern entrance lock gates.

With the remnants of his own unit, and Walton's, and McLagan, Watson headed south again through the warehouses. His blood was up now, even though he felt strongly that his time was too. Unlike his Tommy-gunners he made no effort to keep to the shadows. At one point, thinking they needed to move faster, he turned angrily and asked them: 'Do you want to live for ever?'

George Wheeler, twenty-six, MSc (Hons), had no illusions about living for ever, but he did want to get home.

9. At sea

After the war, when survivors of Operation Chariot looked back on it, many asked why they had been denied a second destroyer to take care of the withdrawal. Corran Purdon wrote angrily in an otherwise congenial memoir: 'The failure to include the second destroyer cost not only the return of the main body of survivors, but the lives of those of our fine commandos and sailors who had to try to achieve their tasks on the Old Mole from flimsy and unsuitable wooden craft carrying vulnerable and highly inflammable extra fuel tanks.'

It was true that John Hughes-Hallett at Combined Operations HQ included two destroyers in a plan presented to Mountbatten on 6 February, but the Admiralty ruled it out and it was not discussed again at a high level. In fact the idea of a second destroyer was never seriously discussed by the Admiralty. It was hard enough to get their Lordships to part with one destroyer. Hughes-Hallett was not a fan of motor launches for this sort of work, but he and everyone else involved were reconciled from early in the planning process to depending on them for the withdrawal, and certainly by the vital meeting of 19 February at which concrete proposals were first put to Admiral Charles Forbes. Except for Forbes, who to his credit told the meeting exactly what he thought would happen to the launches and those forced to depend on them, it was a grand exercise in self-deception.

The deception fell apart in about six minutes. The only launch from the starboard column to land troops ashore was the sixth in line, skippered by Mark Rodier. During the final run-in he had become convinced that he would not survive the night. This disconcerted his number two, Frank Arkle, but somehow not Rodier himself. He piloted his boat into battle a picture of composure even though the first launch in his column had crashed into the harbour wall, the next two had disappeared up river, the fourth had exploded in a giant fireball and the fifth, commanded by the actor Leslie Fenton (who appeared in more than sixty Hollywood films between the wars, including *What Price Glory* and *Boys' Town*, but was now gravely wounded and on morphine), was circling out of control off his starboard bow.

Rodier was last in line but first into the Old Entrance, at about 1.40 a.m. He put Troop Sergeant Major George Haines ashore with a group from 2 Commando, who set off to find and protect Colonel Newman's outpost near Bridge G. Then Commander Ryder came alongside with a loudhailer.

Ryder was a stickler for security, as he'd made very clear. Codewords, including 'Puffin', 'Guillemot', 'Lobster' and 'Porpoise', had been agreed for various manoeuvres and contingencies. 'Ramrod' meant 'emergency withdrawal'. But these were for wireless communications, which were down, and anyway codewords belonged in the battle imagined in Richmond House, not the one raging around the Old Entrance. So Ryder now ordered Rodier in plain English to turn round and pick up as many survivors as he could from the *Campbeltown*. The plan had been for the ship's company and wounded to evacuate via the bow and Bridge G, but that too was for the drawing board. The bow was too high and the bridge was under constant, murderous fire. Beattie and Copland had already realized there would be more chance of getting people out alive over the stern, which the crew was busy sinking with explosive charges so that it would not slip backwards.

Launch 177 came alongside and loaded up with about thirty extra men. They included Tibbits, Beattie and Lieutenant Chris Gough, Beattie's second in command. Rodier cast off and began his run for the open sea at 1.57, although his signal to the destroyers, *Atherstone* and *Tynedale*, waiting offshore that he was on his way was not sent till 2.20. It would be his last.

Beattie joined Rodier on the bridge for a little banter — one captain to another — and to offer suggestions on the best course out. The shoals east of the Charpentier Channel were still easily navigable: there would be fourteen feet of tide till 3 a.m. And, of course, the launch was a surfboard compared with the *Campbeltown*. Did Beattie direct Rodier too far south? Might Rodier have managed better on his own? The night is strewn with similar what-ifs.

The incoming fire was constant and terrifying. Rodier had to steer a slalom course between searchlights and water spouts as the shore batteries that missed the raiders on their way in blasted them on their way out. Rodier got about three miles and was up to eighteen knots when a heavy shell from Le Pointeau on the south shore hit him in the engine room. Petty Officer Motor Mechanic John Rafferty described what it was like to be there:

'Down in the engine room I could hear the gunfire fading and I thought we were getting away with it. The next I knew I was lying on the engine room deck almost submerged in water and in complete darkness. Struggling to the engine room ladder I hoisted myself up, only to find that the hatch to the upper deck would not open. After a lot of banging and pushing it was eventually opened by a survivor who had been sitting on it. The scene I came upon was unbelievable, the deck was overflowing with dead and dying, and hardly anyone unscathed.'

The explosion had smashed one of the launch's two 600hp engines and heaved it onto the other. The steering was gone too. Beattie headed aft to see what he could do and Rodier followed. As he did, the boat slowed and was hit again. Frank Arkle was at the stern, rooted to the spot. 'I can see to this day the funnel folding apart, what appeared to be quite slowly, and the shell bursting in the middle of it,' he said years later. 'And to my benefit poor old Mark was standing exactly between me and the shell and he took the brunt of the explosion.'

Rodier collapsed on the deck. Arkle was peppered with shrapnel down his left side and in the face. 'I was convinced my right eye had been blown out of my head and was hanging down my cheek,' he said. 'I felt there was only one thing to do about this so I plucked it out and threw it overboard.'* Beattie, unwounded, went below to inspect the wrecked engine room with Rafferty.

Two officers were left on the bridge – Lieutenants Christopher Gough and Nigel Tibbits. They had been together on the bridge of the *Campbeltown* on her attack run too, and on the southern dock gate helping the commandos disembark. Like Beattie and Arkle they came very close to making their escape, and were last seen in animated conversation about a job well done.

Six days later Elmslie Tibbits received a letter written in pencil, in rounded cursive, from navy Signalman R. Teeling, a survivor from the *Campbeltown*. It was postmarked the Royal Naval Hospital in Plymouth. 'I should like to tell you what I know,' Teeling wrote, 'and I sincerely hope it may help to relieve some of the anxiety from your shoulders.

'I was with your husband on the bridge right up until the time we hit the lock gate. The captain, Lt Cmdr Beattie, was there too. After we'd hit the gate there was a lot of confusion and bullets flying about. I came down from the bridge with Lt Cmdr Beattie and your husband, helping an officer of the commandos who was wounded down to the deck. That was the last I saw of him. But, and this is the thread of hope I know you will cling to. Remember, I was with the captain all the time during the action and I definitely know that the captain and I think all the officers boarded an MTB [the 177] which came alongside our stern to take some of the crew off. This same MTB was unluckily hit by one of the shells from a coastal battery and consequently sunk on its way out of the harbour. Now, the Germans say Lt Cmdr Beattie is a prisoner of war, so it's quite possible Lt Tibbits is too, together with all our officers who I'm afraid didn't return. I do

---

* Or, at least, he thought he did. Arkle was convinced for many hours that he'd been blinded in one eye, but found out in hospital that the eyeball was still there, undamaged behind extensive swelling.

hope this is true and that you will not be long hearing news of your husband which you must be anxiously awaiting.'

It wasn't true. In due course Elmslie learned through official channels in rough outline what had happened. Then, three years later, she received a letter from Sam Beattie.

'Dear Mrs Henderson,' it began, for she had re-married. 'Very many thanks for your letter – I was so glad to get it, as I wished to write to you and did not know your address . . . I will tell you what happened.' He described Tibbits's role at the wheel of the *Campbeltown*, confirming it was him who had actually steered it onto the dock. 'After that he helped to put the wounded onto [launch 177],' Beattie continued, 'and we started off down river. We were eventually hit, and both engines put out of action, and soon afterwards caught fire. Nigel then was of tremendous help trying to douse the fire, but it was of no avail, and shortly after that, as he was talking to Chris Gough, a burst of machine gun fire came and killed them both instantly – I was more fortunate as I had been standing there only a few moments before, and had moved off to talk to some ratings.'

Like Teeling's, the letter is handwritten. There are no corrections; no signs of hesitation. Perhaps Beattie had written a draft first. He ascribes the difference between life and death to misfortune and is probably right not to overthink it.

Rodier was unfortunate as well: Arkle brought up a big wooden drawer from a chest in the launch's wardroom. It worked well as a flotation device, but Rodier died before he could be lowered into the water to cling on to it. The launch burned for three hours. Beattie, Rafferty and a few others climbed over the rudder as the boat went down and survived till morning, when they were rescued by a German trawler. But most did not survive, and some slipped away into the cold tidal water even if not badly injured, never to be seen again.

Beattie considered this peculiar. Why did some seem to give up and accept death while others clung on literally for dear life? He offered this one-paragraph addendum to his official battle report, written on his release as a POW: 'Benzedrine. This drug was supplied. The men were told of its properties and allowed to take it if they desired. About 50 per cent of the Ship's Company did so. It probably did what it was required to do at the time of the main action in *Campbeltown*, but it is my opinion that the after effects began to show themselves later, and is a probable explanation of several deaths through drowning – the men became depressed when in the water and allowed themselves to drown. I cannot speak from personal experience as I did not take the drug.'

Beattie was on to something. His doubts about Benzedrine were at odds with the official enthusiasm, but they turned out to be sound. There is now an extensive academic literature on the depressive after-effects of amphetamine and methamphetamine – and the Germans saw them first. Millions of German soldiers who went into battle feeling superhuman on Pervitin methamphetamine tablets behaved like zombies the next day, Professor Lukasz Kamiensky writes in *Shooting Up: A History of Drugs in Warfare*. Gerd Schmückle, who fought with the 7th Panzer Division, described the feeling:

'The pills seemed to remove the sense of agitation. I slid into a world of bright indifference. Danger lost its edge. One's own power seemed to increase. After the battle one hovered in a strange state of intoxication in which a deep need for sleep fought with a clear alertness.'

Benzedrine was not as powerful as Pervitin, but Beattie was probably right to worry about it. Long after he filed his report to the Admiralty, a review paper in *The Lancet* concluded that 'amphetamines have been consistently associated with elevated rates of suicide, and evidence suggests a likely causal link'.

The last boat into the Old Entrance was Micky Wynn's. That he'd arrived at all was a triumph of perseverance for his chief motor mechanic, Bill Lovegrove. Lovegrove had left Falmouth still tuning his new wing engine, the 600hp Packard V12 that he'd promised to install before the raiders left for France. Without it, the torpedo boat wouldn't be controllable, never mind capable of forty knots.

A lot hinged on MTB 74. If for any reason the *Campbeltown* failed to ram the dry dock, Wynn was supposed to hit it with his torpedoes. He was not sure the new engine would work properly until dusk on the 27th when he was finally allowed to slip his tow and run in to St Nazaire under his own power. Then, as Wynn wrote in his citation for a decoration for Lovegrove: 'It turned out that everything was perfectly alright.' The torpedo boat hung back so as not to overtake the rest of the flotilla, then surfed in behind it prow high, massively overpowered – until a shell flew through the engine room and Lovegrove was plunged back into crisis mode. It didn't help that he had picked up a painful collection of shrapnel wounds, but they didn't stop him either. This time it was the central engine that stopped working. On no sleep, with no time to spare, in the middle of a furious battle, Lovegrove set about fixing it.

Wynn wrote later: 'It was indeed a wonderful experience to have such courageous men serving under one. It seemed that their own lives did not matter as long as they could achieve what they had set out to do.' Whether it had really come to this is hard to judge because the dead were silenced. Either way the living had their work cut out. Operation Chariot's Combined Plan said Wynn's crew had to be ready for more or less anything:

(a) Should CAMPBELTOWN fail to reach the objective M.T.B. 74 will be prepared to proceed up to the [submarine] boom and fire her "torpedoes" over it at the lock gate.

[or]

(b) Proceed through the Old Entrance Lock (East lock) passing under the footbridge if there is sufficient clearance and fire her "torpedoes" at U-boats in the pens.

[or]

(c) Any other role such as attacking ships alongside. Etc.

(a) would have been Wynn's apotheosis; a mission close to the one his boat had been designed for; a death-or-glory feat to save the day and etch his vessel's name in history. But the *Campbeltown* had reached its objective. (b) might have prompted a triumphant telegram from Churchill to Roosevelt confirming that British forces were indeed 'checking submarine activities at their source' (per the president's message of 20 March). But the East Lock gate was firmly closed. Sailing through it to fire at submarines was not an option. So Ryder ordered Wynn to torpedo it instead.

'The MTB eased off and headed towards the lock gates,' wrote Gordon Holman, the reporter travelling with Ryder on Curtis's headquarters gunboat. 'There was a dull hissing noise which frightened me considerably because I realised she had discharged her torpedoes and, as we were not more than 25 yards from the gates, we stood a fair chance of going sky-high when they hit. I heard them hit the gates, but there was no explosion. It was not until much later that I learned they were delayed-action torpedoes.'

That 'dull hissing noise' was Wynn's sign-off. He spun the boat round and came alongside Curtis again for a drink in the eye of the storm. What they shared is not recorded, but the idea of a stiffener at this point seems entirely appropriate given the genesis of Wynn's torpedo project at a late-night drinking session.

Having drained his glass, like Ted Burt before him, Wynn loaded up with survivors, this time from the *Campbeltown*. He then began his run downriver. Unlike Burt he had five engines, all working, and speed on his side. Even with thirty-six crew and commandos crowding his decks, he was ten minutes from safety.

Ryder watched him go. It was 2.20 a.m. and time to attend to the rest of his flotilla.

It takes two to aim a pom-pom: a layer and a trainer. The layer judges elevation and therefore range. The trainer swivels the gun left or right. They have to work in harmony, and Bill Savage and Frank Smith did exactly that. Savage was the layer, Smith the trainer. They were both from Birmingham; townies at sea who had bonded easily over memories of school, West Bromwich Albion and Aston Villa. On the way in to St Nazaire they had given the guardship hell at its anchorage off the east jetty of the Outer Harbour. Two boats behind, Tiger Watson had heard the hoarse screams of those they hit. Then their own boat, Curtis's MGB 314, turned hard a-starboard to get out of the *Campbeltown*'s way. It circled back to deposit Newman and his team at the Old Entrance, and Smith and Savage – and Curtis – cooled their heels waiting for Ryder to satisfy himself that the *Campbeltown* was set to blow.

At about 2.30 they pushed out, back into the river. Ryder and Newman had seen enough on the way in to agree quietly, after their brief argument, that Newman might be making his own way home. But nothing had prepared Ryder for the scene at the Old Mole – 'the melancholy sight of some half a dozen blazing wrecks'; nor for the decisions they would force on him.

'Good Lord,' someone heard him ask. 'What the hell do we do now?'

It was the only time Curtis saw Ryder stumped. Chris Worsley, the sub-lieutenant assigned to look after the wounded on the gunboat, had no answers. 'I thought of Dante,' he wrote. '"All hope abandon, ye who enter here". The light from burning [launches] as they drifted in pools of blazing petrol, the light from searchlight beams, the streams of multi-coloured tracer coming at us from both sides of the river, and the contrasting hues of our return fire all combined to turn the darkness of night into something which closely approached daylight.'

They watched aghast from the bridge of the gunboat as launch 262 slowed, went alongside 457, was hit, caught fire and sank. Ryder told Curtis to get closer to the mole so Savage and Smith could have a proper crack at position 63. One of the legends of the raid is that they put shells right through the concrete firing slit of the pillbox. Holman, who had a grandstand view, wrote that when Ryder gave the order to fire, Savage 'knew that there was little chance for him once the Germans opened up again' – but that he silenced position 63 with his first shot. When the Germans re-manned it, Ryder withdrew upstream one more time to see if there was any sign of Newman or his commandos. But there was no way back into the Old Entrance; only furious crossfire between the U-boat basin and the *Campbeltown*, possibly from Germans who had chased Roderick's party onto the destroyer and were now shooting at each other.

At three o'clock Ryder called it a night. It was, he said, an agonizing decision. 'We'd been working very closely with the commandos and to leave them behind was very sad . . . but we were faced with the fact that the only two possible places to withdraw were firmly held in enemy hands.' Carrying forty *Campbeltown* survivors (among them Johnny Proctor with his almost severed leg), he headed for the open sea.

It was a nightmare, Holman said. 'There were guns and search-lights all the way . . . getting up a speed of about twenty knots, the MGB ran the gauntlet of fire from both banks. Searchlights held the little vessel in giant beams of light, fresh positions switching on as we came within their radius.' Worsley was at the stern now, making use of chemical smoke floats to hide their position. Once he adver-tised their position instead, forgetting the floats had to be thrown overboard.

In his defence, Worsley was busy. When he wasn't making smoke he made the rounds of the upper deck to see what he could do to help the wounded. At one point he was bending over to attend to a commando propped up against the funnel when a piece of shrapnel passed between the rim of his helmet and his forehead. 'That, I felt, was a close call. On another occasion I found a sea-boot containing a torn-off leg, which I threw into the river . . . I looked around for the limb's former owner and found him lying on the deck near the site of my first action station.'

Eventually the frequency of the shelling slowed. The gunboat was making steady progress, leaving the coast behind, when the shape of another boat loomed close in the darkness. Ryder assumed it was one of his, limping home. He used his loudhailer to tell it to fall in behind, but the reply was a burst of machine gun fire. The pom-pom was the only weapon left on the gunboat in a fit state to fire back. By the time Smith spun it round the angle was too tight, and, anyway, Savage had been hit. Smith saw that he was slumped in his seat and called for water to revive him. The sailor who brought the water realized Savage was dead, 'stove in' from a massive chest wound, and brought a blanket to cover him instead.

For many years most St Nazaire raid veterans thought Savage died earlier, in his battle with position 63. They were encouraged to think so by Holman, who wrote as an eye-witness that the gunner died with congratulations for his shooting 'ringing in his ears'. Not so. In 1992 Frank Smith put it on record in a letter dictated to Chris Worsley and sent to his own brother, Chris Smith, for safekeeping, that Savage was alive until the gunboat was practically clear of the coastal batteries. Smith said Savage died because the boat that killed him was misidentified as friendly. For good measure Smith annotated a picture of the gunboat to show the pom-pom crew had 'no extra protection any place'. And he said the boat's stern-mounted Rolls gun was 'USELESS': 'It never fired more than two rounds before jamming. (I guess it was one of Hitler's secret weapons.)'

Curtis concurred in his official report to the navy that his forward gunners were 'completely exposed'. By contrast he noted that the bridge was well-protected: 'The armour . . . effectively stopped all the shrapnel and Oerlikon shells which hit it.' The miracle of MGB 314, then, which kept all its officers alive, may be less a miracle than a simple cautionary tale about not skimping on steel.

Curtis's recommendation for a posthumous medal for Bill Savage was long and generous, but instead of presenting him as some sort of superman it concluded: 'He was simply a good man, who did – completely – what was required of him when the moment came.' Twice Curtis intervened to prevent Savage being buried in haste. First, out in the Bay of Biscay, he saw to it that Savage was strapped to a bamboo ladder as if injured but alive, so as not to be buried at sea. Instead he was carried back to Falmouth in the ward-room bathroom on the destroyer *Brocklesby*. His great-great-niece said that, wrapped in a navy duffle coat, it looked as if there wasn't a mark on him. On arrival, Curtis personally made arrangements for his transfer to the mortuary and lying in rest.

There were at least three more hours of darkness when Micky Wynn, on the bridge of MTB 74, began his escape run. He had reason to believe he'd get through the night intact. He had the extra weight of twenty-six wounded *Campbeltown* survivors, but less hardware than on the run-in, having fired his two torpedoes. He had the fastest boat in the navy and a dear and dependable friend as a First Officer – Lieutenant Arthur O'Connor of the Royal New Zealand Naval Volunteer Reserve.

Passing the Old Mole he asked O'Connor to bring the engines to full power. They rose to the occasion with a discordant roar: three Packards, two Fords, 4,000hp and underneath it all the satis-fying drum roll of the hull hammering the surface of the water. Lucas Phillips got quite carried away imagining the spectacle, as well he might: 'She was soon racing over the Loire at forty knots, her forefoot high out of the water, her stern settled down into the froth of her yeasty wake, and throwing out high on either hand great wings of flying spray.'

She was too fast, even for the radar-guided guns on the Pointe de Chémoulin. By the time they had a fix on her she was long gone. She flew six miles down the estuary in nine minutes, and it's not hard to picture Wynn and O'Connor staring into the night with half a mind already on the party they had planned for their return to Falmouth.

A few minutes before 3 a.m. Wynn saw two bodies huddled on a life raft. 'We were going [at] full speed . . . thinking we were

24. HMS *Campbeltown* was modified in Devonport naval dockyard to resemble a German torpedo boat.

25. The wooden-hulled Motor Gunboat 314, which led the Charioteers into battle.

26 (*and facing page*). An oil painting of the river battle by the war artist Charles Pears, based on Ryder's account.

27 (*and facing page*). An earlier watercolour of the scene in the estuary as the flotilla came under fire, by Enid Campbell (Ryder's niece).

28. HMS *Campbeltown* hit the southern dock gate at 1.34 a.m. British time on 28 March 1942. Lieutenant Commander Sam Beattie noted she was four minutes late.

29. Wearing only a blanket, Beattie was questioned by his captors after spending a night in the water and being rescued by a German trawler.

30. Despite patches of cloud, a photograph taken by a Spitfire reconnaissance plane on 29 March shows the dock gate, in the bottom-left corner, has been destroyed.

31. Images of Private Tom McCormack, grievously wounded by a grenade, were used by the Nazis to try to show the raid had been a failure. He died two weeks later.

32. Wounded commandos made to wait outside the Café Moderne included (*front to back*) Lieutenant Gerard Brett, Lieutenant 'Tiger' Watson, Private Tom McCormack, Lieutenant Stuart Chant and Sergeant Richard Bradley.

33. Captain Micky Burn (*left*), poet, *Times* journalist, former Nazi sympathizer and lover of the Soviet spy Guy Burgess. Here, he is pictured with Rifleman Paddy Bushe, also of 2 Commando, after their capture in the hold of a German ship in the U-boat basin.

34. Survivors of launch 306 are led away from the quayside the morning after the raid. Lieutenant Ronald Swayne (*right*) and Ordinary Seaman Ralph Batteson support Corporal Glyn Salisbury. Lieutenant Philip Dark, on the left, wears a tie given to him by the 2nd Officer of the *Jaguar*.

35. Churchill called Operation Chariot 'a deed of glory', but Hollywood had to invent a starring role for a Canadian major played by Lloyd Bridges to justify bringing it to the big screen in *Attack on the Iron Coast* in 1967.

clear but suddenly we saw two chaps on a float right ahead of us,' he said. 'And one had in a second to decide whether we were going to stop and pick them up or wash them off their float which would have meant they would have been drowned. So I decided to stop and pick them up.'

The estuary at this point is shaped more like the bell of a trumpet than a French horn: if it opened out quicker Wynn might have been safe, but he was still easily within range of the big 17cm guns at Chémoulin, and an even bigger battery mounted on rails further west at Batz-sur-Mer.

He didn't realize these guns had been shooting astern of him all the way down the river. As soon as he stopped, they hit his boat and set it on fire. Many of the wounded were lost overboard at once. Wynn was blown from the bridge down into the wheelhouse. In his absence, O'Connor gave the order to abandon ship. Lovegrove, noticing his captain was missing, went back into the burning boat to look for him and found him slumped by the chart table, one hand badly mangled and his right eye dangling out of its socket. Wynn seemed concussed. Lovegrove heaved him on deck. 'Then putting his arm around me [he] pulled me into the water and swam with me to a Carley float,' Wynn wrote. 'He saw a rope hanging from it and he lashed me to the float, which saved my life.'

They were in the water for twelve hours, a good number of survivors clinging to the float at first, until cold and exhaustion began to overwhelm them. 'One by one they were letting go and drifting off, and eventually Arthur [O'Connor] shouted to me "goodbye Mick, I am leaving you now". I remember shouting back to him, "do not be a bloody fool, hang on", to which he replied, "It is lovely, I am going, Cheerio".'

By morning there were three left on the float – three out of thirty-six who had been aboard when Wynn stopped the boat. Earlier two more had struck out for the shore, but it was further than they thought. Eric Hargreaves and his friend Len Dennison talked as they swam to keep each other going, but after a while

Hargreaves ran out of strength. 'See you, Len,' he said, and that was it. (Dennison survived by climbing up a navigation beacon and staying there till daylight.)

Dennison, Lovegrove, Wynn and a few others were rescued by another German boat at two o'clock that afternoon. Lovegrove was still up for a fight despite his exhaustion and the cold. As he was hauled aboard the trawler he tried to grab Wynn's service revolver to take on the crew. Wynn, close to collapse, gently suggested the time for heroics was past.

Wynn wasn't given to retrospection but the moment he saw the bodies on the float stayed with him. 'Should one have stopped or should one have gone on?' he asked, forty years after the war. 'One always felt that as a result of trying to save two we lost 33, plus the two we stopped to pick up, and even today there are some nights when it will come back to me . . .'

By 3.30 on the morning of the 28th the launches of the raiding force are strewn across the estuary and out to sea. Eight are sunk or smouldering close to the harbour. Rodier's and Wynn's are burning further out. Six have run the gauntlet of the coastal guns but, of these, three will be scuttled, too badly damaged to get home. And there's one more.

Half past three is the moment to take stock because it's Newman's cut-off point for his commandos; the time when, all being well, the launches will stand by to pick them up from the Old Mole. In the event launch 306 is ploughing west by this time into the Bay of Biscay, clear of Mecke's flak guns, clear of the heavy artillery and making steady progress at twelve knots towards a rendezvous point forty-five miles out, where the *Atherstone* and *Tynedale* will provide protection. The mood on the bridge is tense; below decks it's much worse. The commandos are seething. They have been denied a fight.

Two hours ago launch 306 approached St Nazaire fifth in the port column. Its fourteen commandos were to destroy the outermost lock gates at the southern entrance to the U-boat basin. Ahead, launches 192, 447 and 457 were ablaze. Launch 307, the third boat in the port column, tried and failed to land troops at the mole. The fifth overshot; both eventually withdrew. Ralph Batteson, strapped to the 306's rear Oerlikon gun, saw exactly what the problem was: position 63 was firing at everyone in sight, and even when the boats ahead thought it was silenced it was not for long: 'When it came to our time to get in to try and get our men landed . . . he started firing again in earnest.' When Batteson tried to knock out the searchlights directing the enemy's fire they would switch off, wait and switch back on again. Sub-Lieutenant Philip Dark said there was 'no way' the 306 could get alongside the mole – but it was not his call.

The decision fell to Lieutenant Ian Henderson, commander of the 306 and in peacetime a Lloyd's insurance underwriter. He and Dark received the dubious honour after the war of pen portraits by Lucas Phillips that seemed to go out of their way to emphasize the effete. Lucas Phillips generally liked his heroes tall, swashbuckling and handsome. Henderson, by contrast, was 'fair-complexioned, but premature baldness made him seem older than his 36 years'. He was devoted to his young family, and his ship. Dark was 'a student of both anthropology and art'. For what it's worth, Ryder considered Henderson 'a good-looking chap and a pipe smoker'.

Henderson could have made it a point of honour to force his boat into the mole past the flaming wrecks on either side of it, knowing it would be destroyed and the commandos cut down as they stepped ashore. That might have been the unspoken expectation of Mountbatten, and even Churchill, but to Henderson it seemed futile. Like the skippers of 307 and 443, he withdrew to the middle of the river to work out what to do next. Not for the first time in that terrible half-hour, one of Ryder's commanding officers found himself in a situation screaming for a contingency plan or at least informed initiative. Instead, with no plan and not enough information all he could do was take shots in the dark.

'We circled around for quite a while, firing at various targets and trying to get alongside but to no avail,' Dark wrote. Batteson claimed to have put a few Oerlikon shells through the firing slot in the pillbox on the mole, but somehow it always came back to life.

There were three officers on the bridge: Henderson, Dark and Lieutenant (later Sir) Ronald Swayne of 1 Commando. Swayne was remembered by Micky Burn as a polymath who played the flute, read Proust in the original and survived a plane crash as well as Operation Chariot. He was later a container shipping pioneer. Circling in the river, he was torn. He suggested alternative landing places including further upriver, but Henderson said he didn't know the lie of the shore there; he feared running aground. This was a reasonable worry: it was clear to the naked eye that the shore upstream of the dry dock was rocky. But the commandos weren't to be reasoned with. They could hear those who'd sailed in on the *Campbeltown* blowing up buildings and blasting away at Jerry with everything they had. When Henderson let it be known they weren't going ashore they practically mutinied. 'We were bloody annoyed,' one of them told the historian James Dorrian half a century later. 'We knew what we had to do and we wanted to do it. And here we are, going bloody home!'

Tommy Durrant in particular was furious. He had dreamed with his brother of giving the Germans seven bells for sinking the *Lancastria* and here he was, and Henderson was turning tail. He was borderline insubordinate, said Swayne, and the record suggests that at about this point Durrant decided he'd had enough of waiting for orders. For his own part Swayne had to support Henderson's decision in front of his men. They were all on Henderson's launch. 'But I did think he ought to have tried to go in higher up [or] . . . into the Old Entrance,' he said later. Instead they were withdrawing, with twelve rucksacks of plastic explosive unused on the mess deck.

Henderson proved expert at dodging shells on the way out. 'He knew what he was doing,' Batteson said. He'd slow the ship down almost to a stop and order full speed ahead again as soon as the artillery aimers began to find their range. It was the best he could do without Micky Wynn's speed, and it was enough to see the 306 out of harm's way by the dark hours before dawn.

Batteson was grateful. He'd been at the rear Oerlikon for six and a half hours. Henderson requested sandwiches and cocoa for the ship's company and they could reflect with a little distance on what might have been. It's impossible to know what Henderson himself might have been thinking, for the 306 was not yet free and clear. He was about to arrive at the rendezvous point early – before the destroyers. And he knew he should be ready to come under air attack as soon as daylight revealed his position. He did not know of an extra threat created by the signal sent the previous afternoon from U-boat 593 after its long dive to hide from the *Tynedale* and her depth charges. The signal alerted the German navy to a flotilla apparently heading west, preserving the Charioteers' bluff exactly as Ryder hoped. But it also prompted a full-scale alert at the German naval headquarters in Nantes. Hence the dispatch of five torpedo boats into the Bay of Biscay to hunt for the flotilla.

'Torpedo boat' was a misnomer. These ships were closer in speed and size to destroyers. If the *Tirpitz* was a killer whale they were the barracudas of the German fleet. They were 100 miles offshore when, at 02.51, they received a signal that St Nazaire was under attack. They were ordered to return there immediately at maximum sustainable speed.

Henderson saw them at 5.30, an hour before dawn. Through his night glasses, their phosphorescent bow waves were hard to miss. He stopped his engines and had a quiet word with Philip Dark. Swayne was below decks with his men. 'Dark came along and told me to come on the bridge and to keep dead quiet and to shut up the soldiers, and I did this,' Swayne said. 'Henderson just handed me the night glasses and there were the outlines of three destroyers. I was munching on a sandwich, and it turned to dust in my mouth.'

PART III

After 3.30 a.m.

10. Henderson's call

Through the night glasses, Swayne could see the outlines of three torpedo boats moving fast inshore in single file. They were at most a hundred yards away but the launch was stopped dead in the water making neither sound nor light. There was a chance it might not be seen. Swayne asked Henderson in a whisper what he would do if challenged.

'We shall have to fight, of course,' he said. So this was the moment. Hours earlier he had resorted to reason to save his boat and everyone on it from almost certain death in St Nazaire. Now they faced similar odds and he was resorting to honour.

Unable to finish his sandwich, Swayne spat the rest of it out and went below to bring his men quietly to action stations. Durrant positioned himself amidships with a Bren gun. Batteson returned to the rear Oerlikon, strapped in and held his breath. The three torpedo boats that Swayne had seen steamed past. 'There was another one following up behind and we thought "he's going to go on as well",' Batteson said. 'But just as he got more or less out of distance he must have spotted something.'

The fourth boat was the *Jaguar*, under the command of Kapitän Friedrich Paul. He had surprised the British before, escorting the *Scharnhorst* and the *Gneisenau* on their escape from Brest, and he would surprise them again now.

One version of the story says he thought he'd seen a shadow and requested permission to go back and check it out. Another version says the launch had already been identified and he was ordered to destroy it. Both are half true. In his report Paul referred to the shape off his port bow as a shadow that he could not identify – it might have been a trawler. The captain of the lead ship in his group was taking no chances. 'I received the order via VHF,' Paul wrote. 'Proceed, illuminate . . . and destroy.'

The *Jaguar* turned slowly in the dark. It came up behind launch 306 and switched on a searchlight. Seconds before that Henderson had ordered just enough power from his engines to give steerage way. Paul had him in his binoculars and concluded he was trying to escape. The *Jaguar* was ten times his size and twice as fast but had no interest in a chase. Warning shots from a heavy machine gun crashed into the deck and hull of the 306. In reply, the commandos shot out the searchlight. Another one came on and the *Jaguar* circled the launch off its starboard side. Paul was reluctant to use his biggest gun while there was still a chance of towing a British prize in one piece back to St Nazaire. Expecting her to surrender at any moment he closed on her in a tighter and tighter circle.

Small-arms fire crackled between the two, and the launch got the worst of it. 'People were getting killed second by second, not minute by minute,' Batteson said. 'They were that close. They were within shouting distance' – and they had the advantage of shooting down on a wooden tinderbox from a high-sided steel destroyer.

Kapitän Paul made to ram the launch on its starboard bow. He might have stoved it in if Henderson hadn't turned hard to port so that he was only struck a glancing blow. That was enough to throw several commandos into the water, where they were supposed to know how to swim. Swayne later described his method of swimming training: 'We did that by just throwing them off the gunwales of a whaler. They soon learned.' Except when they didn't. His number two, Lieutenant John Vanderwerve, couldn't swim and was never seen again. Glyn Salisbury couldn't swim either and was left clinging to a railing to stop himself drowning. As he hung there Paul put enough distance between the *Jaguar* and the launch to bring his 4-inch guns to bear on it. He said afterwards he was angry – angry not to have received a surrender yet, angry that when fired at the commandos were firing back, and quite possibly angry that this obliged him to go on killing them.

Something had caught his eye. 'With the telescope I could see that two men were running [aft] towards the depth charges,' he recorded. 'At the same time the British began firing again. I gave permission to fire.'

The 306's survivors denied afterwards that they tried using depth charges against the *Jaguar*, but by that time those Paul had seen were probably dead.

One shell exploded in Henderson's wheelhouse. Another took out his rear Oerlikon, killing a crewman but leaving Batteson somehow unhurt. Most of the twenty-eight men aboard had started the action on deck, where the dead and wounded now had to be clambered over by those who could still move. Durrant saw that the operator of the twin Lewis machine gun behind the bridge could no longer fire it. The Lewis pre-dated the Bren. It was bigger, heavier and more temperamental, but as a regular soldier Durrant had trained on it before the war and he fancied his chances with it now.

He was not a man of many words when few would do. In his last letter home to Green Street Green he'd written:

My dear mum

I have enclosed £20-10-0 as I shan't be needing it where I'm going.

I hope everything is okay at home. I can't tell you where I am. If anything happens you will be notified.

Give my love to Reg Ivy Ruth and David and take care of yourself.

Lots of love
Ever your loving son
Tom.

At about six in the morning on 28 March Durrant called for more ammunition and started shooting.

He'd already been wounded three times but not immobilized. As he found his range, the *Jaguar* continued circling. At this point it had other targets besides Durrant – a direct hit to the bridge knocked Dark unconscious and mortally wounded Henderson, completely severing a leg – but as the other guns on the launch gradually fell silent those on the *Jaguar* focused on the twin Lewis that would not quit.

Twice Kapitän Paul used a loudhailer to implore the 306 to surrender. Twice Durrant replied by shooting directly at him on the bridge. The second time, '[the captain] shouted "no more firing, no more firing, I'm coming alongside",' Salisbury remembered. 'And he came alongside and old Tommy gave him another burst.'

It was, in effect, an act of ritual suicide. The retribution from the *Jaguar*'s machine guns was unforgiving and at last, terribly wounded, Durrant stopped shooting. Swayne was the only officer left who could talk and he surrendered the ship. Paul asked him to promise there would be no tricks. Swayne gave his word, and there were none. The wounded from the 306 were taken aboard the *Jaguar* and given space in the wardroom. Twenty of the twenty-eight who had been ruminating on life and sandwiches an hour earlier were now dead or injured. Durrant and Henderson were still alive but beyond help. The crew of the *Jaguar* offered cigarettes and ersatz coffee, and strips of torn-up bedsheets when they ran out of dressings. Philip Dark, when he regained consciousness, administered morphine to those who needed it on both sides, because the *Jaguar* had none. Paul's First Officer shared a cognac with Dark in his cabin and called the war, in halting French, a beastly thing. Paul paid Swayne the same courtesy and said what they both knew. He never stood a chance.

11. Bridge D

By the time the *Jaguar* reached port, legends were already ripening there about the night before. The English had seized the Town Hall and been seen hurling grenades at the Germans from its upstairs windows. The English had made it all the way to the railway station. Parachutists had been arrested there. The kilted bodies of Scottish commandos had been seen arriving at the morgue – piled on top of each other on a flatbed truck.

It was true that young Nazairiens had been enlisted as stretcher-bearers; bodies – including Tom Peyton's – had washed ashore on the east jetty of the Outer Harbour and the beaches downstream. And, of course, it was true that two tugs in the U-boat basin had been sunk. Anyone could see their superstructures leaning out of the water. But on the whole the French reaction to the night's *son et lumière* was one of confusion and forlorn hope. 'No one dared believe at first,' said Gérard Pelou of the *Défense Passive*. 'Then there was joy, because we thought liberation was near.'

The Germans were still trying to piece together what had happened. Contrary to the assumption of raiders who were dismayed by the truncated air raid, the Charioteers' arrival was an almost complete surprise. Nobody noticed the incoming boats, the official report of Coastal Artillery Battalion 288 admitted bluntly. Even when they were impossible to miss there were only questions – Who? How many? Where? Why? What next? – and sporadic reports that tended to be dismissed as drunken ravings, as Herbert Sohler, the U-boat flotilla commander, had found.

From the start the raiders themselves were the only people in St Nazaire with a clear idea of what was going on. In principle this was an advantage. They knew their targets, and they knew that if the launches couldn't take them home they'd have to walk. The final decision would be Newman's, but it had been explained to them in Falmouth that if left to their own devices they would probably have to try to make a break for Spain. In practice, at 3.30 in the morning, clarity was not much consolation. As Micky Burn put it: 'We were in a trap: the whole of occupied Europe ahead, the sea and the HMS *Campbeltown* behind.' There was an urgent need to spring this trap before the *Campbeltown* blew up, and it was getting more uncomfortable every minute as German port defence troops pushed into the Old Town towards the sounds of fighting.

There were three ways in: across the lifting bridge at the north end of the south entrance to the U-boat basin (Bridge D); across the swing bridge at the southern end of the south entrance to the U-boat basin (Bridge R on the commandos' maps); or across the footbridge over the Old Entrance a couple of hundred metres north of the Old Town Square – Bridge G. All three were supposed to have been destroyed by Newman's men but none had been. Watson did generate tremendous noise for a one-man army in the Old Town, and Roderick and Woodiwiss did even better among the sheds and oil tanks east of the dry dock. But Watson was now awaiting fresh orders, and Roderick and Woodiwiss and everyone else who had been busy north of Bridge G either lay dead or had withdrawn across it.

Micky Burn was among them. He had been delighted to find Newman at his temporary headquarters near Bridge G. 'Colonel Charles was incredibly cheerful and calm whatever he may have been feeling,' Burn said afterwards. 'It was as though we were on a "scheme" almost.' But it didn't mean he was safe. Making his way through the dark grid of warehouses between Bridge G and the mole, Burn was ambushed by three German soldiers. In a sense this was the moment his life had prepared him for. With three guns covering him he was effectively a prisoner. Little did his captors know he'd flattered their Führer in the Osteria Bavaria and shared a dais with the Nazi high command at Nuremberg. Perhaps they wouldn't have cared. Perhaps it would have made no difference to them that this person whom they could barely make out in the moonlight had been FDR's guest in the Oval Office, preceded by his own comical reputation. But it might have made a difference for Burn, who found some chutzpah when it mattered. 'Luckily I spoke German,' he said in a 1974 documentary, without going into detail, 'and I heard them saying *sollen wir ihn töten?* – shall we kill him? – and I thought, "what on earth are they talking about?" I could hardly believe it. I thought I must do something.' So he retreated, hoping to bump into his own side, talking as he went. 'I was saying to them in German, "You mustn't kill me; I'd be a very, very important prisoner."' He gave them a compass and his watch, and backed into Sergeant Major Haines.

As a personality, Haines was Burn's polar opposite: solid, unflashy, utterly dependable. 'He challenged them and they ran away,' said Burn, who pocketed this as evidence that confidence is everything, even in war.

Burn joined Newman's party from the north. Watson joined it from the south and was so stunned by the sight of the burning launches that it was as if his mind had been shunted into a siding. 'Our transport had gone. We stood speechless. For a moment all seemed suddenly silent to me despite the guns which were still firing down the river. Presumably shock had rendered me unconscious of sound during those few seconds.'

Copland, who had supervised the demolition troops in the dock area, was more practically inclined. His mind cycled through the options like an Apollo 11 guidance computer on approach to landing. 'Can we hold this position . . . ?' 'What will Charles decide to do?' 'We can't just give in without making a fight for it, whatever the odds against are.' 'Can we pinch a ship and get away?'

The answer to the last question was no. The only ships visible looking out to sea from the rocky foreshore near the mole were burning. The only ones in the U-boat basin were either sunk or guarding the pens and bristling with guns. As for Charles, the colonel was standing beside Copland with a question of his own.

Opinion is divided on whether it was meant rhetorically but it was this: should we call it a day? And the logic behind it was this: assuming the *Campbeltown* blows up, we have done what we set out to do. Combined Operations HQ made it clear that everything else – the lock gates, the bridges, even the inner gate of the dry dock itself – was secondary. Losses are already high. There is no way home except by fighting against overwhelming odds and the only certain outcome of that is more dead soldiers.

None of this argument was articulated; all of it was obvious. But Copland's response to the question was this: 'Certainly not, Colonel. We'll fight our way out.' And that was that.

There is no reason to doubt Copland was speaking his mind; nor that his reply was as Newman expected. Consciously or not, both were reconciled to more deaths.

Newman invited his adjutant, Stan Day, to join him and Copland for a quiet confab behind a railway wagon to work out the details. They did not have long. If Tibbits's fuses burned down exactly on time the *Campbeltown* would explode at 5 a.m. If the margin of error worked against them she could go at any time. Meanwhile, from about 4 a.m. regular-army units would start reinforcing the relatively inexperienced port defence troops who had borne the brunt of the attack so far. Newman couldn't know this, but he could be expected to expect it. Against whoever was closing in, he had fewer than a hundred men. They consisted of survivors from the teams led by Roderick, Roy, Chant, Smalley and others from the *Campbeltown*; Watson and Haines from the launches, and Newman's own group from gunboat 314. Chant reckoned half of them were wounded, and the casualty count was rising.

During the confab one of the youngest surviving members of Newman's group, Private Frank Kelly, was shot between the eyes and fell down dead. A German grenade landed within kicking distance of Newman and Copland. (It exploded but bizarrely hurt no one.) In the shadows, a group of German port defence troops were seen smoking as if on a break from trimming hedges. 'Their carelessness cost them dear,' wrote Watson; Newman had his adjutant take care of them.

To make any clear decision was an achievement in the circumstances, and Newman complicated those circumstances by asking for ideas to test against his own. Commandos were meant to think for themselves, after all. Bung Denison, a lieutenant from 2 Commando, had seen a seaplane in the river. Why not fly it home? Wheeler, whose mind was always a few quiet steps ahead of most, invited Watson to join him in a small escape group, which he thought would have a better chance than a big one.

He was right, but Watson was in team player mode (as one of a diminishing number of Tommy-gunners he didn't see how he could leave the main group) and Newman was team captain.

In a few minutes Newman made his decision – 'to break inland with the idea of making for Spain'. The main body of commandos would charge Bridge D. Then they would fight or sneak their way out of town into the flat marsh country to the north of the river. After that they would have to head inland and south when safe. Not that Newman was concerned with route finding at this stage, the Spanish border at Irun was 380 miles away. In the Pyrenees it might be easier to cross, but harder to get to. Spain was neutral. If the Spanish authorities chose to play by the rules – and the commandos didn't – the commandos could avoid arrest by calling themselves escaped prisoners of war when challenged. If rumbled as enemy combatants on the run they could be handed back to Vichy France and from there to the Germans. The first friendly speck of land was Gibraltar, a thousand miles away.

In fairness to Newman this was the default plan all along in the event that going home by sea was not an option. It incorporated only one concession to caution, right at the beginning: the commandos would work their way north and south again through the warehouses north of the Old Town Square to take advantage of the cover they provided. The idea was to shorten the dash across an unprotected free-fire zone from 200 metres to about seventy.

This strategy was consistent with that of the whole operation: attack the hardest possible target in the hope of arriving unexpected. It had a certain logic and, as Newman had confirmed by canvassing his men, there was no serious alternative short of surrender. As to his tactics, they were derived as much from rugby as from a training manual. Copland divided the commandos into groups of about twenty and summoned their leaders to receive their new orders. When they arrived behind the railway wagon 'their salutes and bearing might well have been back in Scotland' as if in training, Newman wrote, 'and the orders to fight inland were received with grins which reflected their delight at being able to continue the scrap'. Later he told Lucas Phillips that 'no one seemed at all surprised'.

Why would they be? As Wheeler recalled: 'We were still feeling quite good. Our attitude towards the whole show was that there was a big chance that it would be a sticky one, but we were quite prepared for it. We had been told that if things did become sticky we should try to get out of St Nazaire and make our way back to England the best way we could . . . our morale at the time was excellent . . . we knew what was in front of us.'

And so began what Don Randall of the pumping house demolition group called a drama without a script. In truth there was a script, but it was torn up fast. Burn was told to lead the group back into the warehouses. Roy was to arrange a rearguard. He delegated this to Randall, who complied reluctantly because he wanted to be up front. If he had to play sweeper, he explained, he'd need a Tommy-gunner. He was assigned one who was promptly reassigned elsewhere, leaving the ragged rear end of the column protected by four Colt pistols and a rifle.

Roy himself commanded the middle of the column like a regimental sergeant major. While others used the warehouses and their shadows for cover, he used the spaces between them as a parade ground. 'Scorning concealment,' Watson wrote, he 'strode along in the middle of the road hurling grenades to right and left, his kilt swinging. It was a magnificent sight.' If any Germans saw it they must have been fresh out of ammunition or too stupefied to act. Why else Roy wasn't shot remains a mystery. Contrary to the idea that fortune favours the brave, luck wasn't with the commandos that night, especially not their officers. Only seventeen of the thirty-nine who took part in the raid survived.

For Roy this was a moment of suicidal courage like Henderson's out in the Bay of Biscay, but with a very different soundtrack. Instead of the hushed anticipation of death, Roy and the rest of them fired each other up with banter. They laughed, swore and yelled into the darkness rather than think too hard about what it might be hiding. 'A lot of us had some narrow squeaks,' wrote Corran Purdon of 12 Commando, uninjured to this point. 'I vividly recall that when I trod on a strand of wire and had fallen flat on my face, a German bullet struck the cobbles within inches of my head throwing up sparks and chips of stone, one of which hit my face.' It was the take-that-you-bastards-and-we'll-take-our-chances school of warfare, and it was a team effort. Chant and Newman and others likened it to a charge, by a raucous pack of rugby forwards. Nowadays the analogy would be with a rolling maul – except that this would require precocious half-backs positioned to take all the glory, and one of them was missing.

All of a sudden, Burn wasn't there. He was supposed to be setting the pace with a vanguard of Tommy-gunners but was nowhere to be seen. He 'became detached,' wrote Copland, but it was much more deliberate than that. Burn thought he had a better idea for getting out of this fix, and in the darkness he acted on it. He had explored the northern dockyard up to the far end of the U-boat basin and found few Germans there. In the two rooftop gun emplacements that he was supposed to eliminate he'd found no one at all. And when the Germans had found him, he'd bluffed his way neatly out of danger. Couldn't he bluff them again? It sounded at least as viable as charging a choke point that would clearly be the focus of fusillades of bullets. So he took two men from his own troop, 6 Troop, told no one else, and headed north.

Their route led back up the east side of the U-boat basin. Across it to their left the pens loomed in the moonlight, grotesquely functional and inherently absurd. They were built to last a thousand years, but not by inspiring affection. Since their only intentional purpose was to shelter submarines designed to sink the enemies of the Reich, they also had an unintentional one – to advertise the fact that the Reich would never run out of enemies.

Burn was with two riflemen he knew well from Scotland – Paddy Bushe and Thomas Roach. They ditched their weapons and tin hats, and the white webbing and ammunition pouches they'd been wearing to recognize each other. They were challenged soon after re-crossing Bridge G and somehow Burn managed to keep walking and talking: 'The English have landed,' he said in German; haughty, hard to pigeonhole, with a strange accent and uniform, and just enough about him to make a sentry pause. For a moment his two young companions were able to keep moving in his slipstream, but their luck couldn't last – not when the docks were crawling with soldiers after a destroyer had crashed into the dry dock.

'We strode up toward the [northern] swing-bridge which would give us access into the town and this time were fired on,' Burn wrote in his memoir. Roach became separated, never to be seen alive again. Burn decided to lie low. He would back himself against anyone in a contest of raw courage but he never signed up for gratuitous self-sacrifice. He'd seen enough of life to know its richness; to hold on to his own if possible; and not to sell young Bushe's cheaply. He found a boat moored in the basin where they could hide.

Close to the basin, minus Burn, the commandos briefly lost momentum. Roy and his men came under heavy fire. It came,

Copland said, 'from the most unexpected places', but he had a secret weapon in the form of a commando who actually followed orders. This was Troop Sergeant Major Haines, a farmer before the war, who'd saved Burn's life a few minutes earlier by the simple expedient of telling the three Germans who were threatening him to get lost. 'I called up Haines and told him to take his men forward, contact Donald Roy on the way and then crash ahead with all speed,' Copland wrote. '"Any questions, Sergeant Major?" "None, Sir" came the reply. It seemed just like an exercise . . . Haines pushed on and soon we began to move again.'

Tiger Watson was near the front still bursting with energy, still desperate to prove himself, still angry. He blamed himself for the death of Captain Pritchard, run through with a bayonet in the Old Town. He knew as well as anyone that Bridge D – which he was supposed to have cleared of the enemy – was going to be a death trap when they got there. And now he felt personally responsible for Roy, who was courting death with his march through the warehouses and seemed to have been noticed by a sniper. As they approached a T-junction where they would have to turn left, he saw that a German rifleman kept bobbing into sight at the corner, taking a shot and pulling back again. Watson was trying to keep up with Roy, and at the same time trying to be ready for the German when he next appeared. It wasn't easy, and not only because of the dark. Watson was holding his gun in his right hand and trying to stay close to the right-hand side of the street. The corner the rifleman was using for cover was on the same side, so the angle of fire was tight. Watson never saw much of him except his gun. He got off one burst with his Tommy gun but missed his target.

'When he next bobbed into sight, Donald threw a grenade which seemed to explode right on the required spot. I dashed forward as hard as I could to reach the corner . . . I was about 15 to 20 yards from my goal when the muzzle of a rifle reappeared round the wall. Either the wretched fellow had managed to dodge the bomb burst or another marksman had taken his place. Still running, I squeezed the trigger of my Tommy gun. The magazine was empty. It was too late to stop. I had no idea of how I was going to tackle him but tackle him I must. As I ran I could see the rifle muzzle swing round until I was looking straight at the black 'o' of the barrel. I felt nothing but a numb resignation. I only had time to think "well, this is it".'

Watson went on to study medicine and work as a GP for twenty-seven years. His description of what happened next is a study in detachment – and self-awareness.

'The bullet broke my arm just above the elbow. I was lucky. Had it been four inches to the right it would have gone through my heart . . . I was lucky to have been so close as the bullet had not developed a wobble. Travelling with maximum velocity it just snapped the bone, sparing the main arteries and nerves. Even the exit wound was small and neat. It was almost a clean "through & through". Here was the romantic wound of my boyhood fantasies and it stopped me in my tracks. I dropped my Tommy gun and sat down abruptly.'

Catching up, Johnny Roderick of the first group off the *Campbeltown* ran past to clear the corner of danger, then came back for Watson. He picked him up, and Watson cried out in pain from the 'grinding together of the broken bone ends'. Roderick put him down again, injected a syrette of morphine into the back of his right hand and moved on.

Watson had seen others collect themselves and carry on after being injured, and he hoped to do the same. But the wound, the shock and the morphine had immobilized him. As it dawned on him that he was stuck he decided he would sell his life dearly in a last stand with his handgun. He wondered later if this was a confused memory playing tricks on him – of his father's stories about leading men into no-man's-land in the First World War and telling them 'we'll not be taken!' Another officer, seeing he wasn't thinking straight, took the gun and a spare magazine to give him a better chance of being taken alive. His war was over.

'I lay back and looked at the sky,' Watson wrote. 'Then I looked at the wall at the foot of which I was reclining. It suddenly seemed awfully high. I remembered that the *Campbeltown* was due to blow up at any time now and that I was uncomfortably close to her, and closer still to this wall that might be blown down on top of me. I only felt a vague alarm at this prospect as the morphine was now in full command . . .'

If he'd taken Benzedrine as well his system would now have been high on an even more powerful drug cocktail, but there's no evidence he needed one. Staring into three more German rifle barrels not long afterwards, he felt euphoric as their owners decided what to do with him.

The commandos pressed on without him. Their left turn put them on the east side of the basin, heading south towards the bridge. On their right was open water, and beyond that the U-boat base. Warehouses on their left gave some cover from the enemy troops closing in on them, but not much. They were never not under attack. Bob Montgomery, the captain from the Royal Engineers, got a lump of shrapnel in his bottom when a grenade thrown from the shadows went off near him. Don Randall's party, bringing up the rear, noticed a German unit tracking them down the dock on a parallel street and shooting between the warehouses. One of Randall's corporals was shot in the knee and the same thing happened to Stuart Chant. 'There was no way I could continue to run, or walk even, and I collapsed,' he wrote. Two of his team tried to carry him but he ordered them to leave him in case all three were caught. They propped him up against a shed beside the basin, with a fine view of the bridge.

About seventy commandos made it to the north side of the Old Town Square. There they could pause in the shadow of the last warehouse and draw breath. Ahead was the square itself. Beyond it, the narrow streets of the Old Town. To their right, a thirty-second dash along the south side of the basin with no cover at all, and then the bridge, an asymmetric framework of girders that lifted from the far end on giant cogs. There were machine gun nests near each end of the bridge and one to the south of it in a pillbox beside the lock. Corran Purdon remembered coming under fire from a heavy flak gun too, and one of these was positioned across the basin in front of the U-boat base.

The raid was still barely two hours old. Newman joined Haines and Roy at the front of the column for an inspection of his chosen exit route. They only had to step out of the shadows to draw streams of machine gun fire and tracer. They saw a line of naval guardsmen waiting for them with rifles beyond the bridge. Looking the other way, Haines reckoned fifty more German troops had formed a cordon across the square. There was no time for stirring speeches. Newman stepped back into the shadows and turned to face his men. 'Away you go, lads,' he said, and with little idea whether they would make it to the other side, away they went.

Purdon said they went for it 'like long dogs', meaning presumably as fast and low as they could. He described a hail of enemy fire that erupted as they crossed the bridge, 'projectiles slamming into its girders, bullets whining and ricocheting off them from the cobbles. There was a roar of gunfire of varying calibres and the percussion of potato masher grenades as we neared the far end.'

A grenade exploded at Purdon's feet and heaved him onto Stan Day's back. His left side was numb and wet with blood, but when Day put him down he found he could keep going.

The girders, Wheeler realized, 'were a psychological protection but nothing else, because we could not get behind them'. They are still there and you can see why. Most are on diagonals and would only give cover to a performance artist. More helpfully, it seemed that many of the German troops shot high and wide. The commandos could tell that bullets were hitting the girders high above their heads, and Newman put it down to inexperience; in low light, targets tend to look bigger and closer than they really are, and soldiers who really mean to kill have to learn to compensate.

But there is also the possibility that some of those assembled for the massacre didn't want to be a part of it. Regular German infantry troops had yet to arrive when the commandos stormed the bridge. The soldiers in their place were inexperienced. Consciously or not, they may have aimed to miss.★

This only made the bridge a marginally less murderous place. Some commandos preferred to take their chances clambering hand over hand under the roadway as Chant's men had under Bridge G – but at least one had to be left there with only a morphine syrette for company. Others fell as they ran. 'Lying down there was a sergeant who I knew and I liked at home and he looked pretty ghastly,' Wheeler said. 'I bent down but there was nothing I could do and I thought "well, I'm afraid he's dead," and we went on.'

Amazingly, the choke point yielded. The machine gun posts kept firing but the line of soldiers assembled as a reception committee – probably from Mecke's naval flak battalions – gave way. Most commandos got through even though a third were armed only with pistols and at least a third were wounded.

The charge took a few seconds, but in a real sense it had been three years in the making – one year of humiliation in Norway and France and two of training, probing and frustration. If this was the war in microcosm here at last was a sign it could be won.

Copland emptied a magazine into the firing slit of a pillbox on the west side of the lock. Most of the commandos ran on in search of freedom rather than a fight – and there was a logic to this strategy that was not available to Ian Henderson on launch 306. By the time he and his passengers met the *Jaguar* they were doomed at best to be prisoners for the rest of a war that would continue no one

---

★ If so, they would have been in good company. The claim by the American military historian Samuel Marshall that as few as 25 per cent of US combat troops actually used their weapons against the enemy has been contested, but even if he was wrong by an order of magnitude some soldiers are clearly loath to kill.

knew how long. Everyone who crossed the bridge still had a chance of getting home.

But it was a slim chance. Regular units from the German 679th Infantry Regiment were arriving from a garrison at Escoublac inland of La Baule. An armoured car rolled into position on a slight rise west of the bridge. The commandos split up into several small groups, and one big one led by Newman. Most veered left into side streets between the sea and what is now the Avenue du Général de Gaulle, hoping to lie low if they could not keep moving. Wheeler and a few others regrouped behind a tall wooden fence, thinking they might be able to give covering fire for others crossing the bridge behind them. But a strange calm had descended. All the raiders who could still move had passed through the bottleneck and vanished into shadows. The Germans who had been firing at them seemed happier in the darkness too. Unaccountably, there was no immediate pursuit across the bridge or into the New Town. The battle was over as suddenly as it had begun. 'We did not open fire,' Wheeler said, 'because we could see no one to shoot at.'

12.   The obstacle race

Wheeler's mind turned quickly to escape. 'My feelings were that it would be so bloody awful to be in a prison camp that I felt we just had to get through,' he told debriefers later. After catching his breath behind the fence he tagged along with Newman's group, moving left towards the Outer Harbour and then right again along narrow residential streets towards the centre of the modern town. Darkness was precious and time was short: there were at most ninety minutes before dawn and already every new street corner brought new risk.

Word spread through the group that they should try to stay hidden by using back gardens rather than streets. 'We all barged through a house which had no one in it though it was clean and furnished,' Wheeler said. 'I dumped my demolition charges in the garden . . . [and] we climbed two or three garden walls until we reached a side street.' At this point the commandos were splitting up and regrouping like a single organism looking for the path of least resistance, but it was becoming clear to Wheeler that safety was not in numbers: 'I did not want to be one of a scrum around a doorway.' So he crossed the street from a bigger group to a smaller one, and hid behind a hedge in a front garden.

Newman remained at the centre of the larger group, responsible for its wounded and forced to move slowly. Wheeler's group of six shrank to two: him and Bob Sims, a Canadian-born corporal from the Somerset Light Infantry. Realizing they should stick with the back-garden strategy, Wheeler knocked on the front door behind him. It was answered by a Frenchman who seemed determined not to understand requests to sneak through his back door.

More residents joined the discussion. A German commandant was billeted two doors away, they said. 'They were perfectly friendly, but obviously considered that we had no chance,' Wheeler remembered. 'One of them wanted to go and get a Jerry from the commandant's house. I was still thinking of home-sweet-home however, so I clutched the man and said "Non, non, nous desirons escaper" [sic]! . . . We seemed to be in a world outside their comprehension, and to have set them a problem with which they could not cope.'

They did cope in the end – by letting the two men through and locking the back door behind them. Wheeler and Sims were on their own. Three more gardens and garden walls brought them to a house with an eighteen-inch crawlspace under the ground floor, reached only through a hole on the garden side. It was starting to get light. As they dragged themselves in, Wheeler glanced back to see one of them had left a boot print in the mud outside.

Newman's group had a livelier time of it. His walking wounded included Bob Montgomery with a chunk of metal in his buttock, Corran Purdon, blood-soaked from his grenade blast on the bridge, and Bill Etches of 3 Commando, wounded in both legs and an arm in the battle for the northern dock gate. Despite their injuries they spent the last half-hour before sunrise shinning up walls, falling into hen coops and ducking in and out of alleyways. Just before dawn they found a basement air raid shelter a quarter of a mile inland on the Rue du Croisic. Clean straw mattresses were neatly arranged on the floor. Should they stop and rest? The men were exhausted; some were in danger of bleeding to death. Outside, troops from the Wehrmacht's 679th Infantry Regiment were flooding the zone. Unlike Mecke's scratch units they had combat training and many had experience, too, from the French and North African campaigns. Copland stepped back outside with Newman to assess the risks. 'We were greeted by machine-gun fire from both ends of the street,' he remembered. 'We went back to our desirable furnished residence and let the firing continue.'

For Newman it was a blur: 'I remember going head first through a window into somebody's kitchen – there to see the breakfast or supper laid out on a check tablecloth, and thinking how odd it all was. The next moment we were dashing along the road when an armoured car appeared, spitting fire from the turret on all and sundry – including Germans.'

His official position was still that they were making for Spain. Unofficially he was adjusting to the reality that they had broken out of one trap into another. 'I felt the time for a halt wasn't far away. Every crossroad now seemed to be picketed with an enemy machine gun and movement was very difficult.' He and Copland hesitated in the doorway of the shelter, grenades at the ready. When a few soldiers passed unconcerned he decided they would try to hide out. 'As far as possible wounds were dressed and well-earned cigarettes were smoked,' he wrote. 'I also decided that if we were found in the cellar I would surrender as the wounded were in a pretty bad way and a simple hand grenade flying down the stairs would see the lot off.'

They might have stayed hidden, but for the conscientious Herbert Sohler, commander of the 7th U-boat Flotilla. He was at the U-boat base by 2 a.m. For now his submarines were safe: ballast tanks flooded, sitting under water on the floor of their pens. Their crews were safe in La Baule, a seaside resort a world away from the docks of St Nazaire. Dönitz, who had been driven back to Lorient after dinner, was apprised of the situation. But what was next? The official verdict of the 280th Marine Artillery Battalion that the attack achieved complete surprise was unfair on Lothar Burhenne, who saw it coming and was not believed. But the effect was the same: abject confusion in the middle of the night as Sohler and his subordinates fielded updates and requests for updates from up and down the estuary. By 3.30 a.m. there was talk in the U-boat base that the English were encircling it. Were they? Where were they? But the burning question in Sohler's mind had to do with his own side: where is the army?

The first regular German troops reached the edge of St Nazaire from their base near La Baule at 3.45 a.m. Their commander, Colonel Hans Hugo von Schuckmann, presented himself at the U-Box a quarter of an hour later, with no intention of getting drawn into a messy nocturnal street fight with an enemy of unknown strength.

'My battalion has surrounded the town of St Nazaire,' he told Sohler. 'Starting at first light we will enter the town to clarify the situation.'

Sohler lost his cool. Any delay was out of the question. 'The only weapon we have in the struggle with the English is our submarines. In no circumstances can they be put at risk. If you do not order your battalion into the town at once and something happens to the submarines I shall see to it you face a court-martial.'

Schuckmann outranked Sohler and wouldn't budge, except to order a search of the streets where the English had been seen since charging the bridge. It was not at all what Sohler wanted or expected. As a result of von Schuckmann's obstinacy, he wrote later, 'during the attack there was not a single soldier from the German army in St Nazaire'. He exaggerated only slightly.

As the search got underway the commandos went to ground – Wheeler and Sims in their crawlspace, a group of six led by Haines in a cellar, where they managed to stay hidden, and Newman and his group on their straw mattresses. The shelter was opposite a lighted building where he had considered asking for help. The street was busy, but there was no question of moving the wounded again now. Etches had been given morphine. Montgomery's shrapnel had been dug out of his buttock with a knife but no anaesthetic. A sergeant had been posted at the top of a stone staircase leading down to the shelter, but in truth no early-warning system was needed.

'We heard the Germans in their heavy boots enter the building,' Newman wrote after the war. 'We heard them go upstairs and then what sounded like them leaving again. Just as we thought we were safe somebody shouted something in German and I knew it was all up. I dashed upstairs and tried to indicate that we would surrender.'

At this point Copland expected a grenade. In a startling admission many years later he said the Germans approached 'in a ridiculous fashion', which he put down to inexperience. 'If we had been in their shoes I'm perfectly certain we'd never have taken the risk that they took. We would've chucked the grenades first and asked questions afterwards.' Instead, the commandos were marched upstairs and across the street into the lighted building opposite, which turned out to be the local German headquarters.

A small French crowd had gathered outside and Copland remembered some of them being pushed aside as he was led into captivity. 'We were taken upstairs, searched, questioned – vainly – and left for a little while under guard. A little grey *Feldwebel* [sergeant] stayed with us and was quite pleasant – a last war soldier,' he wrote, one to another.

Newman found the process of surrender humiliating, but he cheered up as more survivors were brought in. It was like a reunion, he said, 'with spirits still high as we all felt that a job of work had been done'. And yet it hadn't. Not yet, anyway. The *Campbeltown* had been brought this far and planted on the dock. Scores of men had been left dead and dying on the streets and quaysides of St Nazaire to make it happen, but the ship had not exploded. There was still time, and in that time there was little else the commandos could think about except their relief at being alive.

Reports came in to their captors from the Port Commander's office:

4.10: Port area and moles cleared of enemy.

4.26: Enemy destroyer at outer gate, big lock. Burning at stern and sinking.

5.45: St Nazaire sealed off by Flak Regiment 22.

5.55: Shipyard police report Normandie lock inner gate heavily damaged . . .

6: English and several Germans found dead.

6.16: *Schlettstadt* reports Normandie lock is slowly filling up.

That message from the *Schlettstadt*, two and a half hours after the infantry arrived, indicated that one or both of the Normandie lock gates were leaking. It wasn't clear to the Germans which gate was most badly damaged, nor if this was the raiders' aim. Didn't they realize they would never do more than cosmetic damage to the massive gates even by ramming them with a ship? The attack was mystifying.

Word that the English were landing had reached the chief surgeon at the German naval hospital in La Baule at 2.42 a.m. His name was Flottenarzt (Fleet Surgeon Doctor) Karl-Adalbert Kraft. His 'hospital' was the dining room of the Hermitage Hotel – the *grande dame* of the sea front.

Like Sohler, Kraft left nothing to chance. As soon as he heard the news of the landing he assumed it was a prelude to something bigger and ordered the evacuation of the hospital. As casualties began arriving from the port, so did indications that this was not a full-scale invasion, and he reversed the order. Instead he had the hotel lobby filled with mattresses. His deputy was recalled from holiday and two more field surgeons were summoned from military hospitals in Rennes and Vannes. They would be busy.

The men Churchill's planners threw at the fortress of St Nazaire had done everything asked of them. Newman had led them into Mecke's kill zones knowing Mountbatten was comfortable with the idea that they might all be lost. All that remained of Operation Chariot now was down to Tibbits's fuses. Then there would be a battle damage assessment by both sides. A reckoning. Survivors, prisoners, wounded and dead would be tallied, but it could not yet be said if it had all been worth it.

Out in the estuary, Bombardier Johnnie Johnson of 5 Commando was floating unconscious in the frigid tide. He'd blown up the southern winding hut with Lieutenant Smalley and hopped a ride on launch 262 for a quick getaway. As the launch went up in flames a few minutes later he'd jumped overboard and struck out for the east bank, thinking wrongly that it was in Vichy France and less hostile than the west. He considered himself a strong swimmer, but when his body washed up on a beach he looked at least half dead. He was carried to a first aid post, where a German doctor revived him with an adrenaline shot directly to the heart.

In the Old Town, Don Randall noticed the hush that fell over Bridge D after the commandos charged it, just as Wheeler did, but from the other side. His rearguard had become separated from the main group when one of his corporals was shot. He had to watch the charge from the shadows where it began. The crush of ordnance, men and girders seemed to him like an explosion in a firework factory. It quickly petered out. 'A few shouts, a motorcycle engine revved, a few shots – then silence.' It was almost as if both sides had to process what had happened.

There was no question of Randall's men mounting their own charge on the bridge, not least because he was not going to leave his corporal behind. Instead, choosing to ignore the fact that he was being observed by dozens of German machine gunners, he walked to the edge of the U-boat basin and stepped into a promising-looking pilot boat with a view to evacuating his soldiers by sea. Never mind that two lock gates and a small army stood between him and open water. Perhaps he could at least hide the wounded corporal in the stern of the boat. But no. 'There was no solution in this,' he wrote afterwards. 'I stepped up, back to quay level, and was surprised to see how much small arms fire was spattering the surface at my feet . . . I had reached a decision: each would have to make his own choices now – the corporal would have to come with me or I would stay with him. I walked back towards the others.'

Eight soldiers stepped out of the darkness into the half-light that played around the basin, covering Randall with automatic weapons and telling him to raise his hands. They could have killed him, as it seems they could have killed many more of those who charged the bridge. Instead they took him and his men across it as prisoners, round the south end of the basin to the U-Box.

Nowadays the U-boat base looks medieval. At the time, it was the height of modernity. 'One of our guards pressed a button in the wall and the door slid smoothly open,' Randall wrote. He and his men spent the rest of the night in cells in total darkness; guests of Herbert Sohler. Later, Richard Collinson and other survivors from launch 192 were brought there from their hiding place under the lighthouse on the mole. He was marched past the U-boat bays as the submarines were re-floated, Sohler having decided the risk to his precious boats had passed. 'The shelters shook and reverberated with the roar of high-pressure air blowing the water out of the ballast tanks amidst shouted commands,' Collinson remembered. It was 'pure Hollywood'.

In reality the Germans were fearful and jumpy. It was two and a half years into the war and many still hadn't fired a shot at the enemy. The soldier who found the survivors of the 192 in the lighthouse on the mole had been visibly shaking as he jabbed a pistol under Collinson's ribs.

Stuart Chant, with a shattered knee and two other serious wounds, had demanded to be left by the basin sometime after 3 a.m. He lay there alone for an hour until joined wordlessly by another British soldier whose name he never knew. After a while they exchanged a few words about what to do. The soldier went off to look for a boat to hide in, and came back. There weren't any. He 'seemed to have a quiet faith in me . . . I felt responsible for him,' Chant wrote. Sometime before dawn three men who he guessed were naval or railway police found them and shot the soldier at close range when he misunderstood an order to put his hands up. He heard 'Hände hoch,' and stood, and died. 'I could not move,' Chant said, 'and I lived.'

Watson, whose comrades had taken his gun before leaving him with his wounds, still managed to get in a scrape. His fighting knife, a Fairbairn–Sykes stiletto with double-edged seven-inch blade, was still strapped to his leg when he was found. His captors not unreasonably thought it might do them harm and were yelling at him as they hauled him into the Café Moderne. Gerard Brett of 12 Commando managed to defuse the tension despite his injuries, by arguing in fluent German that there was no real difference between a fighting knife and the Germans' bayonets.

The café became an assembly point for prisoners rounded up between the mole, the Old Entrance and Bridge D. Watson found Bradley there lying pale and close to death on a stretcher. He'd been picked up where he fell after being shot through the lung. German first-aiders dressed the bullet's entry wound but not its exit. 'Eventually they got the message,' Watson wrote, 'and the bleeding was stopped before he was totally exsanguinated.'

The worst wounds were suffered by private Tom McCormack of Lieutenant Roy's assault troop. He took the full force of a grenade in his face soon after stepping off the *Campbeltown* and somehow lived long enough to be bandaged up and moved around and photographed at every turn. The bandages made him look like someone who could be patched up. In reality, Chant said, half his head had been blown off. 'As he sat with his face clasped in his arms he made the most horrible gurgling noises.' Pictures of McCormack enduring a slow and terrifying death went round the world.

When dawn came the tide was out and the foreshore was strewn with wrecks. Joseph le Pehun, an apprentice dock worker, counted five or six of them on the mud west of the Outer Harbour. One of them 'seemed to have thrown itself at full speed' at a flak emplacement on the Villès-Martin headland, he said. Another lay burned out on the Villès beach. He saw bodies arrive by lorry at the mortuary near his home on the Place de l'Hôpital, and German photographers going to work on it all before breakfast. They knew better than anyone that in the vital business of spinning the war there was a clear first-mover advantage.

Corporal Bob Hoyle of 12 Commando was found hiding in the girders under Bridge D, minus his trousers. He had ripped them off on the *Campbeltown* when told they were burning (in fact they had merely picked up traces of smoking phosphorus from an incendiary shell) and carried out the rest of his mission naked from the waist down apart from his underpants and boots.

The ingredients for a narrative of heroic failure were everywhere. In the mouth of the estuary a German trawler picked up a few hypothermic survivors from launches 177 and 262. A gunboat found the four left alive out of the thirty-six who'd crowded onto Wynn's doomed torpedo boat. Len Dennison had clung on to his navigation beacon with all the strength of youth and was taken off it freezing but unscathed. Wynn and Lovegrove, lashed to their life raft, were at the outer limits of exhaustion. Wynn's eye hung out of its socket and a finger had been practically torn off his left hand. Lovegrove had barely slept since leaving Falmouth and had splinter wounds the length of his right leg. Neither of them had the benefit of the commandos' fitness training, but Lovegrove was still spoiling for a fight. As the gunboat drew alongside the raft he grabbed Wynn's pistol from his belt and yelled at the German crew to put 'em up. Wynn stayed his hand. 'I said, "No, Bill, not now, we're outnumbered this time,"' he recalled. 'And the Germans picked us up. We were treated very well indeed.'

Back on land the wounded men in the Café Moderne were less fortunate. They were brought outside and left to sit or lie on a shallow slope for an hour while the photographers took their fill. Blood ran from bandages round Chant's knees. Brett lay prostrate, shot in both legs. Between them McCormack sat in his kilt, head lolling, a picture of misery, and Tiger Watson stared bravely into the distance, his left arm shattered and the morphine wearing off. He was alert enough to know what was going on. Some of the cameras were from a local Nazi propaganda unit and the first draft of the history of the raid was already being written. 'We tried with mixed success to look both defiant and indifferent,' he wrote later. 'I look more like a sick duck.'

The commandos had inflicted casualties as well as taking them. When Antoinette Loréal opened her shutters on the Old Town Square she saw a decapitated German body in front of the port pilots' office, and a furious German soldier chasing away a French-man who dared to approach it. Some of those who spent the night in shared air raid shelters weren't allowed home until 9 a.m. They found their front doors guarded by German troops and two or three more on every street corner. 'We'd never seen that before and still didn't understand it,' Ginette Guillerme remembered.

The morning was overcast and cool. As it wore on German armoured cars drove backwards and forwards looking for any com-mandos who might still be in hiding, and clusters of British survivors grew in the Old Town, the U-Box and the headquarters on the Rue du Croisic. With each new arrival there was elation, but with every passing minute there was anxiety over the *Campbeltown* — an anxiety that had to be hidden at all costs. Why the destroyer had not gone up was a technical mystery for the raiders. Why it was there at all was a tactical one for the Germans. Perhaps ramming the gate was the extent of the attackers' ambition, and perhaps in a small sense they had been successful. At 8.40 a.m. the Port Com-mander reported that both dock gates were out of action: 'Machine and pump house destroyed. Inner gate leaks. Outer gate tight but unusable.' The report said the water level in the Penhoët Basin, upstream of the St Nazaire Basin and now leaking into the dock, would fall, but only by sixty centimetres.

At last an old army truck came for the prisoners in the Old Town. 'Still hiding our anxiety and fears we were trundled out of the old port, past the U-boat pens, through the town, out into the country and along the coast road,' Chant wrote. The truck was open to the elements. Bradley could feel his wounds reopening with every shake and rattle. Watson remembered locals watching them and hiding their faces in their hands at the sight of McCor-mack's head.

More trucks set off for La Baule from the U-Box, where Col-linson had been surprised by a stream of congratulations from German officers. Many were openly astonished by the audacity of the attack, and their reports were shot through with admiration.

One noted the care with which the commandos' 'excellent' explosives had been prepared. Another said the run-in to St Nazaire had been conducted 'with utmost skill, despite the poor visibility'. A third praised the attackers' use of surprise, secrecy and camouflage. But Collinson sensed the Nazairiens themselves were not sorry to see him go. A crowd lined the street as the prisoners left the bunker. His impression was of 'small, shabby, sombre, black-clad people who were not particularly pleased to see us and were most certainly not going to show any sign of recognition or friendship'.

Younger townspeople tended to remember the night of the 28th as a moment of excitement and hope. Some leaped at the chance to help as stretcher-bearers and one claimed to have directed the attackers' fire – '*Ici les Allemands!*' – but their parents knew any raid would bring risk. They certainly knew better than to applaud the commandos in front of their occupiers.

The only Charioteer who claimed to see signs of a joyful welcome from the French was Copland. As he remembered it, 'all along the route, groups of French people gave us concealed V signs and shook hands with themselves in joy' – although he admitted the joy was carefully concealed from the Germans.

They reached the Hermitage Hotel in La Baule at about ten in the morning. Micky Burn had been left behind and by then was getting bored. He and Rifleman Bushe had hidden in the boiler room of a boat in the basin. With daylight came search parties unafraid of the shadows. Burn could hear their shouts and footsteps on the quayside. He went on deck to see how close they were, and hurried down again to hide Bushe better in case there was to be shooting. Instead there was the sound of boots directly overhead. After a night of nerve-racking inaction Burn had a sense that his big moment was coming. He didn't want to blow it. 'I pushed Paddy into a corner and covered him, thinking "For the first time I am being brave and correct and public school. This is how responsible leaders behave in books."' A pair of Germans appeared in the entrance to the boiler room and Burn surrendered, arms aloft. He and Bushe were marched round the basin, across the lifting bridge and up the Rue du Croisic to the headquarters building where Newman and the rest had spent the morning. They were made to keep their hands up throughout, which Burn tried to turn to advantage by flashing a victory sign for the cameras. He cut quite a dash, uninjured, unbowed, with the top half of his battledress draped around his shoulders like a golfing sweater and his commando trousers held up by suspenders. But it was unclear what victory he was trying to advertise.

On their way round the basin Burn and Bushe saw Sam Beattie, captain of the *Campbeltown*, not to talk to but for long enough to exchange glances. What had happened to the fuses? 'At the latest [the *Campbeltown*] should have exploded an hour ago,' Burn wrote in his memoir. 'It was hard not to show dismay, or seem in a hurry to get clear of her.'

Beattie was being brought ashore with a handful of other survivors from Mark Rodier's launch 177. He had spent many hours in the water and was naked but for a blanket. Behind him the destroyer he'd planted on the dock gate was still there, seeming to claw its way out of the estuary like a wounded beast.

For the Germans it was an object of alarm and fascination. Before first light troops from a local dredging battalion boarded her and came away with files of secret documents including plans and orders for Operation Chariot. They were sent straight to Paris for analysis. As soon as word of the raid was transmitted to German naval command in Nantes, a warning came back that the destroyer might contain explosives. The first inspection party sent aboard by Mengers, the Acting Port Commander, found a German naval officer already there claiming to have searched the ship and found nothing. Two and a half hours later, soon after 10 a.m., Herbert Sohler took a tour of the ship with a posse of admirals, generals and his own submarine commanders. They too saw only the smouldering detritus of the battle. A guard was posted on the dock gate while the VIPs were on board, but when they left dozens of German dock workers and labourers from the Todt Organization – and apparently many with wives and girlfriends – scrambled up for a look. They may have been drawn by rumours of whisky, chocolate and cigarettes free for the taking in the wardroom.

One officer who spent time on the *Campbeltown* that morning was Klaus Ehrhardt, Sohler's chief engineer. His driver must have been clairvoyant or an unusually early eater: around 11.30 local time – 10.30 for the commandos – he suggested leaving for lunch. Ehrhardt agreed, even though he said the idea that a time bomb had been hidden in the hold 'had occurred to no one'.

At this point Beattie was being questioned in his blanket in a back room behind the Café Moderne. What was the point of it all, he was asked in good English. The confusion was genuine. Beattie said nothing; a photograph of the moment shows him smoking and almost smiling in reply.

He was among the last to be brought in from the sea but the last of all were the sailors and commandos of launch 306, dead, dying and dazed. They dropped anchor in the *Jaguar* outside the harbour walls at low tide and had to wait for a tug to pick them up. Ian Henderson's body lay strapped to a stretcher on the deck. Tommy Durrant was barely alive. Philip Dark, who'd been concussed by the shell that killed Henderson, was dizzy with fatigue and hunger.

Ralph Batteson was one of the first onto the tug, helping to transfer the wounded to it from the *Jaguar*. He was there on the deck of the tug at 11.46 (10.46 in Downing Street and on Richmond Terrace) when at last, nearly seven hours late, the acetone in the AC delay fuse dissolved the cellulose disc separating it from the igniter and the Cordtex fuse wire connecting up the depth charges in Nigel Tibbits's bomb. By design, the concrete and steel casing concentrated the blast. So did the great dock gate itself, only a few feet from the four tons of Amatol. With a sudden, terrifying eruption of sound and flame and torn sheet metal, the *Campbeltown* went up.

Batteson felt the explosion as an earthquake that seemed to shake the whole harbour. Dark felt the *Jaguar* shudder from stem to stern. Beattie heard it as a bang that blew the windows in. First Officer Herbert Pflug, asleep on the *Schlettstadt* after a desperate night in the dry dock, woke with a start to find the whole ship tilting and tearing loose from its moorings. On the Rue du Croisic, Charles Newman and his men heard it as rolling thunder and erupted in cheers.

Those who saw the explosion described a pillar of dark smoke rising hundreds of feet above the dock; slabs of concrete and sections of steel hull that were hurled across the U-boat basin as if by a tornado; and the sickening realization that in the debris raining down in a wide circle from the Old Town to beyond the U-Box were the remains of hundreds of dismembered humans. The blast could be heard six miles away in La Baule, where Don Randall was contemplating his mortality and his good fortune, staring at a squashed bullet that had lodged in a hole in his belt, when a loud bang and a shock wave passed through the Hermitage Hotel.

An early report from Acting Port Commander Mengers estimated casualties from the explosion at around eighty. A French account of the raid produced soon after the war by Rear Admiral Adolphe Lepotier put the number at 360. Estimates since then have settled at about 300 dead; nearly twice as many as were killed in the raid itself. They were all German, most of them sailors and port defence troops, many killed with the loved ones they'd brought with them to search the smouldering wreck for what was left in its store cupboards.

The explosion cut the dock gate in two. Its twisted parts were heaved off their foundations and a wall of water rushed into the dock. The *Schlettstadt* crashed into the *Passat* in front of it and both were swept 200 metres up the dock to its northern end. The stern of the *Campbeltown* was swept along with them; her front half had ceased to exist.

In La Baule, Tiger Watson woke from an involuntary sleep to

the shouting of agitated German orderlies and the realization that he'd missed the sound the Charioteers had all been waiting for. The propagandists would try for a few hours to pretend the *Campbeltown* never even made it to the dock, but in a few seconds of merciless destruction Nigel Tibbits had made the story very difficult to spin.

In their hiding place near the Rue du Croisic, Wheeler and Sims heard the explosion and looked at their watches. There were still seven hours to nightfall.

13. Something not quite real

It took sixteen days for news of victory at Trafalgar to reach the Admiralty, conveyed by a schooner, HMS *Pickle*, and a marathon relay of 5 mph post-chaises from Falmouth to London via Penryn, Truro, Liskeard, Bridport and Dorchester. Information about what happened in St Nazaire moved faster but was still hard to come by, especially in the critical early hours when first impressions were being formed. The first signals to reach London about the action of 28 March came via Plymouth from the *Atherstone*, which picked up Ryder and the other survivors from his gunboat at 8 a.m. on the morning after the raid.

Ryder was exhausted. He was lucky to be alive but still torn up about having left so many men behind, and at having to abandon his gunboat – which was now leaking too fast to save. Curtis, too, was upset about the boat. He had spent the winter in her after all, plying the Channel with Savage and assorted spies. Savage was now dead. The gunboat was holed at least a dozen times. As he left her to be scuttled he took with him from the wheelhouse a wooden roundel that he'd grown up with on sailing holidays. It was inscribed with the first line of Joachim du Bellay's sixteenth-century poem 'Heureux qui comme Ulysse' – 'Happy is he who, like Ulysses, has completed a successful voyage.' Curtis's son still has the carving in his Paris home, but neither Curtis nor Ryder knew then that their voyage had been successful (and nor did Gordon Holman, the reporter, who was travelling with a portable typewriter and managed to save that too).

On the 28th Ryder made the best case he could. When the captain of the *Atherstone* commiserated with him, having heard from another officer that the raid had been a failure, Ryder itemized what he knew: that the *Campbeltown* had rammed the dock with its fuses lit; that the pumping station had been blown up; and that Wynn had fired both of his torpedoes at the lock gates in the Old Entrance. 'I don't see why you should call that a failure.'

Ryder's information was fed into Churchill's morning briefing note for Sunday the 29th – but it was hardly the full story. 'Ryder's impression is that the operation was successful, but costly,' the note said. 'The lock pumping station was demolished. The lock itself was dry, and two tankers in it are thought to be damaged. Commander Ryder is certain that CAMPBELTOWN did the trick, and the explosion was terrific.'

In fact Ryder was not certain the *Campbeltown* had done the trick. He thought it had because of a loud explosion he'd heard at 4 a.m. as the gunboat limped out to sea, wrongly assuming this was the destroyer. None of the Charioteers who knew what really happened was in a position to send telegrams that day. They were all prisoners or in hiding. Reconnaissance Spitfires took off from RAF St Eval but cloud over St Nazaire prevented them photographing the dock. It wasn't until the 29th that they found what they were looking for, and then only with a few frames not partly obscured by cumulus.

Those frames were enough. The difference between before and after is easy to spot, even from 30,000 feet, even to the untrained eye. Before, there is a clear line across the entrance to the dock and (because it's empty) there are sharp-edged rectangles of shadow within it. In the pictures taken on the 29th the line is gone and water fills the dock. The news was confirmed in Churchill's Monday briefing note, but by then he already knew. Mountbatten had phoned him the night before 'in great excitement', the moment word came through from St Eval:

Mountbatten: the *Campbeltown* has gone up, Sir.
Churchill (mimicked by Mountbatten in 1974): This is great
    news. This will keep the *Tirpitz* out of the Atlantic for
    the rest of the war.

The *Tirpitz* was at that moment in Trondheim Fjord, a thousand miles north-east of Edinburgh. Whether she would ever have ventured into the Atlantic if the Normandie Dock had been left alone is doubtful. Hitler had resolved that his biggest battleship should stay in Norwegian waters in order to keep the Royal Navy busy patrolling them. It is true that the destruction of the dock shifted the idea of an Atlantic breakout from implausible to impossible; true, too, that this will have brought some reassurance to Admirals Pound and Forbes and their boss, the First Lord of the Admiralty, Mr Churchill. But in the end the Battle of the Atlantic didn't turn on battleships. They could scatter whole convoys by the mere rumour of their presence,* but Hitler had found they were too precious and too costly in fuel to use for more than a few days at a time.

Command of the seas depended on defeating the U-boats, which in turn depended on long-range aircraft. As long as Bomber Harris controlled the use of most Allied air power in Europe, the Atlantic was a happy hunting ground for the U-boats of Lorient and St Nazaire. Once his hold on resources was loosened, all that changed. As Evan Mawdsley has shown,† the number of long-range and very-long-range (VLR) shore-based aircraft at RAF Coastal Command's disposal more than quadrupled in the second half of 1942. They then sank more U-boats in the first five months of 1943 than were sunk by ships and carrier aircraft combined – and more than were sunk in the whole of 1942.

The *Tirpitz*, like St Nazaire itself, was first and foremost a symbol. The real purpose of trapping one and attacking the other was

---

* . . . as the *Tirpitz* showed in June 1942, when Pound learned she was leaving port to intercept the Allies' PQ17 Arctic convoy. He ordered the freighters to disperse and their escorts to withdraw, with disastrous results: 24 of 35 cargo ships were lost.
† In *The War for the Seas*.

to signal to the American public and the Soviet leadership that Great Britain was not a losing partner in the war.

This question of Britain's status was constantly on Churchill's mind, and not out of vanity. It was existential. Stalin had been badgering him for months to open a second front in the west as a condition of the Soviet Union's continued fighting in the east. And in the bleak winter of 1941–2 the Eastern Front had been Churchill's principal defence against an invasion of the British Isles. St Nazaire would play an important part in the case he presented – in person, in Moscow – that the slaughter Russia was enduring at the hands of the Nazis was part of a shared sacrifice that would end in their defeat.

In the same way, St Nazaire played an outsized role in Churchill's correspondence with Roosevelt on the great question of America's entry into the war. In a long and friendly letter on 18 March, Roosevelt gently reminded Churchill that despite Pearl Harbor he still had to deal with isolationists in the press complaining that he was 'dreadfully overburdened'; that he should concentrate on the defence of Hawaii and his east and west coasts; that he should 'do the turtle act and wait until somebody attacks our home shores'.

Churchill knew the subtext better than anyone. Roosevelt always needed evidence to show the turtle brigade that Britain was fighting for herself and for the cause of freedom, not just waiting for America to do it for her.

On 29 March, before he took Mountbatten's triumphant call about the raid, Churchill cabled Roosevelt with assurances that the Admiralty and RAF were working up a new anti-submarine strategy. It would be based on attacking at night, when the U-boats liked to surface for extra speed. He made no promises, though, and had nothing concrete to report except news of Bomber Command's raid on Lübeck. ('Results are said to be best ever.') But on 1 April he wrote again, at length, leading with a few pleasantries and then plunging into 'Dickie's show at St Nazaire'.

Dickie was of course Mountbatten, who Churchill knew had captivated Roosevelt on his trip to Washington the previous year. 'Though small in scale,' he continued, the raid was 'very bracing'. Pretending it was their secret, he noted his recent promotion of Mountbatten to Vice-Admiral, Lieutenant General, Air Marshal and membership of the Chiefs of Staff Committee as head of Combined Operations. The two leaders had been discussing European invasion plans and Churchill assured Roosevelt that Mountbatten would be at the centre of them.

The letter was private. Mountbatten didn't know its precise contents. He didn't need to. The promotions – heartily resented by the other Chiefs of Staff – and the apparent success of Chariot were enough. They were oxygen to his already inflamed ego and more evidence if needed for his lethal theory that the impossible was by definition possible. The theory was almost Mountbatten's undoing. Perhaps the unhappiest legacy of the raid on St Nazaire was that it emboldened Mountbatten to push four months later for a much bigger raid on Dieppe. A thousand young Canadians died there, and the Canadian historian Brian Loring Villa established beyond serious doubt that Mountbatten managed to force the entire Combined Operations machine into action without explicit written authorization from either his fellow Chiefs of Staff or Churchill himself.

Despite Mountbatten's efforts the history of the Dieppe raid could not be airbrushed to his advantage, at least not indefinitely. The story of St Nazaire was different. It was always a glittering prize on his mantlepiece because its main objective was achieved. Even so, it was a contested story from the start, and it was still unfolding even after the *Campbeltown* blew up.

One of the survivors of launch 306 who witnessed the explosion from the *Jaguar* and the tug brought alongside to take them off, Ralph Batteson, had a memory of smoking dust still drifting down around them for several minutes after the blast. It was clear from the bodies and parts of bodies floating with the debris that many Germans had died. Even so, once they had recovered their composure, Käpitan Paul and his crew treated their prisoners with almost exaggerated respect. They were 'extremely courteous and polite,' Philip Dark wrote. 'A large number of them, including all the officers, stood at the rail and saluted us as we shoved off. Looking very bedraggled and without caps, those of us who were afoot could but stand to attention.' Dark had asked for a pair of shoes having lost his boots in the battle. He was supplied after a hasty search with a pair of French rubber wellingtons and, bizarrely, a tie, which he can be seen wearing in pictures taken of the crew as they made their painful way ashore.

Ronald Swayne gave Paul his fighting knife as a token of thanks for the way they had been treated since surrendering. As for Paul, a few days later he tracked Charles Newman down to a prisoner-of-war camp in Rennes to suggest that Tommy Durrant, who had shot up the *Jaguar*'s bridge with his last ounce of strength, be recommended for a high award.

No one ever questioned the wisdom of Henderson's decision to fight. For the men of the 306 it meant a terrifying bloodbath. It bound them together and for some may have satisfied the requirements of soldierly honour. For most it was a simple matter of following orders and having a crack at Jerry when the opportunity came at last. It was tactically pointless but strategically priceless; defiance in a nutshell. Or it would have been if the story had been told and syndicated promptly from the British point of view. The difficulty was that all the surviving witnesses were prisoners for the next three years. The full story of the last stand of the 306 was not told until after their release.

Captivity was harsh, but even more than that it seemed to Philip Dark surreal. They were kept on the quayside for an hour, at the mercy of photographers and a film crew, then loaded into a bus for the half-hour bone-rattle to La Baule. On the way there they paused at a receiving centre where the guards seemed to think they might try to escape. 'They seemed pretty scared,' Dark wrote, 'but any collection of people more unlikely to attempt anything at that point could surely not have been found anywhere . . . What a motley crew we were . . . Men with uniforms torn to ribbons, some with heads bandaged, others with hands and feet blood-stained; some limped or were helped by their comrades.'

They weren't going anywhere except to La Baule, which then as now was considered by Nazairiens 'une ville bourgeoise par excellence'. To make the point, three French women in gay summer frocks gazed down on them from a neighbouring balcony as they filed into the receiving centre. 'It seemed so ludicrous,' Dark wrote: 'men who had been out killing, now wounded and prisoners, heavily guarded by grey-clad Germans, being led into a villa on the front of a fashionable plage; being watched by people who seemed to be of another world, a world of women, pleasure, peace and seaside holidays.'

The next stop was the Hermitage – solid, grand and even more redolent of leisure. Dark shuffled in in a mood of expectancy 'tinged with a sense of hopelessness, and emptiness'.

Not much earlier, Richard Collinson reached the hotel fearing the worst. He estimated later that he'd been in action for at most four minutes from the time launch 192 opened fire until it crashed into the mole. Within a few more minutes he and a handful of other survivors had made it to the relative safety of their hiding place in the base of the lighthouse. From there they had seen and heard only the disaster of the river battle; the crash of artillery, the clatter of machine guns, and the screams of wounded and dying men.

At the hotel he was led upstairs to a suite assigned to captive officers. Newman met him there with a jovial 'Glad to see you're alright, old boy!' – and a swig of whisky from his hip flask. 'I felt quite overcome at this,' said Collinson, 'and the relief of finding many more of our party alive – and more or less unscathed – than I had ever believed possible.'

Tiger Watson was in an altered state. He slowly realized on waking up after the *Campbeltown* exploded that a petty officer in the hotel's hospital wing was threatening to have him and the other prisoners shot. The hospital guards looked angry enough to do it, he said, but he was beyond caring and reckoned his fellow prisoners were too. They were all so physically and emotionally drained, he wrote, 'that being put up against the wall or shot where we lay was a matter of resignation rather than fear'.

The wounded had more pressing things to worry about than life and death. They had the prospect of surgery without anaesthetic. Morphine had been relatively abundant on the raid – Newman had ordered fifty five-dose boxes of single-use syrettes – but in La Baule it was in short supply. This made the chief surgeon at the Hermitage an object of morbid fascination even for befuddled minds like Watson's. He was, Watson later wrote, 'a big man [who] looked like the popular conception of a Prussian with his closely cropped hair and large square head.

'He would enter the room still wearing his blood-streaked rubber operating apron and gloves. He then stalked slowly along the lines of wounded and stopped by some unfortunate. There would be a short colloquy with his assistant and a brief examination. The victim of this barbaric priest was then borne away to be sacrificed, or so it seemed to my overwrought imagination. In reality he was a not unkindly doctor doing his best for his patients.'

By the evening of the Saturday, Kraft had a team of surgeons working round the clock in four-hour shifts. Watson could have been obsessing about any of them, including a hulking senior assistant surgeon named Kozlowski, who had been ordered to stay on at the hospital with one nurse even if everyone else proceeded with Kraft's evacuation order. He was described in the chief surgeon's report as having a reputation for tolerating no nonsense from anyone.

In all, ambulances brought in 115 German wounded and ninety-one British from St Nazaire, the estuary and the beaches. By that day's standards, Watson's broken arm was not serious. He waited hours to be seen. Eventually a different doctor altogether, having tried and failed to show an orderly how to set the arm with wire and bandages, did it himself. 'He was tired and berated the orderly. Then with one sharp, impatient tug he got my arm into the position he wanted. The pain made me gasp, but at least it was all over.'

Stuart Chant had a tougher time. He had shrapnel in his right arm and left leg and a bullet in one knee. When his turn came to be strapped to the table in the dining room the presiding surgeon was, Chant said, a ringer for the actor Erich von Stroheim – monocled, with a billiard ball head, white overalls and the apparently standard-issue rubber apron, as for an abattoir.

A nurse tried ether but it didn't work. 'The next half-hour, or maybe it was an hour, was unmitigated horror and pain,' Chant recorded. The Stroheim lookalike explored all three wounds with long surgical tweezers as Chant lay there awake and screaming. In his memoir he compared himself unfavourably with a Sub-Lieutenant Barham from launch 457 who filched a scalpel from the nurses' trolley to operate on himself in private, without anaesthetic, to remove some shrapnel from his scrotum. Chant feared he was similarly afflicted, rightly as it turned out, but he kept this to himself in La Baule. He confided a few weeks later in a French surgeon, who operated on him only to warn afterwards that 'pour vous, mon Lieutenant, l'amour est fini'. On that at least, the surgeon got it wrong.

There was some confusion among those who went under the knife at La Baule as to whether the German wounded went to the front of the queue. Watson thought that 'quite properly' they did. But Glyn Salisbury, badly wounded in the buttocks on launch 306, thought they either took turns or were all triaged according to how badly they were hurt. 'We were all the same, the Germans and the British together,' he said after the war. 'I had a German in front of me and a German in the back of me.'

Kraft's report said all cases were seen within two days of the raid, but one seems to have slipped through. Perhaps this is because it wasn't life-threatening; perhaps because it was daunting none-theless. After all, if surgery without anaesthetic is traumatic to endure it must be traumatic to carry out. This was the case of Micky Wynn, hauled from the Loire on the morning of the 28th with a finger hanging by its sinews and an eyeball by its optic nerve.

'I think it was two days before they looked at my finger and four days before they looked at my eye, and the eye was actually hang-ing out and it was very painful,' Wynn said after his release. He remembered, as they all did, a guard with a machine gun who accompanied patients to the operating table and stood at the foot of it throughout. He remembered being given a sedative for the amputation of his finger, but not enough, and coming around in the middle of it. 'And when they eventually took my eye out there was no anaesthetic at all, and I was simply strapped to the table with five straps and that was it. Of course all that happened was that you passed out.'

At this point Wynn's interviewer asked if passing out meant he didn't actually experience the pain. There's a short pause on the tape. 'Well, you felt the pain. That's the reason you passed out.'

By Wynn's estimate he would have been strapped to the table to have his eye removed on Wednesday, 1 April. Two days earlier, at 4.30 in the afternoon, the first of the two torpedoes he'd fired at the outer lock gate of the Old Entrance exploded. An hour later the second detonated too.

They had lain on the sea floor at the base of the lock gate for two and a half days longer than expected – two and a half days in which a military cordon was set up round the town and its envir-ons. No trains or trams went in or out. Kapitän Lothar Burhenne of the 809th Flak Battalion said 6,000 German troops were deployed on the south shore of the estuary alone. Then, starting on the afternoon of the 28th, unlucky crews from the Todt Organ-ization began clearing up after the *Campbeltown*'s explosion. 'The whole of the areas on both sides of the dock were littered with legs, arms, heads and entrails,' Ryder wrote, gratuitously. Bodies fished out of the U-boat basin and the flooded dock were piled up beside them. Sawdust was spread on the quaysides to soak up the blood.

The gruesome work continued on the 29th. It was only on Monday the 30th that French workers began returning to the docks in numbers. No one had seen the torpedoes or suspected there was ordnance still to blow. The weapons contained between them two tons of high explosive, and when they went up, rupturing the lock gate and putting the Old Entrance out of action, it was as if the whole town was seized with fear.

Anticipating reprisals, workers in the warehouses north of the Old Entrance rushed for the bridge at the north end of the U-boat basin – their quickest way into town. German troops who confronted them on the bridge saw khaki uniforms and panicked. As it happened, the uniforms belonged to Todt Organization workers, but who was to know they weren't more English commandos?

Early French casualty numbers that day were wildly exaggerated, but police later counted sixteen dead and twenty-six wounded. One reason for the shootings, apart from alarm over the torpedo detonations, may have been a warning that came in to the Port Commander's office that the French were shooting from the windows. Multiple witnesses saw three men shot dead after being ordered into a column and told to march down the Rue de Trignac with their hands above their heads. Bernard Pelven, five years old, was shot through the window of his own kitchen, crouching there beside the stove with his mother. Pierre Marie Hoyet was killed as he closed up his shop. A Madame le Boulicault was shot through the stomach in her home on the Rue du Bois Savary and was dead by the time her neighbours got her to hospital. Around 7.30 p.m. Jules Fouquet, thirty-five, was walking home with his wife on Rue Albert Thomas when witnesses saw at least one German rifleman kneel, aim and fire from a distance of perhaps twenty metres.

A local state of emergency was declared at 7.45. Cafés were told to shut at nine, by which time power was cut all over town. Fouquet, hit twice, died early the next morning.

For Herbert Sohler it was the 28th all over again: another late-night dash to the U-Box to stand guard over his submarines. For Karl-Conrad Mecke there were even a couple more reported sightings of speedboats approaching from the west.

Wynn would have regretted the French casualties, but he would have been delighted by the power of his torpedoes to spread mayhem and confusion. For their own part German authorities had had enough. On Tuesday, 31 March the entire civilian population of the Old Town – about 1,500 people – were moved by bus and *camion* to a nearby prison camp. They were allowed back a few days later, but only to pack. Their houses were then razed to the ground.

George Wheeler was long gone from his hiding place in the New Town. He and Sims ate chocolate, napped and whispered about escape plans until darkness returned on the Saturday. About midnight they set out, leaving their helmets behind. They took only their Colt 45s, a little ammunition, some field dressings and their remaining chocolate. They had resolved to maximize their chances of getting to Spain by minimizing the risks. If that suggests they considered getting caught a matter of choice, that is certainly how Wheeler felt, and in later life he wasn't careful about saying so. As he put it: 'I was not one to put my hands up and say, "please will you take me to Colditz?"'

They would avoid cars and trains and walk only at night, sticking to quiet country lanes. By day they'd hide and sleep. They reckoned it might take three months.

Their first night on the road was auspicious: keeping to back streets and back gardens they slipped out of St Nazaire without seeing a soul. They heard what seemed to be a German dance in progress and resisted the temptation to go in and shoot it up. But they encountered no patrols, no roadblocks, no *cordon sanitaire*. At the time Wheeler simply put it down to luck. Later he wondered aloud if others had exaggerated the extent of the fighting in the New Town before their capture.

This was the night of the 28th to the 29th. That any Germans were dancing is remarkable given their losses that day on the *Campbeltown* – unless the fact that it was a Saturday trumped everything. Even so, Wheeler was perhaps forgetting that his real stroke of luck was not to have been wounded. As Chant, Watson, Montgomery and others found, movement was hard with bullets and shrapnel lodged in painful places. Wheeler and Sims were also lucky not to have been found on the night of the raid. As Randall and Burn could testify, escape was not an option even for the able-bodied when outnumbered by hostile machine guns.

Only three others besides Wheeler and Sims made it out of St Nazaire under their own steam. Every other commando who stepped ashore on the 28th was either killed or captured. Overall, sixty-six of the 265 commandos who set sail – one in four – were killed, and 72 per cent were killed, wounded or taken prisoner. The combined casualty rate for the raiding force as a whole, including navy personnel, was only slightly lower at 62 per cent (169 of 623, or 27 per cent, were killed), compared with 68 per cent for the main Canadian force at Dieppe – but the death rate at St Nazaire was higher than in any other British raid in either war.

That no one who landed on French soil returned to England on the launches or destroyers caused some astonishment back home. Jack Webb, the junior medic who joined the operation just before departure, returned to England in one piece after his launch captain realized there was no way to land. The launch had to be scuttled but the *Tynedale* reached Plymouth with Webb and a few others early on the 29th. A large hall had been prepared in the Devonport naval barracks to feed the entire commando force. 'There were 24 tables set out, each ready to seat 12 men,' Webb wrote. 'We occupied less than two tables; we numbered 18 all told! The emptiness of those other tables was a shock. I was not the only one who, in bed at first night back, wept away the tension until sleep finally obliterated thoughts of our comrades lost in small boats or ashore in a Hell ten times worse than the one we had been through.'

On the Monday, three men from the War Office or Combined Operations HQ – Webb was not sure which – visited the barracks to debrief survivors. One asked if any of them had landed on shore in St Nazaire. There was silence.

'"Surely someone did? No one?" Again there was no response. Questions to individuals confirmed that none of us had set foot on shore in St Nazaire. Then he turned to his companions and said, "We may as well go. These men are no use to us."'

A few days later Charles Newman's oldest daughter, Jennifer, was on washing-up duty in the scullery at her boarding school in Cambridgeshire. Now ninety-one, she remembers quite clearly the moment her headmistress, a Miss Shepard-Smith, 'came bustling in [without seeing me] and said, "Don't tell Jennifer but her father is missing, presumed killed." And I dropped a plate very dramatically.'

The headmistress was horrified. 'She rushed over and said, "I'm so sorry, I'm so sorry",' Jennifer continues. 'I think I was in shock.'

Jennifer's mother probably was too. She was seven months pregnant with her youngest daughter and it would be weeks before they knew her husband was safe.

Before that, a secret German report paid Newman and his commandos a high compliment. They were, it decided, excellent human material (*'Menschenmaterial'*): highly trained, perfectly prepared and completely unexpected. And then the senior staff officers at La Baule paid them a higher one. They arranged to bury the British dead with military honours. A party of about twenty prisoners was invited to attend, provided they gave their word they wouldn't try to escape. A pile of clothes was found from those discarded after the raid, so that the prisoners could look a little more respectable. Razors were offered so they could shave. A

bus came to the hotel and took them along the beach, then inland
a short distance, up a slight rise into piney woods at Escoublac.

'We got out of the bus there, formed ourselves into file and
marched up the road,' Dark wrote. In a field at the top of the rise
a large grave had been dug and about forty coffins laid in it, in two
neat rows. One coffin remained beside the grave, draped in a Union
Jack.

Two or three German platoons were already drawn up to attention, including a firing party. Photographers had been invited, and
members of the public. The British column marched past them,
wheeled right and stopped beside the grave. The funeral service
was performed in German with a Catholic liturgy, and none of the
British understood a word of it. Corran Purdon was among them
and found it 'dreadfully depressing'. He remembered chiefly the
task of lowering the last coffin into the grave, 'gripping the rope
like one possessed as I felt it, slimy with wet mud, slipping in my
hand, and the feeling of relief when the act of lowering was successfully completed'.

But Dark was moved. Some of the civilians had brought flowers,
and the Germans provided a wreath, which Bill Hopwood of 2
Commando, as the senior officer present, let fall into the grave
after the coffin. 'Our hearts were filled with twisted and unintelli-
gible emotions,' Dark remembered, and when the firing party
raised its rifles and shattered the stillness with a final salute he
flinched in alarm. 'Our nerves were a little more torn than our
conscious minds would have us believe . . . We left with an impressive scene imprinted in our memories, coloured by the wonderful
showing of wreaths and flowers but covered with a glaze of theat-
ricality, of something not quite real.'

For Elmslie Tibbits and Cécilie Birney, for the families of Bill
Savage and Tommy Durrant and Ian Henderson, for Bill Gibson's
'Dearest Dad', it was desperately real. They didn't know yet – the
dreaded telegrams took their own sweet time – but it was already
a fact that their husbands and sons were dead. Some had sailed into

battle hoping the odds would favour them and hoping in vain. Some had lost that hope, but not the conviction that the sacrifice was worth it. Eighty years on their graves are still immaculately tended in the field at Escoublac. On ten of them there is no name because the body was impossible to identify. The inscription reads simply: 'A sailor of the 1939–1945 war. Royal Navy. Buried 1st April 1942.'

The aftermath

Three launches made it back to England under their own steam. One of them carried David Paton, the senior medic on the raid, whose first wish on reaching Portsmouth was to phone his wife. Before he could be put through, an incoming call brought an orderly running to the mess where he was waiting with another officer. 'A Mr Winston Churchill was on the line,' Paton recalled. 'Sadly I had to surrender to the infantry officer who had a chat with the Great Man, who wanted to know what had gone wrong. When told that the RAF had failed to show up at all, he nearly exploded.'

The RAF did not fail to show up, but there is little doubt Churchill was vexed by how the air raid had misfired. We know this from his apology to Charles Newman after the war. Over lunch at Churchill's home in Kent, he said he had not wanted civilian casualties to damage his relationship with de Gaulle. He also said that six months later he wouldn't have been so worried about French casualties. But if he was angry at the time, was it with the air force, with senior brass in all three forces for not communicating better with each other, or with himself?

John Hughes-Hallett states unambiguously in his unpublished memoir that Churchill in fact suspended the rule against bombing through cloud cover for the purposes of Operation Chariot. If so, there was no reason for the aircraft not to drop their bombs. No reason except cock-up, that is, and Hughes-Hallett says it was 'through a tragic misunderstanding' that the Prime Minister's instructions never reached the bombers. And yet there is no mention elsewhere of such instructions, and they would have directly contradicted Fred Willetts, liaising between Combined Operations and Bomber Command. Willetts was convinced only a Cabinet decision could overturn the bombing rule, and there was no such decision.

The truth is, Churchill's response to news of Operation Chariot as it trickled in was complicated. Assuming Paton's story about the phone call on the 29th is not apocryphal, that call would have been placed before the one Churchill received from Mountbatten confirming the Normandie Dock gate had been destroyed. Here was Churchill the journalist, working the phones rather than waiting for them to ring. In the process he was getting news of the cost of the operation before news of the benefit. But it was the *fact* of the operation that mattered most.

In his history of the war, Churchill called the raid on St Nazaire 'a deed of glory intimately involved in high strategy'. These were not empty words. In tactical terms he applauded the operation because it was bold and agile. It was the antithesis of attritional trench warfare, which he had come to loathe as Secretary of State for War during the First World War. Like the Battle of Britain, it was also a spectacular feat of arms by the few, not the many. But Churchill was not primarily a tactician. His hope was that these few, dead or alive, could now be made to punch above their weight in the national battle for survival.

How he planned to use them became clear four months later. On the afternoon of Saturday, 1 August, he was driven out of London along the A4, headed for RAF Lyneham in Wiltshire. There he was met by William Vanderkloot, an American pilot from Oak Bluff, Illinois, all of twenty-seven years old. Vanderkloot had recently arrived from Montreal in a B-24 Liberator built for bombing but adapted for long-range passenger flight. The plane had a pair of bunks instead of bomb racks and was nicknamed 'Commando'.

Vanderkloot and Churchill knew each other a little already. The younger man had been personally vetted by Air Marshal Charles Portal, Chief of the Air Staff, on his arrival at Prestwick, the Scottish airport at the east end of the Atlantic air bridge. He had then been introduced to Churchill at Number 10, because he seemed to offer an answer to an increasingly urgent question: how to get the Prime Minister to Moscow.

Churchill needed to go to Cairo because the North African campaign had lurched into reverse and he believed a change of command was necessary. But he wanted to see Stalin face to face as well. On his desk since 3 September the previous year, metaphorically at least, had lain the handwritten letter from the Soviet leader demanding a second front in Western Europe to relieve the overwhelming pressure of the Nazi war machine on Russia. Cables and telegrams in similar vein had been arriving frequently since then.

A second front in Western Europe in 1942 was out of the question. Every scrap of war materiel available to Churchill was being husbanded for a fresh North African offensive; for Bomber Command's assault on Germany's cities; and for the Battle of the Atlantic. For months, Churchill had tried to convey this reality to Stalin without shading it on the one hand or provoking him on the other. The risk in either case was a loss of trust – trust in Churchill as an interlocutor, in Britain as a fighting partner, or both. There were already rumours that Stalin might seek a separate peace with Hitler instead of making a stand at Stalingrad, which Germany's Army Group South was approaching from the south and west. These rumours were all too plausible. After all, Stalin had made a pact with the Nazis before, and since its collapse he had lost close to five million men. A halt to fighting in the East would pose an immediate and existential threat to Britain.

The case against a second front was not easy to make given the losses Russia was absorbing, but Churchill had no alternative. The question was how to make it. He became convinced it had to be in person, even though that meant flying round the biggest war zone in history. He would also have to arrive with a compelling argument; with something to talk about that showed earnest of intent. Operation Chariot, to a remarkable extent, took care of the second of these requirements. Vanderkloot took care of the first.

His strengths as a pilot were navigation and staying calm and wide awake. There were British pilots who flew the transatlantic routes as well, but Vanderkloot had been picked out for Portal by the Atlantic ferry service for his quiet, unassuming manner and superb instrument flying skills. Griffith 'Taffy' Powell, the air commodore who screened him for Portal, was particularly impressed that he had made a special study of Britain's radio navigation beacons. Vanderkloot was resting up between flights at the Savoy Hotel in London when the phone rang in his room to say an RAF staff car was waiting outside to take him to see a VIP – he had no idea whom. A short drive later, Churchill received him in Number 10 wearing a blue dressing gown and smoking a cigar. 'I understand we're going to Cairo!' he said, offering a drink.

Indeed they were. Vanderkloot said it took a couple of minutes to pick his jaw up off the floor but then he busied himself with preparations. His plane's advantages for the trip Churchill had in mind, leaving aside its rudimentary accommodation, were its range and ceiling. Vanderkloot had told Portal he could comfortably get from Gibraltar to Cairo in one hop, avoiding danger by flying most of the way at night over the desert, south of enemy lines. The alternative offered by Churchill's favourite flying-boat pilot involved a huge loop around West Africa, across Equatorial Guinea and up the Nile. This would have required multiple inoculations with potential side effects that worried Churchill's doctor and did not appeal much to the man himself. He was delighted with the Vanderkloot option. It 'altered the whole picture,' he wrote. 'I could be in Cairo in two days without any trouble about Central African bugs.'

Leaving Lyneham on 2 August, they reached Cairo without incident. It was then, and not before, that Vanderkloot was told they would be going on to Moscow. He had no maps for the onward journey and had to make do with a shop-bought Phillips atlas. After several days on the banks of the Nile they continued via Tehran, over the towering Zagros mountains and the Caspian Sea to Moscow, guided for the last thousand miles by the Volga.

On the evening of 12 August, scarcely pausing to unpack in the enormous villa assigned to him, Churchill plunged into talks with Stalin in the Kremlin.

He wanted to get the bad news out of the way first. There would be no second front in 1942. 'Stalin's face crumbled into a frown but he did not interrupt,' Churchill recorded. There would not even be a landing of six divisions on the Cherbourg peninsula. 'There was an oppressive silence. Stalin at length said that if we could not make a landing in France this year he was not entitled to demand it or insist upon it, but he was bound to say that he did not agree with my arguments.'

The first two hours were 'bleak and sombre'. Then, deftly and deliberately, Churchill played the card he had risked so much to bring so far. He explained that while there would be no Anglo-American offensive in Western Europe that summer, there would be one in North Africa. Operation Torch, to be launched in October, would bring victory in Egypt and right along the North African coast, all as a prelude to freeing the Mediterranean.

'To illustrate my point I had meanwhile drawn a picture of a crocodile,' Churchill wrote, 'and explained to Stalin with the help of this picture how it was our intention to attack the soft belly of the crocodile as we attacked his hard snout. And Stalin, whose interest was now at a high pitch, said, "May God prosper this undertaking."'

The hard snout was the French Atlantic coast, and after St Nazaire no one could say Churchill wasn't serious about attacking it. By the same token if there had been no Operation Chariot the argument would have had no force.

After two more marathon meetings, and a visit to the ballet for Vanderkloot with a reception committee from the Soviet Air Force, Commando lumbered back into the air for the return trip. Churchill had a splitting headache from a final night of drinking with Stalin, but the reward was a personal rapport that he believed helped keep Russia in the war.

The B-24 flew back down the Volga and across the Caspian, and refuelled in Tehran and Cairo. On the penultimate leg of the journey Churchill woke at dawn and came forward to the cockpit to find Vanderkloot skimming along at 200 mph barely thirty feet above the Mediterranean in order to stay under the morning mist. Churchill said he hoped Vanderkloot wasn't going to hit the Rock of Gibraltar. The pilot's answers 'were not particularly reassuring', but after three or four hours on instruments alone he flew into clear air as the Rock reared up to the right, and made a perfect landing. It was, Churchill noted, a fine performance.

In the four months after the *Campbeltown* exploded, Operation Chariot hardened into a sturdy utility piece on Churchill's chessboard. It deprived Hitler of a place to repair battleships on the Atlantic seaboard – even if in fact he had already decided to keep them in safer Norwegian waters. It gave the British something to cheer about at last – even if German versions of the raid were quicker to reach newsreels and front pages than British ones, and took time to correct in the public imagination. (They said the *Campbeltown* was blown up before reaching the dock, and that pictures showing the dock gate had been destroyed were fake.) It persuaded Admiral Dönitz to move his headquarters for the German Naval Command Group West to Paris, thinking *he* was the real target of the attack; and it was surely a factor in Hitler's decision to strengthen his land forces in Western Europe in the remainder of 1942 even if he did the same thing on the Eastern Front (adding nineteen divisions in each theatre). But in the end the main strategic value of the raid for Churchill was that it showed the British meant what they said about attacking the crocodile's snout. Given the slightest opportunity – even an opportunity the enemy thought mad – they would seize it and fight to the death. They were not to be judged by Singapore. They were worth having as an ally.

For Mountbatten, Operation Chariot served a more personal purpose: his advancement. His multiple promotions just before the raid gained him a seat on the Chiefs of Staff Committee and infuriated its other members as much as it delighted Mountbatten himself.

General Sir Alan Brooke, Chief of the Imperial General Staff, said there was no reason for his inclusion in the committee, 'where he frequently wasted his own time and ours'. Mountbatten couldn't have cared less. What thrilled him was becoming a Vice-Admiral at a younger age (forty-one) than Nelson had (at forty-two). 'Does that stagger you, as the Americans say,' he wrote in a letter to his daughter, 'or does that stagger you?'

Staggered or not, after St Nazaire Brooke and the others could no longer afford to ignore or belittle Mountbatten. It was too risky. The ancients at the top of the armed forces already had a serious public relations problem in that they were losing the war. They also had a *private* public relations problem in the form of Mountbatten's cantankerous predecessor as head of Combined Operations, Sir Roger Keyes. On handing over the reins Keyes had called the Chiefs of Staff 'the greatest cowards I've ever met', and he talked like that to anyone who'd listen.

Churchill promoted Mountbatten precisely to counter the perception on both sides of the Atlantic that Colonel Blimps were running things at the Ministry of Defence. St Nazaire seemed to vindicate his extraordinary show of faith in young 'Dickie', and soon afterwards Mountbatten won approval for two more raids, codenamed Myrmidon and Abercrombie. One was meant to interrupt rail traffic near Bayonne in south-west France. The other was to be a Canadian-led attack on a coastal village south of Boulogne in the Pas de Calais. Both were duds, but Mountbatten's star continued to rise.

When Churchill needed someone to travel to Washington to explain to Roosevelt his preference for a North African over a European offensive in the second half of 1942, he sent Mountbatten. When General George Marshall visited London in April, Mountbatten was the British military commander he most wanted to see.

The adulation – especially from America – would have swollen any ambitious head, but Mountbatten's was particularly prone to swelling. This was the young thruster, after all, who spent long hours in the spring of 1942 working with Noël Coward on the casting and details of *In Which We Serve*, the film about his time on the *Kelly*, even as he complained to others of being overworked at Combined Operations HQ.

This work was still supposed to be raiding. Just as Churchill was under pressure to open a second front, Mountbatten was under pressure to keep on raiding, especially after the cancellation of Myrmidon and Abercrombie. In the circumstances it would have been surprising if the success of Operation Chariot did not embolden him to push for something bigger and even more spectacular. The obvious candidate, at least to Mountbatten, was Hughes-Hallett's plan for a frontal assault on Dieppe, sixty miles across the Channel from sleepy Newhaven. Codenamed Rutter, the operation was cancelled at the last minute in July because of bad weather and a pre-emptive attack by the Luftwaffe. Even before these hiccups the other Chiefs of Staff had judged Rutter's chances of success to be close to nil – but hadn't St Nazaire shown that with pluck and luck the impossible was possible?

Mountbatten now revived Rutter as Jubilee, and it was a disaster. It had no clear purpose. There was no preliminary bombing. Of 4,000 Canadians who landed or tried to land, 2,700 were killed or captured. Of twenty-seven tanks landed on the beach, not one made it into town. Of 500 soldiers from the Royal Regiment and the Black Watch who landed west of Dieppe, six returned unwounded.

Historians have noted how unfair it would be on the Charioteers to lay any of the Dieppe fiasco at their door. It would indeed, but Mountbatten connects the two raids like a high-voltage cable. Thanks to him, it is hard to imagine the second without the first.

The first two days after Operation Chariot were busy ones for Gordon Holman and Ed Gilling. The two reporters reached

England early on Sunday the 29th and had to work fast to file for that night's editions. Holman was in Plymouth aboard the *Atherstone* by 2:30 a.m. but it was an especially tight deadline for Gilling, who limped into Falmouth harbour at noon on launch 307.

The *Evening Standard* and the *Exchange Telegraph* syndicated nationwide, so Holman and Gilling's stories were all over Monday's papers, although they were far from complete. Like Ryder, they assumed the explosion heard from the *Atherstone* as they escaped was the *Campbeltown* going up, but they couldn't confirm it. *The Times* finessed this by quoting the latest communiqué from Combined Operations HQ in full, including this line: 'A huge explosion, followed by a smaller one, was seen and heard by our returning forces at 4 am, which was the time the delay-action fuses were due to go off.' Above that, for its final edition, the paper carried a confident stand first refuting German claims that the raid failed to achieve its main objective and stating that 'the main lock gates of the dry dock were destroyed'. (Did Mountbatten phone the editor, Dawson, at Printing House Square as soon as he had put down the phone to the PM? It's entirely possible, although Combined Operations HQ was also issuing updates through the night.)

Below the communiqué, dispatches from both Holman and Gilling appeared with – by *Times* standards – a banner headline: 'SPLENDID SUCCESS SCENE OF BLAZING DESTRUCTION'.

'The most daring, and in many ways the most important, of combined operational attacks on the enemy so far undertaken has met with splendid success, but the cost has been high,' Holman wrote. 'Many of the commando troops fought until they were either casualties or taken prisoner . . .

'The motor gunboat in which I was blazed her way past the last barrier before the entrance to the dry dock. She then swung round, and we watched the *Campbeltown* finish her last journey by magnificently shooting up a German flak ship, which she left in flames before speeding up to about 20 knots for the charge into the dock gates . . .

'Colonel Newman jumped ashore . . . Blazing buildings . . . Rapid fire . . . Wounded men . . . Blazing destruction.'

Copy to gladden Churchill's heart.

Gilling wrote that the attack came as a nasty shock to the Germans: 'A fair comparison would be to say that the operation was the same as a German force steaming up the Thames to Tilbury.' He was right about the shock. German reports on the 29th were surprisingly accurate on most points except the big one – the fate of the *Campbeltown* – and they spun the story as a crushing defeat for the commandos and the Royal Navy. But Hitler knew better than to believe his own propaganda and, of course, he was briefed on realities as they emerged. He was curious enough about the kind of soldiers who would volunteer for this sort of suicide mission to send his personal interpreter, Paul Schmidt, to interview them. Schmidt didn't get much out of them – not even Micky Burn, who recognized him from Nuremberg in 1935. But in an admittedly self-serving memoir Schmidt did say he was 'greatly impressed by the complete confidence of all . . . expressed in the prospects of victory, and by the absence of any fanaticism or any suggestion of hatred of Germany'.

Besides being curious, Hitler was angry. How had such a lightly armed force slipped past so many of his defences? He ordered Field Marshal Gerd von Rundstedt, his most senior soldier in Western Europe, to find out. Rundstedt came back with the unsatisfactory answer that no one was to blame, so Hitler told a succession of even more senior commanders to do better, and they argued among themselves. Remarkably, heads didn't roll. Even Gerd Kelbling wasn't punished. He was the U-boat commander who reported seeing Ryder's force heading west on 27 March and thereby helped keep its secret for most of the day. He explained much later to Bill Green, Ryder's navigator, that his signal did get through to German Naval Command Group West but was automatically disregarded as unreliable because he was on his first mission as captain.

Ryder himself did not know for sure that the *Campbeltown* had done the trick until the Monday morning. It was especially welcome news. The previous day, by his own account, he had stepped ashore in Plymouth to be handed a bizarrely spiteful message from the Admiralty. Delivered by an attractive-looking dispatch rider from the Wrens, it was confirmation that their Lordships considered him at fault for the loss of the *Prince Philippe* in the North Channel the previous year. Ryder was exhausted and miserable at having left so many commandos behind. He had imagined this mud-spattered motorcyclist might be bringing congratulations or at least consolation. Instead, a punch in the gut.

It could have been a scene from *M*A*S*H*: the bureaucracy of war stumbling along behind the war itself. It could also have been misremembered by Ryder, whose formal letter from the Admiralty (the Wren could have been bringing advance notification) is dated 10 April. In any case, things were looking up.

Ryder's presence was requested for a press conference at the Ministry of Information in London the following morning. Minutes before it started the Admiralty confirmed the dock gate had been destroyed. Ryder reckoned several hundred reporters attended, which would have been an unusual crush – there were only a few dozen phone lines for the press room's regular users. Against the ministry's instructions Ryder named Sam Beattie as captain of the *Campbeltown*, so the two of them dominated the next day's coverage. Ryder's wife, Hilaré, was doorstepped at their home in Windsor, where she agreed to be photographed knitting and reading, and said she felt 'terribly proud'. Her sisters then arranged for her to go up to town and whisk her dashing husband off to the Berkeley for the night – their treat. She loved it, though what Ryder made of it is hard to imagine. Two days earlier he had led 623 men into a death trap that killed or wounded more than half of them. Here he was back in London with breakfast on a trolley in the swankiest hotel in Knightsbridge and his picture in *The Times*.

The world was catching up. The BBC noted on the Monday that 'the American press today devotes considerable space in praise of the courage and enterprise of our forces engaged in the attack'. It was true: on the 29th the *New York Times* had carried a false German report that the *Campbeltown* blew up before reaching the dock, but it made amends on the 30th with a prominent editorial: 'For sheer daring, the British commando descent on St Nazaire surpasses any similar raid of the war. Irrespective of immediate success or failure, so bold an answer to home demand for offensive action must lift the fighting spirit of the whole British people . . . Such a hazardous venture must have seemed impossible to the Germans.'

Mountbatten could have dictated it himself – and Churchill the pay-off: 'These commando assaults, accelerating in number and power as the Spring advances, serve a double purpose. Each has a tactical objective . . . but all are part of a larger strategy to pin heavy German concentrations on the west front and prevent them from reinforcing Hitler's coming offensive in Russia.'

Ryder didn't like all the attention, but there was more to come. In May, on assignment in Cowes, he was spending the night at a navy mess when most of the other officers there burst into his room to tell him he'd won the Victoria Cross. 'For great gallantry . . . under intense fire from short-range weapons at point blank range,' the citation read in part. 'Though the main object of the expedition had been accomplished . . . he remained on the spot conducting operations, evacuating men from the *Campbeltown* and dealing with strong points and close-range weapons while exposed to heavy fire for an hour and 16 minutes . . . That his Motor Gun Boat, now full of dead and wounded, should have survived and should've been able to withdraw through an intense barrage of close-range fire was almost a miracle.'

Now the congratulations came. Mountbatten wrote that he 'had never had more pleasure in writing to congratulate anybody than in writing to you for your grandly-earned VC'. Philip

Francis, the wireless operator on the *Tai-Mo-Shan*, sent a note suggesting a VC was a licence for farting in trains and kissing girls in hotel lobbies.

The investiture was at Buckingham Palace. Ryder fulfilled his obligations by showing up and talking briefly to the King about the *Campbeltown*, then escaped to Green Park via a side door, alone. The *Daily Herald* counted twenty Ryder family members in attendance and said they had to chase him into the park. He wrote afterwards to Hilaré: 'I am sorry I couldn't revel & wallow in the proceedings etc . . . but I do so dislike that sort of thing. I hope I didn't appear very surly.' In the pictures the press managed to take of him that day he doesn't look surly, but, as ever, he looks strained.

In the same issue of the *London Gazette* (21 May) VCs were announced for Bill Savage and Sam Beattie. Savage had been buried soon after his body arrived in Falmouth, carefully shepherded ashore by Dunstan Curtis. Strapped to a board and covered with the Union Jack, it was loaded onto the back of an open van and driven slowly through town to the chapel of rest. His brother Jack was away on active service on destroyers, where Bill himself had always wanted to be, but their older brother, Roland, came down from Smethwick for the funeral.

The survivors who accompanied Savage's body to Falmouth received a warmer welcome than Webb, Paton and those who returned to Plymouth on the *Tynedale*. Soldiers and sailors alike were taken back aboard the *Princess Josephine Charlotte*, fed handsomely and 'treated like lords', as one lance corporal recalled. The remnants of 2 Commando then headed to Scotland with David Paton. They were fondly remembered there as all-conquering heroes who'd come and go at any hour of the day or night with rucksacks, Bren guns, climbing ropes and insatiable appetites – for food, drink if possible and at all costs the chance to go to war.

Paton described this last leg of their journey:

'We went by bus to Plymouth to see the rest of our chaps who had come home on the destroyers and then by train back to Ayr, where I marched my sorry little commando of 3 officers and 25 men from the station back to our H.Q. for debriefing. The people of Ayr stood in the streets and the women wept as we marched. They remembered us as the rumbustious 400 they had learned to live with for months. We all got a week's leave . . .'

From 2 Commando alone, twenty-five officers and 160 men had set out.

Beattie was by this time a prisoner in a camp of wooden huts on heathland in northern Germany. The Lüneburger Heide is now a nature reserve; hiking country for outdoorsy types from Hamburg and Bremen. It struck most of the Charioteers sent there after the raid as bleak and windswept, useful only for escape practice. But the frustrations of living there behind barbed wire were relieved by the company of comrades and, one day, by the ex-admiral who ran the place. He ordered the prisoners to assemble for an unscheduled parade and had a quiet word with Newman, who in turn, to general rejoicing, announced Beattie's VC.

There was nothing yet for Newman himself. The commandos all had to wait till the end of the war for their decorations. Then recommendations poured in for Newman, and for Durrant. They too won VCs. The total of five for one brief action was unmatched in the war, and for years afterwards many of those who survived it said Tibbits deserved the highest medal too.

Corran Purdon put it in so many words. 'Your grandfather never got the credit he deserved,' he told Bill Tibbits, Nigel's grandson, at the funeral of Bob Montgomery in 2016. 'He should have got the VC.' It's certainly hard to think of anyone who combined devotion to duty and self-sacrifice to quite the same degree, and among the Charioteers the bar is high. The march of history can make triumphs and disasters seem foreordained, but the detonation of the *Campbeltown* was no more foreordained than victory in the war. Hundreds of things could have gone wrong, from the design of the bomb to the setting of its fuses and the steering of the ship – all of which Tibbits in the end took care of personally. He was the difference between success and failure.

His son, Andrew, regrets that initially there was 'no acknowledgement at all that he had died a hero' – although this was probably because there was no official word that he was dead. Elmslie didn't know until June, and it took the Admiralty a full year to confirm. Tibbits was then awarded a Distinguished Service Cross, the third-highest award for gallantry, and the seven-year-old Andrew went to the Palace in a sailor suit to collect it.

Having grown up and grown old without a father, Andrew Tibbits also regrets that the mission wasn't designed differently. 'If they'd had a skeleton crew . . .' he begins, seventy-nine years on. 'If they'd simply blown up the *Campbeltown* and destroyed the lock gate, and had a couple of motor launches that would have shot off down the river within ten minutes of hitting the lock gate, that would have saved a lot of life and would have been nearly as effective as doing all the other things. But that's with the benefit of hindsight.'

Success has many fathers, and once the pictures were in and Ryder's press conference concluded, his superiors stepped forward to bask in a little of his glory. Admiral Forbes, who had forecast the loss of the entire Chariot force, said that in putting the dry dock out of action the raid had been an undoubted success. Alan Brooke, so rankled by the presence of Mountbatten in his Chiefs of Staff meetings, sagely informed the visiting American General Marshall in April that the idea behind raiding was 'to force on the enemy a feeling of insecurity and uncertainty'. Two days later the Admiralty – which in practice meant Admiral of the Fleet Dudley Pound, who had approved Chariot in principle but resisted providing any destroyers for it in practice – stated that the St Nazaire raid had 'a more far-reaching effect than any previous one' and created 'a state of nerves and disorganisation'.

This was true, at least as far as the nerves were concerned. When Wynn's torpedoes exploded on the Monday after the raid, the

German authorities were so concerned about the possibility of a general uprising that they threatened decimation. Mayor Pierre Toscer and his four deputies were shaken from their sleep and marched to a midnight meeting with a colonel of the Wehrmacht visiting from Angers. Townspeople had been shooting at German soldiers, the colonel said. If it happened again a tenth of the civilian population in the neighbourhood in question would be shot without a hearing. Mayor Toscer was to have posters printed to that effect by morning. They were up by 7 a.m.

Pound and Forbes had every reason to applaud the raid. They had dragged their feet over the planning and shouldered little of the personal or institutional risk, yet still they could congratulate themselves on an important piece of enemy hardware put beyond use.

The congratulations didn't reach far down the ranks, though; nor to the bereaved. According to Tibbits family lore, Elmslie Tibbits, finding herself without a husband or an income, decided to pay the Admiralty a visit. As the great-granddaughter of a hero of Trafalgar and the daughter-in-law of a retired admiral, she felt she deserved a hearing – especially now that she was the widow of a hero of St Nazaire as well. 'So she went up to London and said, "I've got a young son and no money – what do you recommend?"' says the son. 'And some commander said, "You've got a nice ring on your finger; you could sell that." She was so disgusted she walked out.'

Elmslie received one month of her husband's salary and went to work in a munitions factory. Tibbits had been cut down by machine gun fire on a launch that carried most of those on it to their deaths. The exact number isn't known because the number Mark Rodier rescued from the *Campbeltown* is not known either. But by launch 177's standards Tibbits was not especially unlucky. His body was swept out with the tide and never found; he is commemorated at Portsmouth Naval Memorial, overlooking the Solent.

It could have happened to George Wheeler at any of a dozen moments. He could have been hit on the run-in aboard 457, jumping onto the mole under position 63, running across the Old Town Square after Philip Walton, running to Bridge G for Tiger Watson after Walton's death, wandering among warehouses in the confusion of battle, or running across Bridge D into the New Town. And yet he wasn't. He was determined to get home. It's tempting to ascribe one to the other, but in the end it's surely pointless. Every one of the 265 commandos on the raid sailed up the Loire facing the same long odds. One in four were killed. Another two in four were wounded or taken prisoner. They were all tough and highly motivated, and some were lucky too, but on the night of the raid there was not much scope for making your own luck. On the contrary, the officers whose job it was to lead by example set one of total defiance. Copland, Roderick, Roy and Newman weren't for dodging bullets. They were quite comfortable with the idea that the bullets would either get you or they wouldn't.

Wheeler went along with it – but then, from the night of the 28th, when he no longer had to take orders, he started being careful.

Once he and Sims got clear of St Nazaire they assumed it would be a long grind home, and this may have been partly because of a different sort of example set by Arthur Boswell and Alf Logan. They will have known of Boswell's and Logan's story from the papers; two guardsmen captured at Dunkirk who escaped, headed south and eventually made it to Gibraltar. It took them sixteen months. In the end the most dangerous part of Wheeler's and Sims's escape took them only sixteen days, but they were still not taking chances. Every day they hid in barns, preferably deep within haystacks. Every night they walked.

'We avoided towns like the plague and walked along country lanes avoiding also the big villages,' Wheeler said. 'We saw no Jerries at all from the time we left St Nazaire till the time we reached the line of demarcation.' This was the line between occupied and

Vichy France, marked by the River Creuse, which they crossed by wading into it up to their chests while three helpful young French women kept a lookout for patrols.

Before the crossing Wheeler and Sims learned to arrive at farms at mealtimes and identify themselves with the only recognizably British things they still possessed – a ten-shilling note and a box of Bryant & May matches. The further they got from St Nazaire, the longer it took to persuade potential helpers that they were truly *évadés* from the raid. But once that message was conveyed they were usually rewarded with food and wine, and hay to sleep in. Early on they ditched their uniforms for black pinstripe trousers and short black coats. Wheeler said they looked like bank clerks.

After the river crossing they were feted by a local landowner and his wife at their chateau. They drank the cherry brandy and green Chartreuse ('Oh, that lovely Chartreuse!') and picked up the pace by taking a bus to Châteauroux. There they fell in with a Belgian teenager who used his fluent French to get them all train tickets to Toulouse. Spanish smugglers walked them over the border in the Pyrenees, where they took off their unsuitable dress shoes and sunbathed for a day. The British consulate in Barcelona supplied fresh clothes and transport to Madrid. Wheeler and Sims tossed a coin for the first seat available in a car heading to the capital, and Wheeler won. Continuing alone, he spent five days in the Spanish capital and six in Gibraltar, and flew home in more comfort than Churchill enjoyed with Vanderkloot; he took a flying boat.

Later in 1942 Wheeler received the Military Medal at Buckingham Palace, explaining to the King that he had not escaped capture; he had evaded it.

Those who were taken prisoner had three more years of it. Some adjusted better than others to the monotony and anticlimax. For Corran Purdon, still only twenty-one, it was not enough to have survived. He signed up at once for any opportunities offered by the escape committee at the camp on the Lüneburger Heide, Marlag und Milag Nord. None paid off, but he tried again when moved to Schloss Spangenberg, an officers' prison in hill country south of Hanover. He and another prisoner made a daring run for it during a play presented by their comrades, and lived off the land and their wits for nine days before being recaptured in a shunting yard.

Stuart Chant tried escaping from a prison on the River Fulda in a cart full of potato skins, but was caught in the act. Tiger Watson helped dig a tunnel out of Spangenberg but in the end he stayed there and studied medicine. (His long career as a doctor and aid worker took him to Iran and all over Africa, but it started immediately after the war working with starving civilians in Germany.)

Philip Dark recorded his prison years in paint. Marlag und Milag Nord was technically for navy personnel, and as a navy man – like Bill Lovegrove, Micky Wynn's motor mechanic – he was kept there until 1945. Prison life was as grey as his captors' uniforms, he said, so he injected colour from his nightmares into his paintings. They were found hidden in the camp after he'd been marched out of it as a hostage a few months before its liberation, and were sold at an exhibition after his death, in 2016.

Dick Bradley recovered from the bullet hole through his lung, to escape four times from camps in Germany and Poland, eventually creeping over a field into Switzerland at midnight in his socks. Chant was repatriated early on account of his injuries and went on a speaking tour of America to prove to any doubters that the British could still fight. And Micky Wynn became a hypochondriac. Sent to Colditz from Marlag und Milag Nord, he decided his only way out was to persuade the authorities he was finished. He spent six months complaining of fictional back pain, which was enough to have him sent to hospital. From there he was allowed home a few months before the end of the war. Under the Geneva Conventions, as a repatriated POW he was not allowed back into active service. But Wynn was not much bothered with conventions. He followed the Allied forces' advance into Central Europe with one goal in mind – to be present at the liberation of Bill Lovegrove.

The man who'd saved his life was still there, unhappy and unwell. His wife had left him for another man – a GI – and years of camp food had sapped his strength. 'I took him with me and we flew straight back to London,' Wynn said. 'He was in a bad way so I sent him to stay at our home until he'd recovered.' The 6th Baron and Lady Newborough, Wynn's parents, took care of Lovegrove on their Welsh estate.

For weeks after the raid, the status of Tommy Durrant, Bill Gibson, Nigel Tibbits, David Birney, Micky Burn and many others was, as far as anyone in Britain knew, the same. They were missing in action. Cécilie Birney, like Elmslie Tibbits, hoped against hope to hear that her husband was a prisoner and alive. Durrant's parents waited in Green Street Green for news of their boy, and Gibson's father waited for news of his in Thornliebank on the south side of Glasgow. As for Clive Burn, Micky's father, he got a letter as if from the King and Queen.

'Their majesties express the fervent hope that you may soon hear reassuring news,' said the note from Sir Piers Legh, Master of the Royal Household. For the royals, Sir Clive was by now a close and trusted courtier in his role as Secretary of the Archives of the Duchy of Cornwall, and his son was fondly remembered for his *Times* coverage of the royal tour of the USA and Canada. So Micky's fate in the war was practically a family matter. In early July, Sir Clive at last received a letter from his son at Marlag und Milag Nord. Their majesties were informed and sent word immediately of their joy and relief. The letter from Germany included a hopeful mention of Bill Gibson, whose fate Micky didn't yet know. Sir Clive had made a point of keeping in touch with all the parents of Micky's 6 Troop men, and he forwarded this section of the letter to Gibson's father, Alex. Four days later came a reply from Thornliebank. Alex Gibson had heard on 7 July that his son was dead.

'I'm glad Captain Burn escaped with his life,' he wrote, 'as he was a great favourite with the boys. They always spoke of him in admiring terms, and my son, in a last letter to me, describes him as a "great and good man" . . . I'm proud of my son, and glad that it was in such a noble attempt that he lost his life.'

Burn Jr spent most of the next three years in Colditz. He set up a school for fellow prisoners, wrote a novel and read up on Marxism. As American troops drew near in 1945 he prepared for a return to journalism by writing two long dispatches for *The Times* that helped found the Colditz legend. He tried not to glamourize the place but couldn't help it. He had to lead with the news, and the news in those final days was that two nephews of the King and Queen, the son of a field marshal, the Polish General Bór-Komorowski, the son of the American ambassador to London and a dozen or so other 'prominents' were being kidnapped from Colditz on Heinrich Himmler's personal orders as human bargaining chips. Burn described the prison as 'dismal and detestable' – 'a fortress infected with the restriction of the human spirit'. He could have been writing about Europe itself, of course, when the Charioteers hurled themselves at its steel gates and concrete fortifications to show that one day it would be free again.

How did they do it? Charles Newman settled down with a typewriter on his return to England in July 1945 and produced a brisk, cheerful account of the raid he'd planned with such precision and survived without a scrape. He got some basic facts wrong. Describing the effects of the *Campbeltown*'s explosion, for example, he said an 'outrush of water from the Dry Dock carried the two vessels that were in her out to sea where they sank'. There was no outrush because the dock was empty; there was an inrush instead. The vessels – the *Passat* and the *Schlettstadt* – stayed inside the dock and didn't sink. But by that time such details were immaterial. The war was won. And, he wrote: 'if we who took part in the St Nazaire operation can look back and say that the raid on the 28th March was the first offensive operation carried to the enemy in Europe, and justifiably think that from that date the country never looked back – if we can do that, then we might be allowed a small measure of reflected glory in that we were the lucky ones to be in at the start.'

One of the last commandos home was Arthur Dockerill; ex-choirboy, plumber, whistler, demolition man. On his return to Ely he wrote to Chant, whose life he'd saved leading the way back up from the pumping station floor, with ninety-second fuses burning in the dark behind them. He got a swift reply. 'My dear Dockerill,' Chant began, congratulating him on winning a Distinguished Conduct Medal and passing on some news of other officers. Colonel Charles was well and out of the army already. Purdon was off to Burma soon. 'I haven't yet seen anyone else but as you say I hope soon we can have a Beano and then see everyone.'

He urged Dockerill not to rush back into uniform. 'Take as much leave as you can: – you'll find out you will need *all* the leave you can get: – I could do with about six months of it right now . . . Give my regards to any of the boys if you see them and especially to your wife. Give me a ring if you are in London and then we will be able to have a drink or lunch. All the best, Stuart Chant.'

The letter is part of a small but cherished collection kept in a box by Duncan Dockerill, Arthur's son. Did the beano ever happen? If it did, Arthur would surely have whistled his way there and back.

Postscript

Clouds sometimes passed over Dockerill's sunny outlook. In fact, his good fortune at having survived the war uninjured perplexed him for the rest of his life. 'He could never understand it,' his son said. 'On Armistice Day he would stay home with tears rolling down his face.'

No wonder. No other raid was as dangerous or daring. Twenty-seven per cent of those who took part were killed. The losses as a share of the number who set out were higher than at Dieppe (19 per cent) or Zeebrugge in the First World War (12 per cent), and many times higher than on D-Day.

These larger events have often eclipsed the story of St Nazaire in popular memory, but there was always reassurance for survivors that their sacrifices had not been in vain. They formed an association, the St Nazaire Society, and in 1949 the reporter Gordon Holman sent a letter for publication in its newsletter. It appeared under the heading 'Do You Remember?'

'For a minute or two –' Holman wrote, 'on the same little type-writer that was hooked out of the motor gunboat before we sank her with our own shells on the way back from St. Nazaire – I am going to set down a few memories.

'Those of you who did not get out until long after, may never have appreciated what an immense tonic your exploits were in those back-to-the-wall days of 1942. Everybody wanted to hear the story first-hand . . . Many could be quoted, but one's memory switches to the youngster from the Navy – Young, his name was – who came back in the *Atherstone* with both arms badly smashed up. He kept away from the doctor for hours so that others could be treated. In front of me is the crumpled piece of paper on which I wrote down his dictation as we went ashore at Plymouth, the message to be sent to his mother – "Back safe, slightly wounded but only arms. Very fit, much love, Charlie".

'If memories fade in these busy, difficult post-war years, do not forget the Charlies – and Toms and Bills and Jacks – who were your comrades; and who, if they live, in the words of Lord Mountbatten, have the right of membership in the most exclusive Society in the world.'

In 1952 Trevor Howard and Richard Attenborough starred in *Gift Horse*, based loosely on the story of the raid. Howard played a captain modelled on Sam Beattie and a gift horse – given by America, not to be looked in the mouth – is what he called his ship. The film might have helped carve a niche for Operation Chariot in Britain's cultural as well as military history, as *In Which We Serve* had done for Mountbatten himself, but the critics panned it and American audiences stayed away.

The full story of the raid had yet to be told, and two writers, forty years apart, assembled the British side of it from interviews and archives. Charles Lucas Phillips was the first, in 1958, writing to dozens of survivors and asking them to put their recollections down on paper. He called his book *The Greatest Raid of All*, and the assessment stuck. James Dorrian was the second. His Herculean *Storming St Nazaire*, published in 1998, collects dozens more personal histories and interweaves them into the most comprehensive portrait of the raid that will ever be written, not least because no one who took part is still alive.

Without the work of Lucas Phillips and Dorrian, Operation Chariot might never have caught the eye of Jeremy Clarkson, the TV presenter and provocateur. As it was, in 2007, he took a break from programmes about cars and made an affectionate and enthralling documentary that brought the story of the *Campbeltown* and her doomed entourage roaring into thousands of living rooms. Finding no archive footage of the *Campbeltown* exploding, his visual-effects team – more famous for their work on *Harry*

Potter – built a seventeen-foot scale model and blew that up instead. The building and destruction of the model wasn't a commercial decision, the team's leader said. 'It was really just the subject matter. It seemed to strike a chord.'

It should not be a surprise that the story of the *Campbeltown* still resonated more than six decades after the event. In that time and since, the war and Britain's role in it have been examined more closely than any other chapter in the country's history. Some episodes, like the raid on Dieppe, have shown how poorly spin stands up to long years of forensic scrutiny. The verdict of history is damning even if Mountbatten never accepted it. Grand themes, including Britain's path to victory, have been re-evaluated in light of new information and broadening perspectives. The end point has not changed but the journey there is dominated less now by heroic narratives of Britain alone and more by the thunder of American aircraft and Soviet tanks.

In this evolving context, Operation Chariot stood firm, a bit like the Old Mole jutting out into the Loire. In the great reckoning of the late 1940s and early 1950s, historians paid little attention to it. Churchill himself gave it one page in nearly 4,000. But as the din of propaganda faded and time brought more detachment, the idea of Britain fighting on alone through the nadir of the war was tested. There were stories aplenty of daring and defiance with backs to the wall, but where was the irreducible proof of the offensive spirit Churchill demanded? It was at St Nazaire.

After the war, survivors of the raid travelled every March to the port where the *Tirpitz* never docked, to toast the memory of those who died. As they grew older they brought children and grandchildren. In 1982, to mark the fortieth anniversary of the operation, the Royal Yacht *Britannia* brought many who would otherwise have had to make the trip by bus and ferry. (Ralph Batteson sailed home in a cabin used by Princess Diana's lady-in-waiting on Charles and Diana's honeymoon, and asked, 'How lucky can you get?') Tiger Watson, one of the longest-lived of the Charioteers, died in 2019, aged ninety-seven. But their families still visit when they can.

The only years since 1946 in which the town has not hosted a reunion of Charioteers or their descendants have been 2020 and 2021, on account of Covid. But French and British flags still fly year round, regardless, next to a memorial to the raiders at the base of the Old Mole, and if you walk along it, out towards the lighthouse, you can still see traces of cement that once fixed the pillbox at position 63 to the cobblestones; a QR code reaching back to history.

It was from here, in 1947, that Newman and Ryder led their men across Bridge D again, this time in orderly columns between pavements packed with townspeople. They were met in the New Town by Paul Ramadier, the French Prime Minister and former member of the Resistance, who thanked them and told them: 'You were the first to bring us hope.'

Later that year the Normandie Dock was reopened. One of the first vessels to use it was the former German steamship *Europa*, now sailing under a French flag as *Liberté*.

Appendix

Appendix 2

OPERATION CHARIOT — COMBINED PLAN
(Short Title: CHAR ONE)

References:-   Chart No. 1104 Bay of BISCAY
     " No. 2646 FRANCE west coast
                BOURGNEUF to ILE DE GROIX
     " No. 2989   Entrance to LOIRE
      River and approaches to ST. NAZAIRE

     Orders for the Passage (Short title: CHAR TWO)
     Orders for the submarine (Short title: CHAR THREE)

Appendix -   A.   Times of High Water, etc.
         ALL TIMES ARE B.S.T.

OBJECT

The enemy is making great use of ST. NAZAIRE as a base for U boats and light craft as well as a port of shipping. The object of the raid in order of priority is to destroy: -

(a) The lock gates and mechanism of the large dock

(b) The smaller lock gates and their installation.

(c) Other key points, such as pumping machinery for the basin, etc.

(d) Any U boats and shipping which may be accessible.

FORCES TAKING PART

2. H. M. S. CAMPBELTOWN

M. T. B. 74

M. G. B. 314

12 M. L.s

2 Hunt class destroyers.

Military Forces

(16 officers and 68 Other Ranks: Demolition parties (from Special Service Brigade.

(25 officers and 136 Other Ranks of No. 2 Commando.

Air Forces

Aircraft detailed by Bomber Command

P. R. U. aircraft after the operation — Admiralty to arrange.

INTELLIGENCE

3. Intelligence will be issued separately.

OUTLINE PLAN

4. It is intended that the force will proceed in company so as to approach ST. NAZAIRE after dark on a moonlight night near high water. A submarine will act as a navigational beacon.

5. The force will proceed up the estuary over the mud flats, CAMPBELTOWN being appreciably lightened to do this. The two Hunts will remain to seaward.

6. The troops will be carried in the CAMPBELTOWN and the M.L.s. On arrival CAMPBELTOWN will ram the outer gate of the big lock and the troops on board will disembark over her bows, then proceeding to carry out their demolition tasks. The remainder of the force will disembark from their M.L.s at selected points in the dockyard area.

7. After CAMPBELTOWN has come to rest, she will be scuttled and the large charge, which is stowed forward, will be fired with a delay action fuse.

8. The whole force will withdraw in the M.L.s after a maximum period ashore of 2 hours or earlier if ordered.

AIR

9. Bomber aircraft will carry out continuous attacks on ST. NAZAIRE during the night of the operation with the object of: -

(a) Detracting attention from the main assault force.

(b) Disorganising local defences and lookout.

(c) Preventing any repairs being made to the docks before the fall of the tide.

COMMAND

10. The operation as a whole will be under the supreme command of Commander-in-Chief, PLYMOUTH, under whose authority combined orders will be issued.

11. Naval and military forces will be under the joint command of two Force Commanders as follows: -

Commander R.E.D. RYDER, Royal Navy, who will command naval forces taking part; referred to as the S.N.O.

Lieut.-Colonel A.C. NEWMAN, No. 2 Commando, who will command the military units.

The Force Commanders will proceed in the CAMPBELTOWN during the passage and transfer to M.G.B. 314 at dusk on the evening of the operation.

12. Air forces taking part in the raid on ST. NAZAIRE will operate under Commander-in-Chief, Bomber Command, in the normal manner. Group Captain A.H. WILLETTS, of Combined Operations Headquarters, will act as liaison officer between Commander-in-Chief, Bomber Command, Commander-in-Chief, PLYMOUTH and Air Ministry.

DATES

13. The operation can only take place between certain dates when the moon and tide are suitable. These are between the nights of 28th/29th March and 30th/31st March inclusive. This is a period of full moon. It is also essential to have calm weather for the passage.

ZERO TIME

14. Zero time will be 0130 B.S.T. and the landing will take place as near this time as possible. Zero time is the same for all nights on which the operation may be carried out.

PRELIMINARY MOVEMENTS

15. The orders for the assembly and training of the force will be issued separately.

OUTWARD PASSAGE

16. Orders for the sailing and outward passage will be issued separately.

SUBMARINE ACTING AS LIGHT BEACON

17. The force will pass position "Z" (46° 48' N, 02° 50' W) at 2230 approaching on approximate course 045°.

STURGEON will be stationed in position "Z" and will act as a light beacon for navigational purposes.

18. The light will be operated by STURGEON in accordance with paragraphs 7 to 9 of CHAR THREE.

19. Both Hunt class destroyers will listen for STURGEON's signal as laid down in paragraph 10 of CHAR THREE. Opportunity to practice inter-communication between destroyers and STURGEON will be made available prior to the operation.

RESTRICTIONS ON A/S OPERATIONS DURING APPROACH
20. During the approach, submarines WILL NOT BE ATTACKED when within 20 miles of position "Z".

THE APPROACH
21. After passing position "Z", the force will proceed on a course direct to the buoy in charted position 47° 7.6' N, 2° 20.2' W passing there at 0030, thence to a position 2 cables to eastward of LES MOREES TOWER (47° 15' N,, 2° 13' W). The force will then proceed up GRANDE Road and then to its individual objectives.

22. It is intended that the approach up the river from the buoy referred to in paragraph 21 should be made at 10 knots; this reduction may be made without signal. Craft must be prepared for alterations of speed without signal particularly an increase when the force is fired on.

23. After passing position "Z", the two escorting destroyers will part company and patrol about 30 miles to seaward keeping clear of STURGEON as she proceeds to the southward. Further instructions for these destroyers are given in paragraph 44.

DISPERAL OF NAVAL UNITS

24. On arrival abreast the extremities of the southern breakwater of ST. NAZAIRE the force will disperse as follows;_

   (a) CAMPELTOWN proceeds towards the big lock gate.

   (b) M. G. B. 314 hauls over to starboard towards PETITE Road.

   (c) Group 1 of M.L.s proceeds alongside the north side of old mole.

   (d) Group 2 of M. L.s proceeds alongside landing steps on both sides of old entrance.

   (e) M. T. B. 74 takes up a position just south of the NAZAIRE shoal.

MOVEMENTS OF CAMPBELTOWN

25. On passing the dispersal point, CAMPBELTOWN will steer to ram the centre of the big lock gate. She should pass about 100 yards off the end of the old mole increasing speed so as to strike the boom off the entrance of the lock at about 15 knots engaging dock defences with all available weapons. As the tide will be flooding it is probable that the stern of the ship will be carried upstream as the bow enters slack water just prior to hitting the net.

26. After ramming the gate the ship is likely to slew across the entrance. It is most important, however, that she is kept against the gate after the first impact irrespective of her position in order to expedite the landing of the troops. This will be done by grapnels and warps and/or by working the engines.

27. After the troops have disembarked, the Commanding Officer will arrange for the evacuation of the crew and having set off the delay action of the main charge, scuttle the ship. The delay action on the main charge will be two hours.

28. The CAMPBELTOWN's crew will be taken off in M.L.s which will lie alongside the north side of the old entrance for this purpose.

M.G.B. 314

29. M.G.B. 314 will land the Force Commanders at the Old Entrance after the troops have been landed and then act as required by the S.N.O.

GROUP 1 of M.L.s.

30. Group 1 consisting of 6 M.L.s will be in the port column. M.L.s will pass close to the end of the Old Mole engaging the shore defences and will round up sharply and go alongside the north side at the steps. After troops have landed M.L.s will secure alongside bows outward under the orders of the piermaster.

GROUP 2 of M.L.s

31. Group 2, consisting of 6 M.L.s will be astern of CAMPBELTOWN during the approach and will come up on her port quarter as she approaches the big lock. M.L.s will proceed alongside both sides of the old entrance using either the steps or ships alongside.

32. Three M.L.s will be detailed to remain alongside the north side of the Old Entrance to embark CAMPBELTOWN's crew and any casualties. When fully loaded these boats will proceed out of the LOIRE and in accordance with paragraph 43. If not fully loaded they will lie off within hailing distance of the Old Mole. The remaining M.L.s of this group will also lie off the Old Mole.

M.T.B. 74

33. M.T.B. 74 will be prepared to carry out any of the following roles if ordered by the S.N.O.:-

(a) Should CAMPBELTOWN fail to reach the objective M.T.B. 74 will be prepared to proceed up to the boom and fire her "torpedoes" over it at the lock gate.

(b) Proceed through the Old Entrance Lock (East lock) passing under the footbridge if there us sufficient clearance and fire her "torpedoes" at U-boats in the pens.

(c) Any other role such as attacking ships alongside. Etc.

OUTLINE MILITARY PLAN

34. The Military Force will be put ashore in three main groups as follows:-

Group 1: Consisting of 17 officers and 69 Other Ranks, will be carried in 6 M.L.s and will land at the Old Mole to execute tasks south of the Old Entrance (Exclusive).

Group 2: Consisting of 11 officers and 76 O.R.s will be carried in 6 M.L.s and will land within the Old Entrance to execute tasks in the sector north of the Old Entrance but exclusive of the dry dock.

Group 3: Consisting of 14 officers and 59 O.R.s will be carried in CAMPBELTOWN and will land at the south end of the dry dock to execute tasks in that sector.

35. The Military Force will be divided into:-

(a) Assault Parties to deal with known defences and to seal the area within which demolitions are being carried out.

(b) Demolition parties each trained for a specific task.

(c) Protection parties accompanying demolition parties to ensure that the latter work undisturbed.

36. It is of great importance that the area within which demolitions are taking place, is firmly held so as to prevent enemy troops from gaining as entry. All bridges, gates or other entrances over which access could be gained must therefore be held.

37. It is equally important that the area should remain sealed during all but the final stages of withdrawal and re-embarkation. Only the most careful signal plan will ensure that this is successfully accomplished.

PRIORITY OF TASKS
38. The order of priority of the tasks allotted to the Military force is as follows:-

(a) The lock gates and mechanism of the large dock.

(b) The smaller lock gates and their installation.

(c) Other key points such as pumping machinery for the basin, etc.

(d) Any U-boats and shipping which may be accessible.

DANGER AREA OF DEMOLITIONS
39. ALL demolition charges, inclusive of those placed inside the destroyer, will be blown in accordance with a careful programme drawn up and agreed by the Naval and

Military Force Commanders. This programme must cover not only the successful completion of the tasks but also the security of naval and military personnel working within the area of those tasks.

PRECAUTIONS ON THE OUTWARD PASSAGE

40. In order to disguise the presence of the military personnel on board the destroyer and M.L.s, every precaution must be taken to ensure that at all times during the outward passage, NO military personnel are allowed on deck unless they are wearing duffle coats or naval oilskins.

TIMING OF THE WITHDRAWAL

41. (a) The Force will be withdrawn as soon as possible after the completion of its tasks.

(b) There is no necessity for the Force to effect its withdrawal as a whole. Individual boat loads may be sent away independently under Naval instructions as soon as their tasks have been completed. (See paragraph 42).

(c) The aim should be to have completed ALL tasks and re-embarkation by 0330 hours.

(d) It must accordingly be clearly understood that the completion of the re-embarkation by 0330 hours is to take precedence over everything except the execution of any major demolition task which may be unfinished at that time.

WITHDRAWAL OF NAVAL UNITS

42. Except as described in paragraph 31 withdrawal will take place from the Old Mole. The outside M.L.s are to be loaded first and will be ordered to shove off as soon as 40 men have been embarked. M.L.s lying off will be called alongside by the premaster.

As M.L.s shove off they will proceed independently to seaward and then in accordance with paragraph 43.

RETIRING COURSE

43. All craft on retiring will proceed at maximum speed until clear of shore batteries. They will then pass through position "Y" (47° 01' N, 2° 43' W) thence on course 248° at their best speed with due regard to fuel consumption.

44. The escorting destroyers will pass through position "Y" at 0600 on course 248° spread 5 miles apart in order to pick up craft which may be in difficulties, take onboard personnel from M.L.s and generally rally the force.

45. Return route for light craft and escorting destroyers is given in the passage orders.

OUTLINE AIR SUPPORT PLAN

46. (a) The critical time is from 0100 – 0300 hours, with the attack at its heaviest scale between 0100 and 0200 hours while the Force is approaching the objective and when troops are first ashore

   (b) From 2330 – 0045 hrs: Heavy bombs.
                                            M.P.I. on the Town.

   (c) From 0100 – 0300 hrs: Maximum number of sorties using light Bombs and incendiaries. M.P.I. on The Town (and NOT the Docks area.)

   (d) From 0300 hrs for the remaining hours of darkness; small raids to prevent the sounding of the ALL CLEAR. M.P.I. in dock area.

   (e) A P.R.U. to be flown at the latest moment prior to the operation in order to ascertain position of shipping in the harbour, etc. These photographs to be given to the Force commanders before sailing.

CASUALTIES

47. Force Commanders will satisfy themselves that each Commanding Officer and Officer Commanding Units fully understands his own individual task. It must be clearly understood by them that they must proceed with their tasks with the utmost determination and speed irrespective of casualties to other craft or units. This particularly applies during the approach.

48. If heavy casualties occur during the approach which are liable to jeopardise the success of the original plan, the decision to send in CAMPBELTOWN alone must be considered, bearing in mind that if this only is done something can be achieved.

ACTION BY CAMPBELTOWN IF EITHER LOCK GATE IS OPEN

49. (a) If the outer lock gate is open the first task for CAMPBELTOWN is to disembark the troops as near the pre-arranged landing place as possible.

(b) If the outer lock gate is open and the inner one shut CAMPBELTOWN should carry out her role on the inner gate as originally planned planned for the outer one having previously complied with (a) above.

(d) If both gates are open, having complied with (a) above, it is at the discretion of the Comanding Officer whether he enters the basin nad expends his ship on the most valuable target he can find or sinks his ship across the iner lock gate sill.

DAMAGED OR BROKEN DOWN CRAFT

50. Light craft which may become damaged during the approach are to do their utmost to reach their landing positions even if this may be some time after the main assault. During this stage other craft will not stand by them and they must fend for themselves.

51. During the withdrawal every effort must be made to get damaged boats out to sea, assisting each other as necessary.

ORDERS FOR THE CHARGE IN CAMPBELTOWN

52. A charge of 24 depth charges is to be placed as far forward as can reasonably be expected to be undamaged by the impact. This charge is to be carefully secured so that it cannot break adrift and fitted with alternative firing methods. The delay action on firing the charge is to be 2 hours.

MEDICAL

53. During the return journey accommodation for casualties will necessarily be extremely limited. It is therefore incumbent on the Force Commanders to make all possible arrangements for the comfort and well-being of wounded. To this end, the following steps must be provided for in the plan: -

   (a) Two M.O.s will be landed with the Force.

   (b) Each sub-group will contain selected N.C.O.s or men who have been given training in advanced first aid. Each individual so trained will carry ashore a small medical haversack.

   (c) Special medical equipment will be issued to all officers. Special equipment will also be carried in each M.L.

(d) Casualties will be transferred from M. L.s to larger ships as and when this becomes possible during the return journey. advance arrangements must be made for their reception.

CANCELLATION OF THE OPERATION

54. If during the outward passage, naval units become scattered by enemy action or stress of weather, and it is not possible to reform without delaying the operation, it is at the discretion of the Force Commander to cancel it. They must, however, inform C. in C. PLYMOUTH if they do so.

Sources and further reading

Anyone who writes about the raid on St Nazaire starts with a debt to James Dorrian and C. E. Lucas Phillips for laying the foundations for an account of a complicated and intense few hours of history. It's a debt acknowledged by Robert Lyman in his more recent *Into the Jaws of Death*, which brings a new and broad perspective to the origins of the raid, and which I acknowledge here. But there are almost as many other voices to listen to as there were participants, and many thankfully left correspondence, recordings and unpublished manuscripts that I hope enrich the narrative.

Survivors' written records that offer vital first-person points of view of the raid include those of Ted Burt, Richard Collinson, Bill Copland, Philip Dark, Charles Newman, David Paton, Don Randall, Bill 'Tiger' Watson, Jack Webb, George Wheeler and Chris Worsley. Among the voice recordings that bring it to life at the Imperial War Museum are those made by Ralph Batteson, Herbert Dyer, Glyn Salisbury, Ronald Swayne, Bill Tillie and Micky Wynn. In addition to plundering material mined for me from German archives I made use of Cabinet and Defence ministry papers at the National Archives in Kew and John Hughes-Hallett's papers, held at the Churchill Archives Centre in Cambridge.

The following list of secondary sources is not exhaustive, but all have been invaluable:

Adkins, Roy, *Trafalgar, the Biography of a Battle* (Little, Brown, 2005)

Batteson, Ralph, *St Nazaire to Shepperton – a Sailor's Odyssey* (Highedge Historical Society, 1996)

Blair, Clay, *Hitler's U-Boat War* (Weidenfeld & Nicolson, 1997)

Braeuer, Luc and Bernard Petitjean, *Raid sur Saint-Nazaire!* (Liv'Éditions, 2012)

Burn, Michael, *Turned towards the Sun* (Michael Russell, 2003)

Chant-Sempill, Stuart, *St Nazaire Commando* (John Murray, 1985)

Churchill, Winston, *The Second World War* (Cassell, 1948–53)

Clayton, Tim and Phil Craig, *Trafalgar – the Men, the Battle, the Storm* (Hodder & Stoughton, 2004)

Dixon, Norman, *On the Psychology of Military Incompetence* (Jonathan Cape, 1976)

Dorrian, James, *Storming St Nazaire* (Leo Cooper, 1998)

Fenby, Jonathan, *The Sinking of the Lancastria* (Simon & Schuster, 2006)

Ford, Ken, *St Nazaire 1942 – the Great Commando Raid* (Osprey, 2001)

Holman, Gordon, *Commando Attack* (Hodder & Stoughton, 1942)

Hopton, Richard, *A Reluctant Hero – the Life of Captain Robert Ryder VC* (Pen & Sword Maritime, 2012)

Kamiensky, Lukasz, *Shooting Up: A History of Drugs in Warfare* (C. Hurst & Co., 2017)

Lavery, Brian, *Churchill Goes to War* (Naval Institute Press, 2007)

Loring Villa, Brian, *Unauthorised Action: Mountbatten and the Dieppe Raid, 1942* (Oxford University Press, 1990)

Lownie, Andrew, *The Mountbattens – Their Lives and Loves* (Blink Publishing, 2019)

Lucas Phillips, Charles, *The Greatest Raid of All* (William Heinemann, 1958)

Lush, Peter, *Winged Chariot* (Grub Street, 2016)

Lyman, Robert, *Into the Jaws of Death* (Quercus Editions, 2013)

Mawdsley, Evan, *The War for the Seas* (Yale University Press, 2019)

Milton, Giles, *Churchill's Ministry of Ungentlemanly Warfare* (John Murray, 2016)

Ministry of Information, *Combined Operations 1940–42* (HMSO, 1943)

Purdon, Corran, *List the Bugle — Reminiscences of an Irish Soldier* (Greystone Books, 1993)

Reynolds, David and Vladimir Pechatnov, *The Kremlin Letters* (Yale University Press, 2018)

Ryder, Cmdr R. E. D. VC, RN, *The Attack on St Nazaire* (John Murray, 1947)

Schmidt, Paul, *Hitler's Interpreter* (The History Press, republished 2016)

Stanley, Peter, *Commando to Colditz* (Murdoch Books, 2009)

Stephenson, Michael, *The Last Full Measure — How Soldiers Die in Battle* (Duckworth, 2013)

Sutton, Chris, *From Smethwick to St Nazaire — the Life of Bill Savage VC* (Smethwick Heritage Centre Trust, 2012)

Wilson, Charles, *The Anatomy of Courage* (Constable, 1945)

Woodham Smith, Cecil, *The Reason Why* (Constable, 1953)

Zeigler, Philip, *Mountbatten — the Official Biography* (HarperCollins, 1985)

Acknowledgements

This book could not have been written without the help of Ann Mitchell, Chairman of the St Nazaire Society and daughter of Captain David Birney. She let me into the Society's archive while museums and national archives all over the world were closed, and not just once. I'm also deeply grateful for expert knowledge shared unstintingly by Peter Lush, James Dorrian, David Tait and Peter Stanley; and also by Luc Braeuer, Janice Dale, Bernard Petitjean and Robert Wynn. Professor David Reynolds came to my rescue in an hour of contextual need, as did Professors James Bainbridge and David Nutt. Charioteers' descendants who trusted me with letters, logbooks, reminiscences and sometimes all of the above included Andrew and Bill Tibbits, Jason Beattie, Caroline Carr, Christopher Curtis, Julia Davies, Jeanne Davis, Paul Durrant, Fiona Read and Peter Watson. Michel Euxebie was a wonderful guide and host in St Nazaire, and Marc Pratt-Yule and Thomas Fuchs explored the Bundesarchiv on my behalf as I never could have done alone. My thanks also to Daniel Crewe and Alpana Sajip at Penguin for floating the whole idea and shepherding it expertly to completion; to Mark Handsley for his copy editing; to James Harding and Katie Vanneck-Smith at Tortoise for giving me the time to write; and Bill Hamilton, as ever, at A. M. Heath.

Most of all, for round-the-clock room service and limitless moral support, thank you Karen. And Bruno, Louis and Enzo. And Chumley.

Index